AF566784

China's Discursive Nationalism

Contending in Softer Realms

China's Discursive Nationalism

Contending in Softer Realms

Bhavna Singh

First Published in 2012

Published by
PENTAGON PRESS
206, Peacock Lane, Shahpur Jat,
New Delhi-110049
Phones: 011-64706243, 26491568
Telefax: 011-26490600
email: rajan@pentagonpress.in
website: www.pentagonpress.in

Cataloging in Publication Data—DK
Courtesy: D.K. Agencies (P) Ltd. <docinfo@dkagencies.com>

Singh, Bhavna.
China's discursive nationalism : contending in softer realms / Bhavna Singh.
p. cm.
Includes bibliographical references (p.) and index.

ISBN 9788182746510

1. Nationalism—China. 2. China—Politics and government—2002- 3. Nationalism—Social aspects—China. 4. Mass media—Political aspects—China. 5. Digital media—China. I. Title.

DDC 320.540951 23

Printed at Aegean Offset Printers, Greater Noida.

Dedicated to my parents
Richpal & Raj

Contents

Acknowledgements

I am fortunate to have received the support, guidance and blessings of many distinguished people during the compilation of this manuscript and therefore it is opportune that I express my gratitude for them. First and foremost, I owe a debt of gratitude to Prof. Srikanth Kondapalli for his immense support, invaluable insights and continuous encouragement. His dynamic ideas and suggestions coupled with concern and cooperation have been a source of moral and intellectual strength for me. His perspicacious knowledge on Chinese affairs has guided the outcome of the present work, and his indefatigable attitude to work has been a constant source of inspiration in my quest for knowledge. His timely guidance on accessing multiple kinds of research material and insistence on field trips has tremendously shaped the quality of this work. It will be apt to say that it would not have been possible for this work to be completed without his constant prompting and encouragement.

I am thankful to Prof. Sucheta Mahajan (CHS/JNU), under whose guidance I developed a keen interest in the ideas of "nations and nationalisms." Her lectures were stimulating and titillated a desire in me to explore the subject more deeply. Prof. Prasenjit Duara and Dr. Abanti Bhattacharya deserve much credit, whose earlier works on the issue provoked and shaped my enterprise. Special thanks are due to Mr. Zang Wentao whose comments provided me with an insider's view on Chinese nationalism. Maj. Gen. Dipankar Banerjee, Prof. P R Chari, Dr. Suba Chandran and Dr. Mallika Joseph need a special mention for guiding me and helping me develop my research skills over the period of my association with the Institute of Peace and Conflict Studies (IPCS).

I also thank Dr. Alka Acharya, Dr. Varaprasad Shekhar, Dr. Ritu Aggarwal and all other faculty members of the Center for East Asian Studies, JNU, who critically influenced and shaped my ideas on several issues relating to China over the period of my study and their great support all through. I extend special thanks to Dr. D.S. Rawat, School of Languages, JNU, who introduced me to the challenges of learning the Chinese language. Patricia Oberoi,

Director, ICS, and Dr. Madhavi Thampi need a special mention, whose inputs on my presentation on "National Identity Formation in China" at the ICS helped me to clarify my conceptual framework on identity issues, and thanks to Prof. Sreemati Chakrabarti, Center for East Asian Studies, DU, for providing me that valuable opportunity.

I also extend my heartfelt affection and thanks to my parents, grandparents and siblings -Vandana and Anirudh, who have been my pillars of strength through thick and thin. I have been fortunate to be endowed with the encouragement of my friends Dr. J Jeganaathan, who painstakingly went through the script to point out any errors of content or argument, Rishu Arora, Namita, Neha and all my peers and colleagues at IPCS as well as Dr. Jabin T Jacob, now with the ICS, who helped me in clarifying my thoughts and shared their perceptions on various issues related to Chinese polity and foreign policy. Thanks are also due to Rajiv and Pratibha at the CEAS, JNU, who have also been of immense support.

I appreciate the generous help given to me by the library staff at JNU Central Library, IDSA Library, Sapru House (ICWA) and Nehru Memorial Library at Teen Murti in collection of research material. I am earnestly indebted to the CEAS staff, the SIS office staff and specially Harish Sir, who made things easier and less bureaucratic by their instantaneous help and support. I am collectively thankful to the Center for East Asian Studies, professors, the Indian Government and the IPCS for providing me opportunities for visiting China during my research work as a part of the Indian youth delegation and as part of my work and conferences, which enriched my perceptions of the Chinese people and their culture.

Needless to say, any inaccuracies of facts, arguments and judgement are mine alone.

Bhavna Singh

Abbreviations

BOBICO	Beijing Olympics Games Bid Committee
CCP	Chinese Communist Party
CCCPC	Central Committee of the Communist Party of China
CCTV	China Central Television
GONGOs	Government Operated Non-governmental Organisations
GMD	Guomindang/Kuomintang
IOC	International Olympics Committee
MFN	Most-favoured-nation
NATO	North Atlantic Treaty Organisation
NOC	National Olympic Committee
NTDTV	New Tang Dynasty Television
PLA	People's Liberation Army
PRC	People's Republic of China
ROC	Republic of China/Taiwan
SARFT	State Administration of Radio, Film and Television
UN	United Nations
UNEP	United Nations Environment Programme

Note on Spellings in the Text

Chinese personal names are given surname first. Pinyin has been used for Chinese words.

1

Introduction

The formation of supra-national and regional identities like that of the European Union and the emergent West Asian community has ushered in a prescience of nationalism becoming a passé phenomenon. In fact, regionalism has been sought to emerge as an alternative mode of identity formation in the twenty-first century. Nonetheless, a closer assessment of contemporary dynamics reveals that nationalism still continues to be a persuasive steering force in contemporary social formations, especially in China. Nationalism (minzu zhuyi)[1] as an ideology has refused to cave in or render itself redundant in face of the forces of globalisation. Despite the creation of supra-national spaces and multi-variant ethnoscapes, the desire to belong or relate to or possess a community-bound consciousness has continued unabated, manifested mostly in the garb of 'nationalism'. An urge to retain a group identity when faced by external threats has been best appeased by a propensity to associate with a history of culture or what is termed as "collective memory."[2]

While nationalism might not suffice to explain the contemporary realities in some parts of the western hemisphere any more, specifically a centripetal Europe, its influence is considerable in the eastern part of the world. These nations which are emerging out of their colonial pasts to assert their new found sovereignty have massively relied on nationalism as a saviour over the past few decades, meanwhile the colonisers seem to be experimenting with the supra-national paradigm. Moreover, there are several movements which are still striving to achieve the identity of a state. Thus, it will be more apt to comprehend the international system of nation-states in terms of an existential binary of nationalist and post-nationalist paradigms juxtaposed in defining political and group behaviour among states. The late twentieth and early twenty-first centuries in the Chinese developmental trajectory provide substantive validation to the fact that the near-term future is definitely not going to be devoid of nationalist moorings.

The contention between national or regional entities will be more prominent though. Since a linear progression of modernity entails that certain stages of development might be transcended as a result of skip-over to futuristic forms of development. Ergo, an East Asian identity might be explored vis-à-vis a strong nationalist tenor amongst the East Asian nations. This contention also transpires into a struggle between the notions of interests of an individual and that of the community. An East Asian Community will be difficult to establish in the near-term since the strong national identities have not yet been superseded for a larger community interest.

Drawing comparisons between the relatively developed West and the rising East, it is important to bear in mind the significant differences in their growth patterns historically. Nationalism in China has assured the protection of national interests despite contradictions with the global ethos, witnessed particularly in instances like that of the Carrefour demonstrations and the Tibetan Uprising. The levelling of societies/states which was projected in a rhetoric of *"one world, one dream"*[3] was undoubtedly restricted to the idea of progressing together however, spearheaded by China, as nationalism implicitly beckoned a "first our nation, followed by the rest" approach.

The outstanding extravaganza witnessed during Beijing Olympics in 2008 provides a case in point for the swelling national pride that is bolstering nationalism in China today. With a euphoric public opinion escalating on the jargons of a "rising China" or "the next superpower", the patriotic fervour is being ceaselessly refurbished. The Chinese masses are experiencing vicarious sentiments through the achievements and accomplishments of their sports representatives which effectively reinforce the nationalist discourse. The threat to nationalist underpinnings in form of globalisation has been rendered ineffective primarily because global spaces have become yet another arena for reiteration of nationalistic impulses. Many scholars believe that globalisation has beguilingly facilitated the transition of nationalism from an ideology based predominantly on "a pursuit of national interests between nations on the territorial realm" to a "quest for an identity based on symbolic realms" albeit without undermining the sovereignty of the state.

The nature of interaction between nationalism and globalisation in the Chinese geo-polity and international behaviour has left many aficionados swelling with pride, mostly the Chinese Communist Party (CCP) leadership and dumbfounded others, to whose imagination it was incomprehensible to see a communist country endorsing nationalism as its dogma. The beginning of the twentieth century saw the communist ideology bourgeoning in China while the nationalist elements remained relegated to the backdrop. With the ascendance of party politics between the KMT and the CCP, the elements of nationalist ideology were seeped in even the communist regime, since it acted as a mortar for sustaining the social fabric of the nation.

This seepage occurred through a slow transformative process of interaction between the political and the cultural spheres in China. Since progress began to be associated more with opening of the economy and economic development, globalisation opened up different forums for interaction of cultural and political spaces and led to regeneration of the nationalist ideology. The emergence of alternative spaces as a result of globalisation led to a high level of interaction between the foreign policy stratagem and nationalism as an ideology. These alternative spaces often referred to as the public sphere[4] have tremendously contributed to the discourse of nationalism in China.

The public sphere which functions as the springboard for propagation of ideologies and formulation of public opinion has itself been largely redefined by the impact of globalisation in China. It provides more scope for expression of dissent and access to alternative sources of information today. In fact, the larger gamut of public sphere like "dance, drama, the media, music, song, speech, poetry, literature, opera, fiction and above all sports" are by far the most effective tools of understanding the role and progression of nationalism in the Chinese society.[5]

Contemporary China witnesses one of the most aggressive deployments of new symbols and cultural repertoire for the purpose of weaving its national fabric. The folklore celebrations for instance, create an arena, "a social context" into which these ideas are concretized.[6] Government units and scholarly associations combine forces to promote symbols of Chinese culture, and arrays of organisations contribute to the effort by producing books, movies and material artefacts. Ostentatiously, these activities occur in a larger international framework; nevertheless, an "intensely national" tenor is inherent within the manner of articulation. Further, the growth of dissenting organisations—the Falun Gong and technological developments viz. the increasing access to Internet and hi-tech gadgets, which make the state management of opinion a cumbersome process, provide both an impediment as well as an opportunity to the discourse of nationalism. The manifestation of nationalism thus occurs in softer realms or what can be better understood as an element of China's soft power projection.

The turn of the millennium has also portended a major shift in the discourse of Chinese nationalism given the paradoxes of contemporary realities. The process of "eliciting future hopes for the destiny of a nation" along with seeking its legitimacy in the nation's history has gained ascendancy in the rhetoric of the nationalist discourse, something akin to the "manifest destiny" syndrome of the US. It is no more only the "wounded or reactive nationalism" that had erstwhile been the motto of the Chinese government, which is identified as the overarching trend in Chinese nationalism but the developmental and assertive face of a nation that now symbolizes its identity. A prominent role is being played by the entrepreneur class and the netizens, who are increasingly getting involved in the issues of the state, while the peasant based nationalism of the early 1930s and 50s has been relegated to the background.

The international implications of China's renewed nationalism are also significant. Buttressed with the unceasing discourse of nationalism, China's rise is becoming a concern for the international community. Many have drawn parallels between the rise of China and that of Nazist Germany, pre-Second World war Japan,[7] in terms of fascist proclivities or the cold war era Soviet Union in terms of nationalist underpinnings under authoritarian regimes, but this does not suffice to explain the future course of Chinese nationalism. Most nations make a conscious effort to learn from histories and the Chinese strategy of "making use of history to serve the present" will hopefully inhibit it from repeating the mistakes done by these authoritarian regimes. However, this does limit one from considering Chinese nationalism as a form of political extremism.

Being an *"image conscious nation"* the management of discourse is heavily influenced by China's strategy of peaceful rise whereby it wants to project itself and be perceived by others as a "responsible power." The post-Mao and post-Deng China today stands tall on its feet under the new generation leadership of Jiang Zemin and Hu Jintao who have remarkably utilised the maxim of nationalism in both domestic and international arenas. The most palpable tenet of this new nationalism is the paradoxical existence of a collective-coercive agency of the state, which incinerates the identity of an individual for communitarian aims, simultaneously with a parallel citizen-sponsored patriotic ardour, which challenges the state orchestrated nationalism at every step.

The crux of this tussle lies in the state's attempts at homogenization and the citizen's efforts at retaining their individual identities. The dynamics are played out in a very interesting manner; the citizens provide blind support to their government in face of international pressure or calumny, on the other hand, the same citizens do not refrain from open criticism of the government when their individual rights are encroached upon. This is largely a result of the meta-narratives constructed by the Chinese state. For instance, the discourse on the "century of humiliation" and the endorsement of popular maxims like "cutting of the Chinese melon" has abetted the state's efforts in retaining its hold on the psyche of its masses.

It is however essential to bear in mind that the Chinese state does not officially endorse the usage of "nationalism" in its political parlance though it might outrightly use it as a strategy. The official phraseology recognises only "patriotism" (*aiguo zhuyi*) as a glorified ideal. A detailed analysis of the speeches of the prominent leaders and the party suggests that patriotism has often been adduced by the state as a stronger psychological tool. This was most prominent in Mao's dictums and his attempts to garner popular support for his struggles based on patriotic appeals to the citizens. And though Mao has been castigated for many of his maverick endeavours, the CCP leaders even today continue to use this strategy practiced by their great helmsman to gain legitimacy and support from the masses. To aid a better understanding of the trajectory of Chinese nationalism, it is imperative to outline a basic definition of what one means by a nation or how is nationalism to be construed in various international contexts. For the purpose of drawing an analogy on how these concepts have evolved historically certain basic tenets are being explored.

Nations and Nationalisms

Incessant attempts have been made to understand the elements constituting a nation and in this process substantive literature has been assembled. However, there is still no consensus on an *a priori* definition of a "nation": who constitute it in terms of homogeneity? And what levels of association with the state can be termed as patriotic or nationalistic? How far is the role of dissent accepted within a nation? And what is the basis of acceptability within a nation: race, ethnicity or citizenship? There are two main strands in the extant literature on nations as political units and nationalism as a phenomenon: first, those who endorse a primordial nature of nations and nationalism, that is, nations have persisted since the very beginning and second, those who believe that these are modern constructs engendered from birth of a system of nation-states as a corollary to the industrial developments in the sixteenth century.[8]

To the first group belong scholars like Clifford Geertz, Anthony D. Smith and Edward Shils who postulate that the nations have a primordial origin which "spring from cultural "givens" of kinship"[9] exhibiting a centrality of language, ethnicity and religion. Geertz analyses the formation of a nation through a jostling experience between the search of an identity and the modern imperatives of progress. The modern states become susceptible to disaffection given primordial loyalties. Smith argues that "ethnie" remains at the core of a nation and those groups who have their own ethnic solidarity are more likely to develop a nation.

This argument can be accepted as far as the contemporary sub-nationalisms in China are concerned. Since the separatist movements in Tibet and Xinjiang are inspired by such solidarities of different ethnicity and common culture striving for political recognition. However, given the strong current of the overall state nationalism, these remain only in a budding stage without realizing their full potential. Thus, the presence of "ethnie" does provide a basis for group consciousness but is not necessarily the single determining force. It remains to be seen what the future of such ethnic movements will be China. However, it is not the intent of this work to delve into the sub-national tendencies.

On the other hand, scholars like Ernest Gellner, Eric Hobsbawm and Benedict Anderson believe that these are modern edifices ushered in the wake of modernisation and urbanisation. There are differences amongst modernists on whether the nation forms the basis of nationalism or if it is nationalism which leads to creation of a national identity. Gellner, for instance, believes that "nationalism invents nations where they do not exist..." while Smith argues that "nations create nationalism."

In one of the earliest efforts, Earnest Renan in his essay "What is a nation?" questioned the idea of a single race or language as being identified with a single nation. It is the national/collective will which is reflected in the cultural memory of a state that becomes the basis for its nationhood. However, his was a highly euro-centric vision and he believed that the Asian countries were not capable of developing into nations. China was deeply steeped in the concepts of divine right of theories and the emperor's claims to being the son of the heaven for it to make space for a collective will. Thus, nations as entities were confined to Europe according to him.

However, he did believe in the hybridity of various ethnicities which would ultimately form the basis of a nation and emphasized on the necessity of "forgetting" or "selective remembrance" for any nation to regenerate itself. In this sense, he believed that "Nation is a daily plebiscite" where there is a constant effort of chaffing the non-identifiable and stressing what can further contribute to a national memory. Nations were not to be eternal entities rather could be created and destroyed given the determination of a collective will.

Even Marxist historians agree that it is industrial capitalism that has led to the emergence of nations and nationalism. In his quest to respond to "why so many people are ready to make considerable sacrifices in the name of the nation,"[10] Anderson argued how print capitalism brought about the creation of an "imagined community" which became the springboard of nationalism. The creation of a sacred language amongst vernaculars and the tremendous dispersion through the commercial revolution became the manifestation of "nation-ness." However, it is critical to note that in the analysis of the modernist scholars "China" is treated more as *aberration* than as a part of norm.

Others argue for a multiplicity of perceptions within a nation. For instance, Max Weber believes the nation to be a "prestige community" derived from the material interest of the state as well as a sense of "irreplaceable cultural value." He makes a distinction based on the perceptions amongst different social strata primarily the elite and the common masses. Other scholars have also criticized the "myth of modernity" and the overemphasis on identifying the birth of a nation through making a distinction between modern and pre-modern nations.

It is plausible according to them, that the seeds of a nation may have remained dormant in the past, while they might easily constitute themselves into a full-fledged identity spurred by a transformative event. Continuities exist as a by-product of traditions and heritages from the past which coalesce over generations. These critics also point out that nations can emerge from all kinds of social and economic milieu as evident in case of Quebec and Eritrea and many times in circumstances where no ethnic or cultural memory existed at all.

For the purpose of simplification, a nation can be simply recognized as "a community of people composed of one or more nationalities with its own territory and government"[11] or as a "*territorial unit having corresponding sovereign political units and bound by a common consciousness of identity among its citizens.*"[12] A similar debate exists on the issue of defining and understanding nationalism. Prominent among them are the definitions cited by Elie Kedourie, Gellner, Hobsbawm and Anderson. Kedourie attributes nationalism to the rise of secularism whereby it is seen as a doctrine which replaced the church. It is construed as a "product of European thought" and a homogenizing force which acts through the power of ideas. Nationalism is seen as filling the vacuum brought about by collapse in the transmission of traditional values and the rise of a restless, secular, educated mass which does not have access to power.

Most scholars perceive nationalism as an ideology invented by political elites in order to legitimize their power against revolution and democratization. Hobsbawm and Gellner strongly support this conviction. Hobsbawm believes that "technological revolution has been the harbinger of such *social engineering.*"[13] He further mentions the invention of public ceremonies to serve the intent of the state; this is particularly relevant in the Chinese case where sports, cultural symbols and cinematic representations are used to buttress and regenerate nationalism.

A heavy reliance on print capitalism or technological revolution will, however, prove counter-productive in analysing how nationalism functions. Though Anderson makes a strong case for how an "imagined community" could be devised by nationalist discourses, the same print technology could also be dispersed to other elements in the society undercutting the homogenous tenor of nationalism. Thus, these conceptual frameworks need to be cautiously applied when attempting to understand the course of Chinese nationalism. Again for the purpose of simplification and convenience this work adheres to the definition of nationalism as a "presence of a relationship between nation and state that obtains when the people of that nation identify with the state."[14]

Contemporary Perspectives on Chinese Nationalism

China has been conventionally observed through the lens of a civilisational state. Hence, a susceptibility to define the nation as a homogenous entity has overridden the heterogeneous tenors of multiplicity in theoretical discourses.

The Westphalian[15] model which was best kept in abeyance by the traditional Chinese state and observers at large, earlier when situating China within the larger world-politics and nation-state order, is now agreed as a relevant and appropriate frame of reference. This is largely due to the shift in the Chinese discourse of borders and states from a frontier based-tributary state system to the modern system of boundaries and allies. While the symbolic notions of China as being the core and the other nations being the periphery reflected in its *Sino-centrism* model of international relations still remains but it has been modified to accommodate the geopolitical realities.

The contemplations and theoretical debates on Chinese nationalism were largely restricted to a dichotomous understanding of either an "aggrieved defensive nationalism" or a "confident and proud nationalism" previously.[16] But the emergence of new dimensions with the opening of economy and reform has forced sinologists across the globe to take into account the role of political structures and their resonance in face of onslaught by miscellaneous genus of dissent engendered in the Chinese and global public spheres.

Despite several attempts at deconstruction and consequent reconstruction of the chronological transmutation of Chinese nationalism, there still remains a serious lacuna in understanding the relationship between nationalism and the institutions and processes which engender it. Various conceptualisations of Chinese nationalism have been made which can be understood by clubbing them under the framework of Western perspectives, Chinese perspectives and perspectives from other countries (South Asian Nations).

Western Perspectives

In association with the traditional debate on nations and nationalisms, Chinese nationalism has also been studied by Western scholars in terms of whether it is intrinsically based on primordial moorings or is an offshoot of the modern nation-state apparatus. The earliest assumptions underlying the characterisation of modern Chinese nationalism have been viewed through the phraseology of "culturalism to nationalism" progression.[17] Under this rubric scholars like James Harrison, Joseph Levenson,[18] Joseph Whitney, Hugh Seton-Watson, Selig Harrison *et al* have postulated that "traditionally the Chinese self-image was based on a common historical heritage and shared beliefs, mostly Confucian and was not associated with the nationalism that is largely regarded as a modern phenomenon based on the Westphalian system of nation states." The conventional understanding of Chinese nationalism, more or less, focussed on the ambition of Chinese nationalists to recover the lost glory of China's historical empire.

The problem of applying the "culturalism" thesis and the lack of a confirmatory definition on nationalism in the Chinese prodded further debate. Lucian Pye questioned the basis for China being considered a modern nation-state and rather argued for understanding China as "a civilization pretending to be a state." He views Chinese nationalism as "confused," "content less" and "incoherent" as the Chinese people not only face difficulties adapting to the institutional norms of the modern nation state system but also are unable to articulate a "clear and firm sense of the unique values and ideals that their nation should stand for in the world." His understanding of the phenomenon is, however, inappropriate and limited.

Though the Chinese may have expressed an initial inhibition or unwillingness in accepting the norms of the modern nation state system, the nationalism exhibited by the Chinese people in the recent times is definitely organised, anti- "the other" and engendered with all strength of a mass movement. In a similar vein, Ross Terrill, visualises Deng Xiaoping and his successors as displaying a blend of "nationalism and developmentalism of nineteenth century self-strengtheners."[19] Terrill repeatedly invokes the Leninist nature of the Chinese Communist Party, the autocratic traditions from Chinese dynastic history and the People's Republic of China's (PRC) increasing control of previously non-integrated peripheral lands to assert that the PRC is not a real nation but "is indeed an empire of our time, as out of place as a fish in trees." This interpretation of China as a "nation" also does not hold ground given the complexities of contemporary nation-state system.

Some scholars have attributed Chinese nationalism solely to being an anti-imperialist nationalist tradition of the early twentieth century. For instance, John Fitzgerald argues that the key factors that gave rise to Chinese nationalism were the repeated aggression against China by the Western powers, and their control over different parts of China since the times of the Opium war of the 1840s.[20] But this explanation cannot suffice to explain the contemporary dialectics of Chinese nationalism. Since the past decades have been marked by a huge modernisation drive, the nationalism debate has also been moulded by the study of the linkages between development and nationalism.

This link-up also meant that nationalism began to be seen as a political tool of the state to amass and maintain power. Henrietta Harrison delves into the transformation of nationalism into an ideology that never meant a simple allegiance to the nation or nation-state.[21] He postulates that ever since the late nineteenth century Chinese nationalism has been a means by which people made claims for political power at both the lowest and the highest levels of Chinese politics. This was also substantiated by the use of symbolism to provide legitimacy to the party.

Recent deliberations on the nature of Chinese nationalism have been initiated in the backdrop of a "China threat" syndrome, a perception moulded primarily by the Western intelligentsia. The economic burgeoning of the Chinese economy has stimulated a "threat" perception, which in the Western perspective needs to be "contained." This threat is conceptualized within the repercussions from the transcendence of the Chinese economy from the second tier to the first tier according to Immanuel Wallerstein's theory on a single-capitalist world economic system.[22] The Western literati has been influential in shaping the discourse that given the nature of influence of Chinese nationalism on its foreign policy since 1979, China in the twenty-first century would become more like Germany and Japan of the nineteenth century. That is, as an economically strong power it will embark on the path of military and foreign aggression resulting in the destabilization of global power structures.

The progression of Chinese nationalism has also been related to the global hierarchy of nation-states. In this context, Thomas Metzger and others have emphasised the continuity of the Chinese tradition in modern Chinese political thought and hence have underscored the particularity of Chinese ideology and institutions.[23] Modernist scholars like Harumi Befu, believe that the notion of a cultural core got projected into the eighteenth century as an anti-imperialist Cultural Revolution.[24] Rebecca Karl, in her book, *Staging the World, Chinese Nationalism at the Turn of the Twentieth Century*, observes the significant break when modern China broke away from its imperial past and relates China's particularity to the structure of global capitalist modernity.

Instead of conceiving of modernity as a level playing field for various nations, Karl emphasizes the hierarchical nature of global space in the modern world and links the emergence of nationalism in China with the dynamics of global capitalist spatial relations. She contends that Chinese nationalists developed nationalism as they viewed their position in the world-system, a position that entailed struggle against imperialism and colonialism. Since Chinese intellectuals established their nationalism based on an awareness of their structural location in global space; they naturally supported other anti-colonial movements from similar structural locations.[25]

Contradicting Anderson's view, she cautions against the tendency of conflating the nation with the state. She further criticizes Anderson's argument that nationalism emerged with the demise of traditional social forms and with the development of a homogeneous notion of time, which was associated with print capitalism. According to her, the problem is that "in deconstructing the a priori nation (whether culturally or politically understood), local studies tend to see nationalism as essentially irrelevant to local practices, thus tending to reinforce the synonymity of nationalism and the central state (or the pursuit of one)."

Like the post-colonialists, she also contests the teleology associated with modernization theorists, who assert that pre-modern societies must emulate modern ones. The temporal categories of modern and pre-modern are not useful when discussing nations in the global capitalist world. All regions in the capitalist world-system can be considered "modern," and one has to explain elements associated with pre-modernity in certain regions, such as the lack of liberal institutions, in relation to dynamics of the global system.

Karl shifts the emphasis away from the narrative to economic and political relations. So, while post-colonialists associate the dominant nationalisms with Western narratives and seek to find indigenous non-nationalist alternatives, Karl grounds nationalism in global power relations. Non-western nationalisms specifically Chinese nationalism, are not just instantiations of a Universalist discourse, rather, they emerge, as elites understand relations of domination in a new global order.[26]

However, all assumptions made by Karl cannot be accepted in totality. While she accurately points towards drawing non-temporal dimensions to understand the phenomenon of nationalism, she negates the intertwined nature of the Chinese state with this ideology. Since, China has for long exhibited a Party state tendency, the grounding of this concept in China has to relent to the uncompromising authority of the state, which is primarily the reason why Duara attempts to seek the alternatives to state nationalism in indigenous and plural identities.

Many scholars correspondingly highlight the dangers of a jingoistic Chinese nationalism. David Shambaugh, for instance, claims "a succession of Chinese governments have periodically stoked xenophobia for their own purposes—from the boxer rebellion at the turn of the century to Chiang Kai-shek's 'neo-fascist manifesto' in the 1930s, to Mao's cultural Revolution." Thus, he argues that such a manifestation of Chinese nationalism could produce severe consequences for the world at large.

Christopher Hughes in his book, *Chinese Nationalism in the Global Era*, dwells on the discursive nature of the concepts of nationalism and globalisation. He alleges that China's much-vaunted "peaceful rise" is shadowed by a resurgent nationalism that has become a key factor in the ruling party's political calculations.[27] The resurgence can be seen as a bottom-up phenomenon, with popular opinions constraining the options open to the decision makers. While China's leaders and scholars present a view of the peaceful rise of China, the popular writers captivate the burgeoning commercial market by speaking ominously about "China under the shadow of globalization", or despairing over the lack of national self-confidence revealed by the proliferation of signs advertising "China's long island" and the "Manhattan of the East."

New social groups which have been formed due to the "reform and opening up" under Deng Xiaoping and the Three Represents of Jiang Zemin, have provided an ideological justification for the emergence of an *elitist techno-nationalism*.[28] A belief that science and education can "rejuvenate the nation" is fuelling the decisions of the leadership. Thus, the Chinese Communist Party has allowed this new class that comprises technical personnel, entrepreneurs, and managers of public and non-public and foreign enterprises to join its echelons.[29]

The growing discontent amongst the intellectuals, who vie for democracy and identify with increasingly iconistic student demonstrations such as the Tiananmen Square incident, requisites proliferation of nationalist politics into the broader discussions of key policy areas, especially as the Internet and a commercialised publishing industry have opened up new spaces for dissent. Much of the political leadership is perplexed with the need for balancing popular demonstrations and foreign policy issues. Most considerably, discomforted by how it is reflected in the China–Japan relations, Bruce Cumings observes that "to be ... a Chinese nationalist was to be anti-Japanese" for any lay citizen of China. Allen Whiting also notes that the events of 1989 catalysed a brief period of assertive nationalism in China aimed against the West.[30]

Delving further into the international repercussions of Chinese nationalism, Richard Bernstein and Ross Munro warn- "driven by nationalist sentiment, a yearning to redeem the humiliations of the past, and the simple urge for international power, China is seeking to replace the United States as the dominant power in Asia."[31] Similarly Samuel P. Huntington states that the Chinese have increasingly put forward their intention to resume their historic role of "the pre-eminent power in East Asia" and "to bring to an end the overlong century of humiliation and subordination to the West and Japan." James Lilley agrees with this position while stating that "there is a rallying cry for Chinese everywhere ... that after a century of humiliation and Mao's social and economic experiments China's time has come ... it will rise in the world to the place it deserves."[32]

Even a early as 1964, David E Apter anticipated that China would resort to nationalism and political leaders in socialist countries may turn to "greater nationalism" in order to compensate for weakness in solidarity and identity. He believed this would occur since nationalism has an ability to incorporate primordial loyalties "in a readily understandable synthesis" and thus provide for the needed identity and solidarity. He suggests a "substitutive capacity" of nationalism which was effectively utilized by the CCP leadership.[33]

However, the cultural aspect of the Chinese civilization can hardly be ignored if one has to understand China's resurgence as a nation. The resurgence of cultural nationalism in China is strongly evident in its foreign policy agendas. Soren Clausen sheds light on the deconstruction and reconstruction of culture and redefines how culture operates in the Chinese case. He believes "that culture is a set of understandings and consciousness under active construction by which individuals interpret the world around them..."[34] The deconstruction of "cultural nationalism" occurs under certain circumstances and traits that exemplify the new culture. Globalisation reaffirms the role played by culture in the spread of nationalism, as postulated by Arjun Appadurai, and global cultural flows move in a number of "non-isomorphic paths" thus, creating a complex interplay between global cultural homogenisation and disjunction.

The different levels of discourse on cultural nationalism in China are constructed in the shape of a pyramid where official party declarations and ideological guidelines remain at the top level, a bit below them is the "authoritative discourse" conducted by the main national media, directly or indirectly under the official control, further below is the section of less established intellectual rebels who provide scope for a much broader cultural debate involving art, literature *et al.* And at the bottom remains the popular culture that gives the space for mass-opinion building.[35]

Over all, most Western sinologists agree on the fact that Chinese nationalism has been an integral part of the nation's polity and economy since its very inception. The fast paced transformation from an oft-quoted "semi-periphery" to a "rising super-power" bulwarked by the entrepreneurial elite[36] not only rescinded the future of socialism in China but also debunked the notion of a one-trajectory (same stages of development) growth for all nations believed by many scholars previously.[37]

Besides the renewal of the cultural aspect of nationalism, several scholars are also foraying into other factors which might explain the spread of nationalism. Edward Friedman makes an interesting observation on the political geography of Chinese nationalism. He believes any polity contains competing nationalisms given the difference in experiences among people who identify with different historical roots hence pursue variant agendas—both economically and patriotically. Their perceptions of situating the nation differently in the region and the world lead them to compete for their identities in a political arena.[38]

He configures that Chinese nationalism underwent different phases of transformation depending on its movement from region to region that it moved from southern China to the northern areas and was manifested in a change of perspective from a pro-Japanese approach to an anti-Japanese approach. With each movement the nation was re-imagined. In contrast to the south's anti-British and anti-Manchu nationalism the northern antagonism of the Japanese is a recent construction. This northern nationalism was spearheaded by an anti-American sentiment by Mao as the leader of the movement. Mao's nationalism was meant to legitimise his aim to see socialist China becoming a world power. He categorises the territorial spaces into a five-region zone: the north, south, east, and west and centre, and construes Chinese nationalism as moving in between these directions at different times according to different needs.

To summarize, the earlier concerns gyrated around defining Chinese nationalism through categories like atavistic nationalism, patriotic nationalism, developmental nationalism, reactive nationalism, xenophobic narcissism, futuristic politicization, jingoistic nationalism and irredentist nationalism and most overarching, as ethnic and cultural nationalism. Sinologists today have begun to deliberate on the repercussions of nationalism on state behaviour and its capacity to work as a tool for covert nationalist goals. But the contemporary scenario can be best explained by James Townsend's argument of the presence of more than one nation or potential nations in a state today and the fluctuating nature of loyalties that different communities exhibit towards the nation at different times.

He accurately surmises that "nationalist movements and doctrines rise and fall, expand and contract, and change their statements about what the nation is or is going to be ... the official nation is mainly one of aspiration, not social reality." While Townsend's assumption that popular nationalism was not so strong and less intense than the state made believe could hold true for the time period he was considering,[39] it can be argued for the contemporary realities that modernisation and globalisation have enlarged the sphere of influence of nationalism from the elite to the local masses and hence has provided a populist character to the movement. It is possible to suggest that "culture" has resurfaced as one of the most influential sites of generating nationalism, if not the mainstream identity of regurgitating those ideas.

Chinese Perspectives

While an inherent bias would be reasonably present in any analysis by a citizen of a country when considering issues of national pride and patriotism, several Chinese scholars have attempted to steer clear of such limitations. In tandem with above-cited bifurcations, the Chinese historiography too operates within the dichotomy of "ethnic" or "modern" genesis of Chinese nationalism. While some sinologists expound the cultural basis of Chinese nationalism others reiterate the modernity of the same, i.e. a consequence of imported European enlightened ideas. In her seminal work, Maria Hsia Chang, one of the earliest scholars on study of Chinese nationalism, argues how a stable economic and political structure provided the opportunity for redirecting China's efforts towards defining new goals for its domestic and international policies. She defined this nationalism as an "irredentist nationalism,"[40] which was characterized by a desire of an existing state to retrieve lost territories and ethnic kin. It was a post-state phase of nationalism that was activated when a sovereign state which was already in existence became strong enough to articulate and press its territorial claims.[41]

The opening of the economy during the 1980s brought along several Westernizing influences, which the layman citizen had aspired but the government felt threatened by them and began a struggle to preserve its legitimacy. This was evident in the suppression of people's opinion in incidents like the Tiananmen Square, which was in turn justified by the media under Deng's leadership as an implicit threat to the state, while negating the critiques by the Western nations as ostensible lack of democracy in China. Explaining its origins, Jisi Wang observes that Chinese nationalism stemmed from a "long-standing pride that was frustrated by Western and Japanese conquering of China in the modern history."

Other recent scholars situate the nationalist discourse within China's attempts to establish itself as the *numero uno* power in the international system. Ying-shih Yu observes how the rise of a new Chinese nationalism is aimed at "replacing the dominant position of the West in the world and making the twenty-first century a Chinese century." Wang Yi Wei believes that in an attempt to seek a new identity as a responsible country, China is attempting to gain a candid and inclusive national spirit, harmonious national character, and a moderate sense of national pride. And under the new framework "of the nation, by the nation, for the nation" it is trying to adapt to the compulsions of the "nationalization stage, modernization stage, internationalization stage." He further asserts that to shape a new Chinese national identity through modifying the so-called new nationalism is merely to continue the myth of Chinese nationalism in the new era.

As the largest developing country and a rising world power, China has to achieve modernization and internationalization at the same time and keep the whole nation united on the basis of the three compulsions of historical traditions, international trends, and world identity. For this purpose, the new nationalism is manifested in the garb of building a harmonious world of lasting peace and common prosperity.[42] In his lecture on "the revival of Chinese nationalism," Gung Wu Wang argues that Chinese nationalism has many faces, and "the most common face concerns questions of polity and stresses the recovery of sovereignty, the unification of divided territory, and national self-respect."[43]

While Wang calls this the most common face of Chinese nationalism, Tianbiao Zhu avers it to be the ultimate goal of Chinese nationalism that is Chinese nationalism seeks and constantly endeavours to preserve national independence. To reach this goal, the state has to protect its territorial integrity, promote a good image of itself in the international community, and engage in economic development in order to build comprehensive national power. These are key state interests and are the means to reach the goal of nationalism. As far as the manifestation of nationalism is concerned in the foreign policy dimensions, he believes that it has been a state constructed nationalism that aimed at building amicable relations with stronger nations for obtaining resources and technology for domestic economic development right since the establishment of the PRC.

The shift to nationalism as a result of pragmatic considerations was also evident in China's behaviour. Suisheng Zhao in his book, *Chinese Foreign Policy: Pragmatism and Strategic Behaviour*, emphasises how in the 1990s China's leadership abandoned Marxism for pragmatic nationalism, which he defines as "a commitment to avoid dogmatic constraints and adopt whatever approach proves most effective in making China strong."[44] Dogmatic constraints have been construed to mean 'Marxism-Leninism' and 'Mao Zedong' thought that were impeding the process of China's development.

Pragmatic nationalism is seen as an alternative to nativism and anti-traditionalism, the two competing currents in Chinese political thought. While, Zhao defines "nativism" as seeing China's problems as caused by foreign imperialism and that China must look inward to reassert traditional values in order to recover its rightful place of world leadership. On the other hand, "anti-traditionalism" is viewed as a strand that holds Chinese tradition as a burden that must be abandoned completely in order for China to embrace the foreign-imbibed strengths of modernization. He demonstrates that the policies of Jiang Zemin and Hu Jintao have both employed nationalism as the most practical and effective way to assemble domestic support for building a modern Chinese nation-state.

Lei Guang in his article *"Real Politik Nationalism"* characterizes Chinese nationalism as fusing real politik ideas and ideals in a fervent quest for national identity and power. He defines that real politik nationalism symbolizes a severe threat to China, not in terms of the country's unique culture or history, but as a key tool of breach of the prevailing norms of the nation-state system, whose key dimensions include sovereignty, territoriality and international legitimacy.[45] He links the rise of nationalism in China with the demise of communism in Soviet Union in the early 1990s, which is when the Chinese government shifted its focus away from communism and towards the rhetoric of nationalism. Thus, along with Thomas Christensen he argues that the essence of the Westphalian system has been integrated into the Chinese nationalist discourse.

The fusion of political realism and nationalistic aspirations in formulation of real politik nationalism is a palpable change, which visualises sovereign control as an important *leitmotif* of Chinese nationalism. And this change can be best understood if one restrains from associating Chinese nationalism as primarily an anti-western movement. In this regard, an evaluation of China's foreign policy in comparison to other Asian countries like India may provide a larger dimension to the study of Chinese nationalism. Further on, Simon Shen in his attempt to reconstruct Chinese Nationalism treats it as a non-unitary and segmented movement practiced by different people for different reasons. However, her study is a comparative analysis of the role of nationalism in Sino-American relations and thus cannot be generalized for the purpose of understanding the phenomenon at large.[46]

Deliberating on the role played by nationalism in the economic integration of the Chinese nation, Leong H. Liew and Doug Smith agreed on the role of nationalism as providing a motivation for the "modicum of cooperative behaviour among economic actors in China's economy, while it was in transition from central planning to market economy." On the other hand, Mobo Changfan Gao visualised the emergence of a neo-nationalism based on the twin foundations of Western conceptualisation of post-colonialism and post-modernism whereby China is believed to have skipped the stage of modernity experienced by the West and made a leap into the post-modernist structural paradigms. Though Mobo successfully raises these questions, he is unsuccessful in providing satisfactory answers.

An intriguing development in the study of Chinese nationalism has been the emergence of populist Chinese opinions on their state and nationalism on the Internet. Yang Jianli[47] commenting on the various facets of Chinese nationalism, surmised that on one hand it is quite pragmatic, on the other, it is fostered by "vassal nationalists" who are China's elites working in congruence with the party.[48] He categorizes four kinds of nationalism in contemporary China: Pragmatic, Vassal nationalism, Popular nationalism and Human rights patriotism.

Xuefei Ren analyses the relationship between architecture and nation building in the age of globalisation centring on the debates and controversies about the National Stadium, the main sports venue for the 2008 Olympics in Beijing. He argues that nationalism, along with the cultural ideology of global consumerism, drives the production of flagship architectural projects in China. The dilemma between nationalism and global consumerism has led state politicians and bureaucrats to opt for a global architectural language to narrate national ambitions. The study conducted by him reveals the rationale underlying the search for global architecture among political elites in China, as well as its mixed consequences for local cultural discourses and politics.

Thus, there are perceptive differences within the Chinese scholarship on how to understand nationalism within this Asian behemoth. Though themselves bound by inherent expectations of nationalist visions several authors have felt free to opine about the elitist nature of contemporary Chinese nationalism, while others have endorsed the state's view of anti-western nationalism. Unfortunately, the literature on Chinese nationalism is largely restricted to Western and Chinese perspectives and there are very few scholars who fall out of this division and have contributed to the corpus. It is however essential to take into account these few voices from the Indian sub-continent.

Alternate Perspectives

Chinese nationalism provides a dynamic sphere for academic research as witnessed from the previous discussion. Of the smaller cluster of sinologists in India, Prasenjit Duara provides a nuanced view of Chinese nationalism. His work is pivotal since he suggests the possibility of perceiving a nation through "multiple narratives" engendered within local, national and transnational levels, that is, in terms of a "bifurcated conception of history." He attempts at a deconstruction of the larger corpus of understanding of the Chinese nationalism and argues that nationalism in China is not simply a modern phenomenon. Under long periods of foreign rule in the twelfth century, segments of the scholar class in China had already begun to advocate a notion of the Han community and fatherland (*guo*), bringing together state and people.[49] However, this proposition seems to be best defining the roots of forming a nation and not nationalism as an ideology or principle. Recognizing this flaw, he revised this definition in his later work that the system of nation-state that now prevails in China cannot sustain itself solely based on the conceptualisation of a "Han" nation.

In his book, he contends that the novelty of the modern nationalism lies in the 'world-system of nation states' that has manifested itself on a global level and sanctions the nation-state as the only legitimate expression of sovereignty and also enables a swift transition to a modern capitalist society. The global *institutional* revolution has produced its own extremely powerful representations of the nation-state wherein the political identity shifts between different loci and nationalism is best seen as a relational "identity."[50] He underlines the significance of looking at *class* as a historical category, as a "trope" that constructs a powerful representation of the nation. For instance, in China, Li Dazhao imagined the "nation in the language of a class"—the Chinese people were a national proletariat oppressed by the capitalists. This conception got extended to the domestic scenario during the Cultural Revolution and instigated an attempt to shape a nation in the image of the idealised proletariat.

Similarly, he further deliberates on the elevation of Mao Zedong to a "role of the supreme theorist" and the creation of a Chinese model of revolutionary transformation in the late 1930s which led to embodiment of "nationalist distinctiveness" in a model of class struggle. He also suggests that the Chinese history came to be influenced by the enlightenment mode by the early twentieth century and the Chinese intelligentsia developed a progressive history modelled on the European experience of liberation from medieval/autocratic domination. In the historiography of modern China, the project of "defining the national product" preoccupied most of sophisticated historians that revolved around the three terms—"race, nation and history."

The global discourse of social Darwinism and the anti-Manchu's politics of the republican revolution forced a *conception of the national community* that was made of the Han race (for instance Liang Qichao, Fu Sinian and Minzudi Guomin are some scholars who argue in favour of this discourse). This unity is historically embedded through the traditional perception of being a cultural nation/civilisation and its links with Confucianism. While conceding a relative attempt of debunking the nationalist histories by Ellie Kedourie and Benedict Anderson, Duara expresses suspicion about the "novelty of the mode of consciousness" that forms the basis of their understanding. He agrees with the primordialists in stating that the incipient forms of identities which may or may not develop into a nation were present from historical times.

He further extrapolates the quandary of accepting historical representations as such, based on Paul Ricoeur's discourse on time and narrative, which seeks to understand historical facts within the realm of temporality and traces left from the past. He observes the May 4th Movement which engendered a specific break from the past was also not devoid of a leadership (Sun Yatsen) which relied more on traditional organisational forms to build the nation and became victims of the radical nationalists' rage, who saw no value in the past. The aftermath of the movement saw a deliberate attempt to visualise the "formation of a Chinese nation by remaking the people" through anti-religious campaigns.

Tracing the campaigns from the New Policy reforms (*Xinzheng*) to the republican revolution, the GMD/Kuomintang phase, and into the present, he depicts how various political groups tried to manoeuvre the writing of history to their own advantage. He also deduces that the effort to make the "people" in the image of the new world and the nation had extremely destructive implications for the rural community. The anti-Manchu campaigns of the secret societies were appropriated as an ideology to devise complex strategies of bringing together two parties and the clash between the tradition and the modernity at this juncture calls for an understanding of dispersed meanings in a wider historical context.

The conspicuous absence of a civil society in much of twentieth-century China can be seen as triumph of the discourse of the global system of nation-states.[51] The state led reforms curbed the spirit of individualist dissensions which are now under the scrutiny of a new generation of scholars. He believes that the provincial narratives of the nation and the progressive decline of the Maoist narrative of "great Han, anti-imperialist nationalism" which celebrate minority histories and disparage a unified national tradition have created one such space. Recapping the need to separate culture from political propitiation he has proposed culture as a tool to oppose modernity. He is however perplexed that nationalism as an ideology, today, is most threatened by the needs of transnational capitalism and multi-culturalism. He restrains his analysis to the narrativization of concepts wherein the power groups who continue to shape history, bring about a transformation.

In this much congruent argument, he has vociferously argued for the need to question linear—totalizing histories and administered—"culture" as a tool to discover new Chinese nationalism. However, this alternative for evaluating contemporary nationalism seems to be a critical failure in his conception. While culture can form a part of this endeavour, it cannot solely determine the spatiality of contemporary Chinese nationalism.

Abanti Bhattacharya also traces the course of Chinese nationalism and observes that it has become a product of its own historical experience of culturalism and Marxism–Leninism. She believes that in the post-cold war period it has further become associated with the quest for comprehensive national power.[52] Most of this literature however, focuses on defining the nature of Chinese nationalism and understanding how it fits into the larger understanding of nationalism. It is being attempted here to understand the *modus operandi* of Chinese nationalism.

Discursive Frameworks and Chinese Nationalism

Though as a state China boasts of a much more monolithic-constitutive base in terms of the Han majority, than any other contemporary nation, yet it struggles to establish its legitimacy due to the manner in which it handles internal dissent and international calumny. Thus, it is within this process of the redefinition of its state structures and international behaviour that the contemporary Chinese nationalism is remoulded. There is a need to avoid juxtaposition of contemporary Western concepts strictly according to their definitions while observing their functioning in the Eastern civilizations, which exhibit myriad forms of identity formation and a relatively different phase of the development cycle.

In the backdrop of the innovative global-local spaces, the present work aims to evaluate the impact of *a century of humiliation (bai nian guo chi)* followed and overlapped by a parallel *century of nationalism* on the institutions functioning within the Chinese Public sphere and thereby study the advancing notions of Chinese Nationalism. It will be interesting to observe the changing dynamics of nationalism by monitoring the interaction between the public spaces created by the forces of globalization. In particular it is imperative to see if a redefinition of nationalism is emerging, which besides economic development, is being buttressed through the "media" in China. Second, how is this metamorphosed nationalism *"managing, realigning and curbing"* the dissentions and contradictory spaces created by global onslaught. Third, how is the nationalistic rigour being enhanced by the deployment of soft power techniques like the public culture of sports and cinema?

The collective agency of the government has been trying to institutionalize a structure resulting in the incineration of an individual's identity and the prioritisation of community over an individual. But how far has the state been successful in doing so. The individual identities are not necessarily obliterated though the regeneration of discourse on nationalism through movies and sports shapes them to a large extent on a day-to-day basis. Further on, nationalism engenders in form of a strong psychological commitment by the citizens towards their country and hence it is a collective quest of transiting from an imagined community to a real community under the aegis of a leadership. The multiple histories congregate into one single whole as they describe the functionality of nationalism through a state's behaviour and come to be clubbed under what I argue as "Discursive Nationalism" borrowing the framework of Michel Foucault's Discursive formations.

Discursive, etymologically speaking, is often adduced in reference to a style of writing and speaking, something a structural which moves meanderingly from one sort to another. However, Foucault's delineation of relations in the field of discourse will be most appropriate to contextualize this work. Discursive nationalism is a system whereby I study the phenomenon as a thought which is reconstituted on the basis of a definite discursive totality. The circumference of analysis treats both the statements and the intentions of the leaders in terms of both conscious as well as unconscious activities. It presupposes the existence of "semi-silence" that precedes the articulation of a discourse.[53] Discursive formations signify both the latent as well as the manifest dimensions of a phenomenon. Thus, any articulation or argument contextualised within this paraphernalia seeks to observe the existence, functioning, reciprocal determination and transformation of the institutions and processes in a given outline, in this case: China.

Nationalism as a discursive practice consists not only of traditions, observations, heterogeneous practices but also a corpus of knowledge which transcribes a series of descriptive statements in a recognisable play of metaphor.[54] Hence, print-capitalism as a cradle to the genesis of national consciousness does not solely manifest nationalism; it becomes the primary tool of the discursive formations. The creation of languages of power[55] is not in terms of making the Chinese Mandarin a powerful language, in this case, or for that matter any other language, but the use of the language for the purposes of achieving the goal of national aims and ambitions (who or what might determine these aims is a different matter altogether).

Thus, while making Mandarin the official language might be done for the purpose of convenience of print or official convenience, it is the act of imposition on those who do not adhere to its ethno-cultural apparatus that it becomes an accomplice of nationalist agendas. The realm of discourse also engenders as well as elicits a social consensus and a psychological commitment from the people involved in its dispersion. What is important to decipher is the manifest discourse which is not so visible overtly and is believed to be articulated in the "semi-silence" that precedes any event.

Besides dwelling on the malignant or benign nature of this nationalism it is imperative to study the ***processes and institutions*** which come into play for the manifestation of the same. The CCP leadership has provided strong sustenance for uninterrupted governance by effectively eliminating power struggles in the political arena. Though there are officially eight parties in China, the CCP has continued to hold monopoly over the government structures and decision-making processes. The strong influence of personalities in the Chinese-nation building is also tremendous and gives a wider perspective on the shaping of the nationalist discourse by Chinese leadership.

The following chapter deals with the conceptualisation of Chinese nationalism through the perspective of prominent Chinese leaders who moulded the discourse over the past century. Being at the apex of hierarchy these leaders have wielded unprecedented power to shape or distort the pattern of national culture building according to their convenience and understanding. And for this purpose they have not only relied on the traditional tools of war and foreign policy but also technology and cultural influence. The intent is to study the continuities or the disrupters and the points of diffraction in the self- and world view of the Chinese through the discourse of their leaders. In this day and age when complex interdependence between technology and dissemination of ideas has been established it becomes necessary to gauge the changing face of public sphere in contemporary times for which the model propounded by Habermas remains the benchmark. Thus, the third chapter takes into account the electronic and print media as a tool of state for whipping up nationalism.

The fourth chapter analyses the manifestation of nationalist sentiments in the discourse of cinematic presentations through observing the use of cinema as a tool of articulation of national sentiment via the interpellation of the implied national spectators instead of the point of consumption in the Chinese scenario. It further tries to fathom how the Chinese audiences construct their identity in relation to the various products of the national and international film and television industry. Though the entire chapter is based on essentially primary sources, the observations on the causal relationship between nationalism and cinema is largely circumstantial. The fifth chapter dwells on the impact of sports as a spectacle on the nationalist discourse of a nation via a case study of the recently held Beijing Olympics. Finally, certain conclusions are drawn based on the observations made during the course of the research in the sixth chapter.

The work sets out with certain basic premises, notably; the metamorphosed kind of nationalism is managing, realigning and curbing the dissensions and contradictory spaces created in the wake of global onslaught. This nationalistic goal is being achieved mainly through manifesting the soft-power techniques of creating a cultural ambience of peaceful rise of China. The metamorphosis of the temporal dimensions of China's rise, which is becoming a concern for the international community, is jettisoned through an endemic discourse of nationalism.

But, it is not the intention to make an extensive study of the Chinese film or sports industry and therefore the work is restricted to a certain number of movies or sports events depicting nationalism at their best, that too produced in the past few decades. The work will also be limited in terms of taking into account only one case study, that is, of the Beijing Olympics along with a cursory glance at the history of sports development in China. Within this framework, the study analyses how far China will be able to achieve its goals through the power of attraction or soft power and use it as a tool to further its nationalism on an international stage.[56]

NOTES

1. The closest Chinese adaptation reads *minzu zhuyi,* which can be translated as *minzu* meaning ethnicity and *zhuyi* meaning love. Thus the word literally means love for ethnicities and not necessarily love for one's country. Therefore, there is a contestation on the usage of this word. Various scholars argue that it should instead be *Guojia zhuyi* which can be understood as love for one's country.
2. Benedict Anderson, *Imagined Communities: Reflections on the Origin and Spread of Nationalism,* Verso, London 1991, p. xiii.
3. This was adopted as the official theme of the Beijing Olympics delineating a more internationally accommodative stance.
4. A term popularised by Habermas and which is still nebulous and emergent in the Chinese polity. Though it is highly debated amongst scholars whether to construe the Chinese cultural spaces through this terminology, but it still remains the only effective frame of reference to understand the growth of alternative spaces.
5. The present work deals with sports, cinema and the Internet as part of the Chinese public sphere and does not take into account all kinds of public spaces.
6. Sue Tuohy, Cultural Metaphors and Reasoning: Folklore Scholarship and Ideology in Contemporary China,' *Asian Folklore Studies,* 50 (1), 1991, pp. 189–220.
7. Masako Ikegami, 'China's grand strategy of peaceful rise—a prelude to a new cold war?' in Hsin- Huang Michael Hsiao and Cheng-yi Lin (ed.), *Rise of China: Beijing's Strategies and Implications for the Asia-Pacific,* Politics in Asia series, Routledge, Taylor and Francis Group, London & New York, 1991, p. 44. The author observes that Japan in the 1930s showed a similar pattern to current China: the economy was entirely controlled by the *Zaibatsu* closely tied up with the government while currently the absolute majority of Chinese enterprises are controlled by the CCP elites; in the state apparatus the military was in position to exert influence in state decision-making just like the PLA's role in the Chinese politics; severe income gaps and poverty in the rural areas caused much social tension, which eventually harboured extremism and 'super-nationalism'.
8. For a more detailed account of the debate on how nations and nationalism emerge, see Hutchinson and Smith, *Nationalism- Critical Concepts in Political Science,* Volume I, Routledge Publishers, London and New York, 2000; Eric Hobsbawm, *Nations and Nationalism since 1780,* Cambridge University Press, London, 1990; and Ernest Gellner, *Nations and Nationalism,* Basil Blackwell Publishers, Oxford UK, 1983.
9. Hutchinson and Smith, *Nationalism- Critical Concepts in Political Science,* Volume I, Routledge Publishers, London and New York, 2000, p. xxvii.
10. Anderson, no. 2.
11. According to the commonly known encyclopedic definition.
12. Dittmer and Samuel, "In search of a theory of National Identity" in Lowell Dittmer and Samuel Kim (ed.) *China's Quest for National Identity,* Cornell University Press, London and Ithaca, 1993, p.13.
13. E.J. Hobsbawm, *Nations and Nationalism since 1780; Programme, Myth, Reality,* Cambridge University Press, London, 1990, p. 10.
14. According to the definition given by Lowell Dittmer and Samuel Kim.
15. A system of modern nation-states formally recognized as per the Peace Treaty of Westphalia signed in 1648.

16. David Shambaugh (ed.), "Introduction," in *The Modern Chinese State*, Cambridge, University Press, Cambridge, 2000.
17. James Townsend, "Chinese Nationalism," *The Australian Journal of Chinese Affairs*, 27, January 1992, pp. 97–130.
18. Joseph Levenson, *Confucian China and Its Modern Fate*, University of California Press, Berkeley, 1958.
19. Ross Terrill, *The New Chinese Empire*, Basic Books, New York, 2003, p. 74.
20. John Fitzgerald, "The Nationless State; Search for a Nation in Modern Chinese Nationalism," *Australian Journal of Chinese Affairs*, 33, 1995, p. 76.
21. Henrietta Harrison, *China, Inventing the Nation*, Bloomsbury, USA, 2002.
22. Mao also accepted such a three world conceptualization wherein he believed the US, and the Soviet Union belonged to the first world, Japan, Europe, Australia and Canada to the second world and China, India, the African countries and other Asian countries except Japan belonged to the third world. Source: 'On the question of the differentiation of the three worlds, Mao Zedong on Diplomacy (1998), Foreign Language Press, Beijing, p.454.
23. Thomas Metzger, *Escape from Predicament: Neo-Confucianism and China's Evolving Political Culture*, Columbia University Press, New York, 1998.
24. Harumi Befu (ed), *Cultural Nationalism in East Asia: Representation and Identity*, University of California, Berkeley, 1993, p. 1.
25. Her book consists of an innovative interpretation of Wang Xiaonong's Beijing opera, *Gua zhong lan yin*, which deals with the crisis of the Polish nation. Karl provides the first and the only remaining translation of the play in an appendix, and deals with the views of Chinese intellectuals about Hawai'i, the Philippines and revolution, the Boer War, late Qing pan-Asianism, and reform and revolution in Turkey.
26. Viren Murthy, "Staging the World, Chinese Nationalism at the Turn of the Twentieth Century," *China Review International*, 9(1), Spring 2002, University of Hawaii Press, pp. 157–63.
27. Christopher Hughes, *Chinese Nationalism in the Global Era*, Routledge, New York, 2006, pp. 7–14.
28. A term initially used by Richard Samuels to explain the Japanese strategy of linking economic development with the state security.
29. Christopher Hughes, 'Chinese Nationalism in the Global Era,' *Open Democracy News Analysis*, 17 April 2006, Online URL: *http://www.opendemocracy.net/democracy-china/nationalism_3456.jsp*
30. Lei Guang, "Realpolitik Nationalism, International Sources of Chinese Nationalism," *Modern China*, 31(4), October 2005, pp. 487–514.
31. Bernstein & Munro, "The Coming Conflict with America," *Foreign Affairs*, 76, March/April 1997, p. 19.
32. Zhao Shuisheng, "Chinese Nationalism and its International Orientations," *Political Science Quarterly*, The Academy of Political Science, 115(1), Spring 2000, pp. 1–33.
33. David E Apter, "Introduction," in Apter (ed.), *Ideology and Discontent*, Free Press of Glencoe, New York, 1964, pp. 24–28.
34. Soren Clausen, "Party Policy and 'National Culture': Towards a State-Directed Cultural Nationalism in China?" in Kjeld Erik Brodsgaard and David Strand (ed.), *Reconstructing Twentieth Century China: State Control, Civil Society and National Identity*, Clarendon Press, Oxford, 1998, p. 256.
35. Ibid., p. 260.
36. James Petras, "Past, Present and Future of China: From semi-colony to World Power?" *Journal of Contemporary Asia Quarterly*, 36(4), 2006, p. 435.

37. Terence K Hopkins, "The World system of Capitalism, Past and Present," in Walfer L Goldfrank (ed.), *Political Economy of the World-system Annuals*, Vol. II, Sage Publications, p. 22.
38. Edward Friedman, "Where is Chinese Nationalism? The political Geography of a moving Project?" *Nations and Nationalism*, 14(4), October 2008, pp. 721–38.
39. The primary sections propagating nationalism have been considered to be the elite and the government officials by Townsend. Maria Hsia Chang concurs with his viewpoint.
40. Irredentist nationalism was first conceptualized by Hedva Ben-Israel in Naomi Chazan (ed.), *Irredentism and international Politics.*
41. Maria Hsia Chang, *Return of the Dragon, China's Wounded Nationalism*, Westview Press, USA, 2001, p. 205.
42. Yi-wei Wang, Seeking China's New identity: The Myth of Chinese Nationalism, *Fudan Journal of the Humanities and Social Sciences*, 10(4), 2008.
43. Wang Gung Wu, *The Revival of Chinese Nationalism*, Lecture Series 6, International Institute for Asian Studies, Leiden, 1996, p. 8.
44. Suisheng Zhao, *Chinese Foreign Policy: Pragmatism and Strategic Behavior*, Armonk, New York and London, Me Sharpe, 2004, p. 253.
45. Lei Guang, no. 30, pp. 487–514.
46. Simon Shen, *Redefining Nationalism in Modern China: Sino-American Relations and the Emergence of Chinese Public Opinion in the Twentieth Century*, Palgrave Macmillan, Basingstoke, Hants, 2007.
47. The founder of 'Initiatives for China' who served a five-year term for observing labour unrest in China.
48. Yang Jianli, "The Facets of Chinese Nationalism," Editorial, *Washington Post*, 5 May 2008, Online URL: *http://www.washingtonpost.com*
49. Prasenjit Duara, "De-constructing the Chinese Nation," in Jonathan Unger (ed.), *Chinese Nationalism*, M. E. Sharpe, Armonk and London, 1996.
50. Prasenjit Duara, *Rescuing History from the Nation—Questioning Narratives of Modern China*, University of Chicago Press, USA, 1995, p. 9.
51. An interesting juxtaposition made by him is a discussion of Gandhi whom he finds quite effective at countering the dominant ideology of the state by preserving the local. However, "in an effort to displace history, he banished historicity itself." Duara contends that a historian's task is to "banish history, but at the same time rescue it" as well.
52. Abanti Bhattacharya, *Chinese Nationalism: The Impact on Policy*, Unpublished PhD Thesis, Jawaharlal Nehru University, New Delhi, 2004.
53. Michael Foucault, *The Archaeology of knowledge*, Tavistock Publications Ltd., Routledge, UK, 1972, p. 28.
54. Ibid., p. 37.
55. Which according to Anderson is a result of standardization of the dominant dialects of the particular ambience.
56. Keohane and Nye, "Power and interdependence in the Information Age," *Foreign Affairs*, September-October 1998, pp. 81–94.

2

The Nationalist Stalwarts

With a ceaseless rhetoric on loyalty and state-centric behaviour insulating the contemporary praxis, associating with the nation has become the predominant determinant of the sense of self amongst the Chinese. In this sense, nationalism in the Chinese historical trajectory is an overwhelmingly "lived" experience and not a visionary ideal. While the traditional endowments primarily reckoned "patriotism" (*aiguo zhuyi*) for the motherland/fatherland and a personal dedication to the son of the heaven, the modern conceptions rely on the effectiveness of nationalism as an "ideology" to wield the consolidating purposes of the state and fabricate an identity which rejects the individual for the larger commune.[1]

Nationalism in China has been engendered in different forms at different times. Even though originally, it was the peasants who instigated revolutionary nationalist movement, it was the state that crystallized this doctrine later on. Impeccably, one of the striking features of Chinese nationalism was the steering of the nationalist agenda by the CCP. One could speculate and contend that China's left was also its right, but the quandary is out of scope of the present work for now. An effective analysis of the growth of nationalism in the twentieth and the twenty-first century China, prerequisites an investigation of its historical dimensions and scrutiny of the incidents that were by and large considered of nationalist dispositions.

The metamorphosis in the nature of Chinese nationalism remained closely intertwined with the situational needs of the nation. It can be considered remarkably different from nationalisms in other nations as it provided a parallel space for both statist and ethnic discourse. These two have never been entangled in a rule of contradiction in China, as was perceived in the case of European nationalisms. The earliest instances of nationalistic impulses were traced to the formation of a Chinese identity under the Qin-Shihuang unification in 221 B.C. whereby feudalism was abolished, political power was centralized and all territories were unified into a single state.

This allegedly led to the construction of an identity based primarily on a cultural renovation beginning with "A hundred Schools of thought" movement in which contending schools tried to influence the standards of the dynasty as well as through the efforts of Confucian scholars like Sima Qian-who recorded the old legends and the oral histories in a single tome entitled *"shiji"* (Records of the Historian)[2] and tried to spread an ideology which would bind the civilization together. The works of these scholars overwhelmingly embodied ethno-centric discourses and propagated stable governance based on a system of loyalties and responsibilities.[3]

However, the nature of unification under Qin-Shihuang is highly criticised for its ethno-cultural cleansing and political suppression. Thus, national integration was achieved at a heavy cost to cultural legacies of the past. Given this reason, the nationalist agendas under Qin-Shihuang are contested and not considered an intrinsic part of the Chinese nationalist heritage. Yet, his contribution is culogised and used to stoke up nationalist sentiments as and when the need arises.

The discourse further stresses on the recognition of *huaxia*, the Chinese people based on cultural identity or the *Hanren* (an ethnicised version)/*hanzu* and recognises the birth of a consciousness of being one community as opposed to the identity of the "other." The nature of state was virtually authoritarian and filial piety and submission to political ruler were the normative ideals for the entire society. But, the formation of a Chinese identity leading to the birth of a nationalist consciousness is a far-stretched argument. The polity throughout the ancient times was based on an inward-looking state apparatus that did not work in tandem with any state-system or exhibit a need for recognition as one entity by outsiders. Thus, there was barely any consciousness of a nation-state or nationalism.

Certain beliefs, however, provide a thread of continuity in the development of nationalist rhetoric. For instance, even in ancient times it was the educated elite, which spearheaded the national conscience and was believed to possess the critical faculties to remonstrate an errant emperor.[4] They were influential in shaping the religious and political discourse on all matters of China. In the realm of state-building, these scholars adduced the rationale of *"tong bao"*[5] that is "siblings from the same womb" to explicate the basis for Chinese identity. Yet, this proposition provided an indication only of the feelings of "community" and not the formation of a nationalist identity. Moreover, it exposed the non-territorial notions of the Chinese empire, an adherence to which has become the main cause for many of China's conflicts with its neighbouring countries today.

The primary understanding of the Chinese identity was based on the conceptualisation of *"Sino-centricism"* as postulated by John King Fairbank, wherein the Chinese considered themselves as the only true civilization and all outsiders were regarded as barbarians. Foreigners who wished to establish trade with China had to kowtow before the ruler of the 'middle kingdom', a verbiage from which it derives its name: *'zhong guo'* and carry on activities according to the emperor's will and rules and regulations. This belief has persisted over the last 2000 years of its history and is responsible for the image of China that one sees as a coherent identity today.[6]

Besides the Sino-centric view, the construction of the Chinese identity also ensued through the glorification of national heroes. Prominent among these figures were Genghis Khan, 1210–1227 and Kublai Khan, who were acclaimed for their territorial conquests and reformative zeal. The Chinese empire gained much prominence and glory under these monarchs. But the territorial expansion did not correspond with a consolidation effort and hence the empire remained loosely built.[7] Garnet opines that the absolutist tendencies of the state that came to prominence under these sovereigns were accentuated after the Mongol interlude.[8] Till then, the polity and society that was established at the end of the eleventh century to the disappearance of the Ming Empire did not exhibit any drastic changes.

The nationalist underpinnings during the Manchu or the Qing dynasty (1644–1911) were by and large instigated in the economic realm. The sixteenth and seventeenth centuries witnessed severe financial crisis under the Ming rulers. Although the Manchu regime was able to bring the popular insurrections from peasant troops under control, it could not reign in the corruption being infiltrated into the various ranks of state infrastructure. In addition, a growing presence of foreign influence on the statecraft began to be felt. In retrospect, towards the end of the Qing dynasty two major strands of nationalism emerged. First, the proponents of ethnic nationalism who aimed at overthrowing the Qing government and replacing it with a republican state and second, advocates of cultural and political nationalism who planned to preserve the Qing government and transform it into a constitutional state.

With the enhancement of foreign trade the Chinese economy was pulled into the mercantilist system of trade, albeit as an unequal partner. The East India Company's intervention into the court politics of the Manchu empire further accentuated skirmishes between the company and the local merchants who were being made to suffer huge losses in trade. These losses prompted anger among the local people who entered into war with the foreigners. Given the technological superiority and finesse the foreigners defeated the Chinese repeatedly. The *century of humiliation*, as it commonly came to be viewed, surfaced with the Opium wars in 1840–42 and 1848 and came to an end with the establishment of the PRC in 1949. The feeling of dishonour and stigma that this series of events embedded into the Chinese psyche was deep enough to leave its imprints on many of the foreign policy decisions till date.

Samuel P. Huntington provides one of the preeminent descriptions of the nature of interaction that took place between the Western imperial powers and the Eastern colonies during this period. He surmises that given the nature of civilisational difference between the East and the West, the East had an inherent advantage in its mercantilist spirit while China was inherently disadvantaged given its non-modern structures. Though China never came to be fully colonized but the impact of its interaction with the Western countries during this century was highly detrimental to its national interests. Edward Said, in his book "Orientalism", also made a distinction between the *oriental* and *occidental* to explain the inherent clash between the East and the West. This clash was manifest in the unwillingness of the Chinese rulers to deal with the Western powers on an equal footing, which led to imminent disagreements and thereafter to war.

Discourse of the Century of Humiliation

The Opium wars (1840–42 and 1848), it is largely believed, were a culmination of the resistance offered by the traditional Chinese identity or its *Sino-centric behaviour*, that was unwilling to recognize any other nation at par with it or what Tan Chung described as the *"brave new world."* It is also argued that the Opium war was possibly a tragedy of the "agrarian and bureaucratic" Confucian China's failure in adapting "itself to the commercial, industrial and nationalist revolutions brought about by free trade."[9] The British traders were lured by the lucrative opium exchange for Chinese tea and silk and wanted to take advantage of the opportunity at any cost. While the Chinese were determined to not let the foreigners defile their traditional trade architectures.

The Opium war brought the Chinese face-to-face with the reality of the notions of modern nation-states which were exhibiting renewed fervour to foster their respective economic domination. Through a series of treaties the Western powers extracted concessions from China to tilt the balance of trade in their own interests. The sense of humiliation was instilled deep and long-lasting given the nature of colonialism in China; it was carved into different "spheres of influence" or to put it axiomatically—the "cutting of the Chinese melon" was shared by all strong imperial powers of the contemporary period.

The *treaty of Nanjing* imposed derogatory clauses like—it ceded Hong Kong to Britain in perpetuity, opened Xiamen, Fuzhou, Ningbo and Shanghai ports to foreign trade, and abolished the Hong system, freeing British merchants to deal directly with their Chinese counterparts and most of all levied a war indemnity of 21 million silver dollars, which was the first of its kind known anywhere till then. The political integrity of China was debased further with the *treaty of Wangxia* with the US, which introduced the most-favoured-nation (MFN) clause and the right to extraterritoriality,[10] both of which had a devastating impact on China's sovereignty.

The *treaty of Huangpu* concluded with France also invoked the MFN principle and the Chinese agreed to lift the ban on Christianity, opening China to proselytisation by French and other Western missionaries. This was perceived not only as an attack on the economic system but also on the cultural values which had been a crucial part of the Chinese identity. The *treaty of Tianjin* placed the diplomatic relations between China and Britain at an equal footing and by 1864 the British nearly monopolized all foreign trade in China. The humiliating impact of these was evident in the Taiping Rebellion, which was inspired by Hong Xiuquan who employed a mix of traditional and radical ideologies to verbalize his dissent towards the state.

The military superiority of the foreigners exposed the redundancy of the traditional customs and social order and paved the way for formation of new social and political formations. An anti-imperialist nationalism, which would enable the Chinese to recover their lost honour was set off due to the privileges extracted by foreigners and the exploitation of the indigenes visible to all. According to official statistics, more than 12 million indentured labourers were sold to various parts of the world from the mid-nineteenth century through the 1920s. These labourers were put in "pigsties" in Shantou alone and more than 8,000 of them were coaxed, abducted and done to death.[11]

The racial nature of the imperialist ideology further helped in developing a rhetoric that was extremely ethno-centric and xenophobic in content. It is quite remarkable that this essence of formulating a homogenous discourse was visualized by Zhang Zhidong[12] as early as at the end of the Qing dynasty: "it is humiliation at the hands of foreigners that provides the conditions under which the apparently incommensurable positions of dogmatic conservatives and radical reformers can be reconciled."[13]

Though the identity of a Chinese nation did not crystallize at this particular moment, it paved the way for China's transition from an empire to a territory-based nation-state. It ingrained a feeling of being disparaged by the Western nations and an urge to establish itself in the future years.

The Taiping rebellion that erupted in 1850 recognized the increasing threat from foreign forces to the Chinese. The Taiping leaders voiced the idea of creation of a Heavenly Kingdom of peace[14] (*Taiping tianguo*), which reflected the desire of the people to embrace their traditional culture. But, despite the acknowledgement of threat from a foreign culture and colonial dominance, the Taiping rebellion did not make any efforts to oust the foreigners.[15] It remained by and large an indigenous revolt against the Manchu-led government by the loyalists of the Ming dynasty. Nevertheless, it led to indigenous reforms like inclusion of Han Chinese governors into provincial armies.

The dichotomy of "*ti-yong*"[16] articulated by Chinese leaders of late finds its precursor in the strategy adopted by the Manchu emperor Tongzhi, who retained "Chinese learning as the fundamental structure" while adapting "western learning for practical use" during this period.[17] The absence of a truly nationalistic strategy to overcome the problems posed by the Western imperialism resulted in the suppression of nationalistic impulses by the Manchu government that wanted to keep the Han majority under control. The attempts to reform their strategy failed due to anxious behaviour of the Manchu rulers and thus became one of the main reasons for China's defeat during the Sino-Japanese war in 1894–95.

The Sino-Japanese war invoked unprecedented nationalist responses and put the final nail in the coffin of a fading Empire. While Japan had suffered similar humiliation at the hands of the imperial powers earlier, it managed to overthrow the yoke of imperialism and modernize along the lines of an industrial power. The Meiji restoration fuelled Japanese desire for empire and as a result they started expanding in their Asian neighbourhood. As a weak neighbour Korea invited its attention, but, at this time Korea enjoyed a vassal kind of relationship with China, which brought Korea under its protectorate and the aggression against Korea drew China into a direct conflict with Japan.

The imperial Japanese army modernised on Western model, quickly overwhelmed the Chinese forces. The Sino–Japanese war ended in 1895 with the *Treaty of Shimonoseki*, which declared Korea's independence, opened four inland cities, ceded the island of Formosa (Taiwan) and the Liaodong peninsula in Chinese Manchuria. As a result of this treaty Japan earned 230 million *Taels* of silver in extortion money, which was four-and-a-half times of its annual national revenue. China's losses resulting from the destruction and looting by the Japanese invaders during the war were incalculable. This defeat at the hands of a small country, which had earlier looked at China as its cultural mentor, completely wobbled the Chinese self-image. Not only it exposed the weaknesses of the Chinese empire to the other nations, it skewed the Chinese belief in their traditional customs and made reform necessary.

The war modified the discourse of the nationalist stirrings. By way of enunciating heroes and traitors the Chinese historical literature began to intensely deify or stigmatize the actions of certain individuals. For instance, Li Hongzhang,[18] who gained notoriety for his diplomatic blunders during the war, was dubbed as an unforgivable traitor.[19] Similarly, due to the Sino–Japanese war, the entire Manchu government was held responsible for the nation's humiliation and a movement was initiated to overthrow the inefficient rulers. Commissioner Lin,[20] essentially a commendable patriot, was also condemned for providing inappropriate guidance to the emperor during the wars, more as a scapegoat for the Chinese political structures. Cultural–national icons were created who were either to be or not to be emulated by the Chinese masses.

It should be noted that the Sino–Japanese war forms one of the foremost arenas of contestation even today when issues of foreign policy are under purview. It has also emerged as one of the most engaging themes of depiction in the contemporary cinema on nationalism. The war was followed by several peace reforms such as the "Hundred Days Reform" and the Boxer Rebellion, which nonetheless, proved ephemeral. Yet such futile measures paved the way for the Revolution of 1911 that was to codify the first doctrine of Chinese nationalism. Spearheaded by intellectuals, who witnessed their country's gradual disintegration under the pressure of Western imperialism, several societies were set up to create political awareness about the state and the Chinese nation and the need for radical departures.

The nationalism witnessed during this phase was mostly of *reactive in* nature and *popular* in essence. The resentment against the foreigners was displayed in public sphere by stoning and beating the Western traders and oaths of exterminating all who worked inimically to the interests of the Chinese.[21] Still, there was little consensus on the way of systematic tackling of these foreign aggressors amongst the various sections of society. In a retrospective analysis the seeds of an idea of nationalism had been sown but the transition of this idea to a determinative ideology was yet to sprout.

The narrative of Chinese nationalism hereafter was much influenced by the "personality factor", whereby all those policies began to be endorsed by the nation that were formulated by a single individual who was their established leader. An ideology propagated by the mass leader came to be regarded as the ideology of the nation and the leader assumed the "face of the nation." Every phase, which could be distinguished from another based on certain attributes, was juxtaposed with the influence of a leader, thus acronyms like Mao's era, Deng's era became pervasive in Chinese historiography of nationalism. This however, does not imply that the forces of social evolution in Chinese history were centred on a few individuals. There were various processes and influences which determined the course of development which would be dealt with subsequently.

Sun Yatsen: The First Modern Patriot

Sun Yatsen[22] was the first intellectual to realize the significance of a binding ideology for his country. He diligently worked for the betterment of his country and as early as 1894, petitioned the Qing government for reform. Not receiving any appropriate response he set up his first revolutionary organisation—the society to revive China (*Xing zhong hui*) in Honolulu with a support base of Chinese expatriates.

His constant efforts and the martyrdom of his followers led to the establishment of the Republic of China in 1911. However, he soon realized that the country still lacked a national consciousness without which it was unfeasible to rule and the country would soon crumble under warlordism and become unruly. He attributed this dearth of nationalism to not only the suppression by the Manchu empire of such sentiments, but also to the Chinese traditional attachments to family, clan and geographical region, which he described as "loose sheets of sand."[23]

Hence, in an effort to find ways of bringing all Chinese together, he began to articulate his understanding of the Chinese identity and nationalism. Many scholars believe that he saw in the Sino–Japanese confrontation an opportunity to sow the seeds of an incipient nationalism which would assist in the realization of his ambitions for China.[24] He postulated the *san min zhuyi* (the three principles of the people): those of nationalism (*minzu*), people's livelihood (*minsheng*) and democracy (*minquan*). His promulgation of the nationalist rhetoric was largely comprehended as a functional response to an array of problems besetting underdeveloped nations[25] or sometimes as a revolutionary nationalism that impressed upon him a "historic mission" of uniting China into a homogenous unit.

He believed that nationalism lay at the core of the existence of the Chinese people. It was essential to "save the nation" and forestall racial destruction. His understanding of the Chinese identity was embedded in the racial discourse of the "*ethnie*." He believed that China was an inbreeding historic or nation-race sharing a common biological heritage, economy, language and culture. He further made a distinction between a nation based on a race and a nation in terms of a state.

In his book *San-min zhuyi*, he emphasised the significance of the demographic strength of the nation for the purpose of maintaining their existence in the "social law of evolution."[26] He also supported the expurgation of individual liberty for the purpose of assimilating Chinese people into the nationalist discourse. He alleged that understanding societies through the theories of cosmopolitanism or the social contract theory of the state would be pernicious as they would reduce the state to a simple aggregate of contracting individuals, fragile and insubstantial.[27] He prodded the people to give up individual liberty in favour of organization, discipline and loyalty. He did not want this ideology to impinge upon individual rights of equality and liberty as he recognized these as cornerstones of democracy.

The characterisation of China into a "hypocolony"[28] of foreign capitalism was a central theme of reference within his construction of Chinese nationalism. He rejected the Marxist theories of class struggle and contended that the fundamental struggle in history was that of conflict between sovereign nations. He believed that an economic class, unlike a nation, was not an organic community capable of surviving in and of itself in a competitive world. A parochial tinge was implicitly evident in this formulation as he held that nationalism would be in course of time be led by enlightened and disciplined elite (educated).[29] He advocated an innovative type of Chinese democracy for the purpose of building the nation where the ultimate control would be in the hands of the people themselves.

For the common people he advocated the philosophy of a "new man" who should be prepared to "sacrifice for the public welfare, even to the extent of giving up of his life." This had to be achieved according to Sun by renovating the traditional Chinese virtues, primarily that of "loyalty" (*chung*). He also recognised the need for economic modernization and beckoned the common people to collectively work for the benefit of the nation. According to Maria Hsia Chang, Sun's nationalism was a developmental nationalist ideology that had its genesis in his personal experiences of an "assaulted intellectual." Much of the development of Sun's conception was derived from his Western education that did not adhere to the classical Confucian views of the Chinese education. Not having been brought up in China, he continued to be perplexed by questions of identity.

He was further influenced significantly by the ideas of prominent scholars like Homer Lea who in his book *The Valour of Ignorance*, supported the Darwinian theory and prodded Sun to assume the undisputed leadership of his people in times of increasing political instability. Lea was also responsible for the militaristic influence on the state since he proposed that "National existence is governed by the law that the boundaries of political units are never ... stationary—they must either expand or shrink. It is by this law of national expansion and shrinkage that we mark the rise and decline of a nation."[30] Sun also conceded that sometimes violence could become an inalienable part of the process of reconstruction and rejuvenation of a nation.

Sun's inference based on Homer Lea's proposition demonstrates that he was not averse to using help from foreigners as long as the final benefit accrued to his nation. Moreover, several times he tried to raise funds from his activities abroad to foment revolution in China. Another intellectual who influenced his ideology was Liang Qichao, who propagated that conflicts among nations were as natural as struggles among men. Civilization advanced through national competition and a nation's strength depended on the vitality of its people.[31] Despite this comprehensive vision for his country, his emphasis on removing the Yuan Shikai clique from power led to a condoning of the Japanese threat that was threatening the Chinese masses in a major way. Moreover, alluding to his political weakness he found solace in a Pan-Asian dream where he envisaged China and Japan working together for their larger interests rather than competing at jingoistic levels. He brought his manipulative powers to better use when he was able to strike a bargain with the foreign powers instead of becoming their straight partner in the later years of his campaign.

His conceptualization and comprehension of the national and international concerns was prescient in many ways as it was one of the earliest articulations of a firm belief in the existence of a nation and its consciousness. However, his understanding of nationalism was far from perfect. Sun's emphasis on modernisation was limited to the extent of it being utilized for strengthening the economic fabric of the nation, while materialistic business sentiment was disparaged vehemently. He envisaged a Chinese sovereignty based on "nation-state capitalism" (*guojian shehui zhuyi*) wherein a strong government would lead development and make the nation corruption free. Though he supported a private economy he wanted it to be strictly regulated by the state. Comparing in futuristic terms, this proposition proves a remarkable continuity that is evident in contemporary times which allows a mercantile business class to emerge but is still not willing to give them a free hand. (Nonetheless, they function today as one of the major factors in the nationalist strategy).

Interestingly, Sun's conception of nationalism is often compared with the extremist ideologies of Hitler and Mussolini who by the nature of the consequence of their aggrandised nationalism acquired notoriety. Moreover, though Sun conceived martial rule as an inalienable part of his construction of a democratic China, it was reduced to the stance of being at the initial stage (*Junsheng*), while for the end purpose of establishing a self-governing democratic nation (*Xianzheng*) peaceful means were to be adopted. The martial rule followed by authoritarian regimes (*Xunzheng*) would only officiate to rule out the feudalistic tendencies, which were responsible in his view for the retrograde thinking of the Chinese people.

His conception also contributed to the contemporary theoretical debates by providing an alternative to the dependency theorists and anticipating a viable transition to democracy among colonial nations. Around this time the party and various other literary movements capitalized on Sun's image as a true nationalist to promote images of modern cultural ideologies.[32] However, Sun's death in 1925 precipitated the dissolution of his revolutionary Chinese Nationalist Party into several contending factions. Hereafter, Chiang Kai-Shek, the commander of the new Kuomintang (Guomindang/GMD) army assigned himself the task begun by Sun of suppressing warlords and unifying China. By 1928, Chiang succeeded in uniting the warlords under the nominal leadership of the nationalist regime.[33] Sun's contribution to the birth of the nationalist ideology remains immense and he has come to be revered as the "father of modern China" for his contribution to the solidarity of his homeland.

Chiang Kai-Shek: The Forgotten Nationalist

Chiang Kai-Shek held the position of the commandant of Kuomintang's Whampoa Military Academy and succeeded Sun Yatsen in his party position after his death in 1925. He was popularly referred to as the Generalissimo (Chairman of National Military Council) of the Nationalist government of the Republic of China from 1928 to 1948. Since his rise to power was constantly challenged by the communist group, his initial efforts at uniting the Chinese masses were clubbed under the maxim of "first internal pacification and then external resistance." In the later years, he moulded one of the significant phases of Chinese nationalism by leading the Chinese forces against the Second Japanese aggression.

He believed that the French Revolution and the American independence movements of 1789 and 1776, respectively, greatly influenced the upsurge of nationalist thinking in third world countries and formed an intrinsic part of Sun's doctrinal edifices.[34] He endeavoured to comply with Sun's wishes and started the Northern expedition with an aim of unifying China. He also established the nationalist party's control over Manchuria in 1928. However, he soon realised the non-sustainability of war and pointed out:

> "Any country that spends 80 percent of its annual revenue on its military establishment is bound to go bankrupt. If its military expenditure amounts to as much as 90 percent of its annual revenue, then it will surely be faced with possibility of total collapse...In our case, with military expenditure exceeding 80 percent of our annual revenue, nothing is left for national reconstruction... it is only by reducing our expenditure that we can hope to stabilize our national economy. Without a stable national economy there can be no social and political progress."
>
> —*Chiang Kai-Shek*, December 18, 1928[35]

For some time he remained considerably dependent on the Soviet Union for economic support, but as soon as he realised the harm that the Soviet intentions of class struggle in China would do to his country, he became averse to Moscow's insistence on this issue. His plans for disbanding the army in view of the economic future of his country, however, provided an opportunity to the Red Army which mobilised its resources and led several revolts and weakened the organisation of the GMD. Thus, Chiang faced a strong dilemma in deciding his national priorities. To check the communist threat, he encouraged a friendly stance with the Japanese who vowed to help him in ousting the communist elements. To bind the nation more cohesively, Chiang revived the state cult of Confucius and in 1934 launched a campaign, the so-called *New Life Movement*, to inculcate Confucian morals. He often applied Chinese nationalism as an ideology to dub the communists as traitors to the nation and asserted "patriotism requires anti-communism, anti-communism requires unity."

When the Second World War ended, Chiang again concentrated all his efforts to remove the communists from usurping the power at centre. But unfortunately, the Sino-Japanese war II had completely stretched the resources of GMD and in the civil war that followed, the Communist party emerged victorious. As the GMD was forced to move to Formosa (Taiwan), the nationalist discourse of mainland China was monopolised by the CCP which renounced all efforts made by Chiang towards national unification and brought out its own new conceptualisations. Chiang continued his struggle against communism from Taiwan and stressed the need for "counterattacking the mainland to rescue compatriots", "avenging humiliation and restoring the nation" and "recovering the nation"s territory." However, his nationalist visions remained unfulfilled as return to the mainland became increasingly difficult for him.[36]

His understanding of nationalism in terms of a "Greater China", nevertheless, left a significant legacy to the Chinese nationalist discourse. He often counselled the masses to "solemnly and righteously strengthen the nation, and remain calm in adversity," which are still palpable in the discourse of contemporary Chinese nationalism. However, his move away from the mainland has often led to him being seen as a traitor to the mainland and hence, his mention is rare to find in the list of Chinese patriots. Even though contemporary leaderships envision the unification of Taiwan with the mainland, the caveat lies in the inability of coming to a common understanding of which ideology is to prevail. While the CCP visualises the unification under its own tutelage, Republic of China or Taiwan claims to be the original nationalist party and hence some sections of the Taiwanese leadership want the unification to be carried under the ROC banner.

The May 4th Movement and its Implications on Nationalism

The May 4th movement of 1919, which upheld the modern notions of Science and Democracy as two prominent values in the formation of a national identity, can be seen as the first among mass movements stewarded mostly by the educated intelligentsia for building a modern nation capable of resisting imperialism and stand-up proud among the nations of the world.[37] It significantly contributed to the building of the nationalist discourse during the early twentieth century by shifting the focus of reform from the peasants and workers to a new leadership. It derided the principles of Confucianism and believed it should no longer be the national essence (*guocui*). At the same time, many Chinese traditional practices were marked as hindering China's advance into the modern world.[38]

As against the populist agrarian nature of the nineteenth century movements, this movement witnessed the leadership being takeover by the educated youth. The immediate cause for pouring out of student discontent was the presentation of a set of demands by the Japanese to Yuan Shikai, the Chinese President, which meant the recognition of a Japanese sphere of influence. Despite immediate measures taken by Yuan Shikai to gain support for its cause from the allied powers, Zhang Zongxiang (a minister who negotiated the Japanese loans) surrendered many concessions to the imperialists. This embittered the feelings of the populace at large and led to the May 4th movement where large number of students, most of them belonging to the Beijing University under the chancellorship of Cai Yuanpei, marched through the streets of the city. This can be construed under the larger external threat theory of nationalism, which maintains that any external pressure unites the citizens of a country to respond in a collaborative manner.

They demanded that Qingdao be returned to China, and raised several slogans like "China has been sentenced to death!" "Boycott Japanese goods!" "Protect our country's soil" "down with the traitors."[39] The demonstrations were at the beginning peaceful but later descended into violence as the movement progressed. They spread from Beijing to Shanghai and later to other cities in the interior. The nationalist rhetoric and popular sentiments were voiced by several radical scholars, for instance, Chen Duxiu of Beijing University who stated:

> "What we love is the country in which people take their patriotism to oppose oppression by the people; it is not the country in which the government uses the people's patriotism to oppress other people."[40]

The movement of 1919 also demonstrated a radical attack on the values and morality of the imperial state. The most significant contribution of the movement however, lies in the fact that it became the dais for formative personal–political experience for a new generation of leaders who were a part of the student elite at this time and were to dominate the political scene of the Chinese scenario till as late as the 1980s. For instance, Mao Zedong also started his political career as a radical young recruit of the Beijing University at this particular time. Second, the movement aided the process of transformation of the idea of nationalism to an ideology through propitiating a culture based on print capitalism.[41] It called for liberation of the youth and women and rejected the use of classical Chinese for writing to be replaced by the colloquial Chinese. It can also be regarded as a milestone as it was a precursor to the formation of the CCP in 1921 in Shanghai.[42]

The Second Japanese Invasion of China

A decade of reconstruction and modernization followed in the 1920s to overcome the instability that had come about in the early twentieth century. Developments in agriculture, industry, banking and infrastructure paced at an unprecedented rate to prepare a ground for a self-sustained "takeoff." However, before this goal could be fully achieved, yet another wave of Japanese imperialism washed away China's hopes for a brighter future and all material resources had to be diverted to ward off the Japanese threat. Popular protests began in response to the Japanese attacks on Manchuria and Shanghai in 1931, which included propaganda groups visiting towns around Shanghai and shouting slogans, speeches and handing out leaflets.

Chiang Kai-Shek's policy of "first pacification and then resistance" came increasingly under criticism.[43] The Chinese Chamber of Commerce legislated to boycott the Japanese goods, while the protests came to be closely associated with the CCP cadres. With the final outbreak of the war, the presumably divisive policies of Chiang's government were abandoned and a national unity became perceptible. The Nanjing Massacre, more famous as the "Rape of Nanjing" set the stage for a tremendous wave of anti-imperialist nationalism. The Japanese aggression (1937–45) under the command of General Matsui Iwane accounted for terrible atrocities and economic devastation of the Chinese people. The renowned economist Cheng Chu-yuan considered Japan's invasion of China as nothing short of a "holocaust" that retarded China's growth and industrialisation by at least half a century.[44]

The "War of Resistance" exposed the Kuomintang's (GMD) bankruptcy and gave an opportunity to the CCP to showcase its patriotism and takeover the nationalist mantle in China through gaining massive support from the local peasantry.[45] Popular literature and caricatures reflected the popular sentiments, which reinvigorated nationalism. The most prominent manifestation of these sentiments was the growth of local self-defence forces. However, the nationalist struggle was phenomenally weakened by the eruption of a civil war between the nationalists and the communists. The CCP became the main instrument for politicized nationalism hereafter making the Nationalist Party redundant and Mao Zedong emerged as the undisputed leader of the Chinese nation.

Mao Zedong and His Brand of Nationalism

Nationalism found a privileged propagator in Mao Zedong who recognized the organizational power of nationalism and used it judiciously to draw a fractured society into the semblance of a modern nation in response to external threats especially from Japan and the US.[46] Though he recognized it as one of the most powerful "exports" from the West, he strongly embraced it in his task of nation building. His passionate rhetoric of patriotism elicited an extreme form of loyalty from the people towards their nation and the state. While one could sum up the nationalist discourse under Mao in the axiom of "the Chinese people have stood up", Mao's conceptualization of nationalism was to a large extent a disjointed and inchoate ideology which required further streamlining and remedying.

Mao's emphasis on spread of this idea among the masses in the countryside led to extension of the strong propaganda into the interiors of the country. It was paradoxical that though it was the Nationalist Party which was revered as the national party of China in the international arena; the CCP increased its hold on the masses and began to replace the GMD. While formulating a strategy against the Japanese aggression, Mao delivered speech on "the communist" outlining three magic weapons which would lead the Chinese revolution. He proclaimed, "we have come to understand through eighteen years of experience that united front, armed struggle and party construction are the three magic weapons of the CCP that will defeat the enemy in the Chinese revolution."[47]

When Mao assumed command he became a vanguard of nationalist ideas and revamped the philosophical outlook of the ideology to be in sync with the paradigm of a leftist regime. It can be credibly attributed to Mao that his was the first effort to juxtapose nationalist repertoire with leftist doctrines as in most cases abroad it had been the right-wingers who had heralded the cause of nationalism. Through the 1930s and 40s Mao and the CCP were deeply influenced by Sun Yatsen's ideals. Like Sun, Mao yearned for a renewed China capable of resisting imperialists and maintaining a dignified sovereignty. For this purpose he said, "to study the development of this old culture, to reject its feudal dross and assimilate its democratic essence is a necessary condition for developing our new national culture." He stressed that the new culture could be *"opposed to all feudal and superstitious ideas."*[48]

In his view, a communist who was perceived to be an internationalist also ought to be a patriot. The presence of the two qualities together was not to be regarded as a contradiction. He charismatically appealed to the masses by impressing upon them:

> "We are at once internationalists and patriots, and our slogan is 'Fight to defend the motherland against the aggressors'. For us defeatism is a crime and to strive for victory in the war of resistance is an inescapable duty. For only by fighting in defence of the motherland can we defeat aggressors and achieve national liberation"[49]

His appeal to the masses was voiced as an anti-imperialist rhetoric which denounced the GMD as the running dog of imperialism. In an impressive speech at the People's Political Consultative Conference, he exhorted that:

> "the Chinese have always been a great, courageous and industrious nation; it is only in modern times that they have fallen behind…we have closed our ranks and defeated both domestic and foreign oppressors through the people's war of liberation and the great People's revolution, and now we are proclaiming the founding of the People's Republic of China…Ours will no longer be a nation subject to insult and humiliation. We have stood up. Our revolution has won the sympathy and acclaim of the people of all countries. We have friends all over the world."[50]

Mao endorsed Marxism-Leninism as the new state theory and censured Sun's nationalistic programmes soon after he assumed chairmanship of the CCP. He visualized the world as being divided into two camps: on one side were the "progressive" socialist states led by the Soviet Union and on the other side were the "decadent" capitalist-imperialist countries with the US as their mentor. Mao believed that China must "lean to one side" by joining the socialist camp by which China will be able to enhance its prestige and reach the goals it had set for itself.[51]

Calling for the Chinese people to be true revolutionaries he said, "in the international sphere we must firmly unite with the Soviet Union, the People's democracies and the forces of peace and democracy everywhere, and there should not be the slightest hesitation or wavering on this question. At home we must unite all the nationalities, democratic classes, democratic policies ... prestigious revolutionary united front already in existence."[52]

Inspired by Stalin, Mao adopted the command economy where the state was to determine production, control costs, fix wages, and set prices and capital assets were to be generated through forced savings of the people. However, by 1956-57, Mao had started asserting that China must evolve its own indigenous model of development, rejecting the Soviet model on the one hand and the Western model on the other.[53] He further appended the notions of class struggle and espoused a *"continuous revolution"* in which all were bound to participate.

Mao evinced a firm belief in the elements of will power and mass enthusiasm, which could transform the Chinese economy. He redefined class as a state of mind—whereby even entertainment of capitalist thoughts was enough to dub someone a capitalist.[54] He juxtaposed the struggle of the CCP with the struggle for a nation with an advanced culture and sought mass support on that behalf.[55]

He was, however, dismayed by the unsuccessful nature of socialist experiment in the Chinese state and postulated that as long as capitalism remained in the world, its pernicious influence could seep into socialist China and contaminate the masses resulting in antagonistic contradictions between the unpolluted "people" and the infected "enemies of the people." This belief led him to be constantly vigilant against corruption of the self and for this purpose he undertook several campaigns to instruct the masses as well. In the 1950s land reforms were carried out, the Three- and Five-Anti movement, the Hundred flowers movement, the Anti-Rightist campaign and the Great Leap Forward campaigns were meted out. The most sweeping of all, the Great Proletarian Cultural Revolution (GPCR) beginning 1966 evinced Mao's vision at its climax and attempted a sui-generis solution for bringing about the final culmination of his new democratic revolution.

All these programmes though launched in earnest did exemplify certain eccentricities in the formulation of his socialist ideology. The large scale displacement and disparagement of higher officials to the countryside created what is today lamented as the lost generation/or the lost decade. While the economic burgeoning of the late 1950s convinced Mao of the invincibility of concerted effort of human resources in creating leapfrog over the Soviet Union, he overlooked the inherent limitations, which were present in the form of unskilled labour and backward technology. Though he envisioned better living standards for the peasantry by proliferation of the industrial development to the rural centres adopted in the garb of creating backyard furnaces, the manifestation did not testify a pragmatic approach.

The failure to achieve his ends and the events that followed led to relinquishing of his post to Liu Shaoqi who along with Deng Xiaoping introduced certain capitalistic measures to revive the economy. Disenchanted by the turn of events Mao recalled his decision and transferred power to the Gang of Four and the Red Guards. A period of instability and internal as well as external crises followed. The early 1970s brought about a reassessment of the foreign policy as well as internal exigencies. Under the direction of Zhou Enlai appeals were made to foreign powers for capital assistance and technology transfers. The period also embarked a rapprochement with the US.

Thus, although Mao formulated an effective doctrine of nationalism to whip up public sentiments he was unable to put it into effect successfully. His understanding of nationalism was inextricably linked with the Marxist-Leninist ideology. The legacy that post-Mao China inherited lacked the zeal and fervour that aids a nation in consolidating itself into a homogenous self. The industrial as well as social base for the hoisting of nation had all but eroded. The new leadership clinched to the developmental mode of nationalism to revitalise the essence of nation building. Metaphorically speaking, an infantile nationalism was reborn from the ashes of a dying phoenix.

What must also be mentioned here is the uncompromising spirit displayed by Mao on questions of spatial dissent. The infiltration of the PLA cadres in Tibet right in the beginning of Mao's period augmented the unresolved crisis of assimilating minority identities and a phase of territorial expansion which exhibited certain traits similar to the Western imperial powers. Throughout the period of his Chairmanship of the CCP, Mao reflected national interests as the top most priority by attempting to create a definable border with most of its neighbouring states. Thus, though in political discourse he maintained the civilizational travesty of the Chinese predicament, slowly he had initiated the transition into a realm of statist behaviour which was in congruence with the norms of international state standards.

His legacy as a nationalist has come under heavy scrutiny by recent scholars who are revising their perception of Mao based on the availability of new resources that have come to light after years of state enigmatic behaviour. The revisionist historiography is now beginning to establish that Mao's ascendance to power was largely due to favourable circumstances and not due to a shrewd stratagem adopted by him. Neither did he have any empathy for the village masses in the initial years of his struggle for power which derived from his childhood experiences of despising manual labour. In fact, the red army exploited the peasantry as bad as the foreign aggressors and looting, smashing, burning was synonymous to Mao's approach as far as the countryside was concerned.[56] It is in the context of the Hunan peasant movement that Mao is believed to have remarked – "A revolution is not a dinner party, it needed violence. It is necessary to bring about a reign of terror in every country."

Even after he occupied the ramparts of the CCP leadership, his approach remained highly parochial and inexplicable to the masses.[57] His tenure was adjudged to have led to maximum damage in terms of population loss in comparison to even the First and Second World Wars deriving from the losses of Cultural Revolution and other marches. And though the peasants were allowed to be a part of the revolution, the rural cadres were looked down upon.[58] Despite these shortcomings he played a significant role as an articulator of anti-imperialist nationalism which has won him a place on the dais of Chinese patriotic stalwarts.

He was able to garner mass support based on his fascinating speeches. For instance, in his greetings delivered on behalf of the Central Committee of the CCP to the "National Combat heroes and of Model workers in Industry, Agriculture and the Army," he praised them as models for the entire Nation.[59] He outlined the build-up of a powerful national defence force and a powerful economy as the two major tasks of importance, for which closer ties of unity and concerted efforts were required from all sections of the people.

Mao even went to the extent of criticizing Han chauvinism, stating that such ideas which exist to a serious degree among many Party members and cadres are manifested in the relations between nationalities and hence need to be corrected.[60] His most significant contribution remains in the form of a Party Supremo whereby he guided the formation of a unified party base and strengthening the ideology that was to carry forward the nation-building task. And though Marxism-Leninism formed the basis for his reign, nationalism also prerequisites a unifying force amongst the masses whose function was fulfilled by this ideology during Mao's era.

Deng Xiaoping and His tête-à-tête with Nationalism

A political conundrum confounded Deng Xiaoping when he came to power in 1978. The inefficacy of Marxism-Leninism to resolve China's political quandaries inevitably led to a quest for a new ideology, at the same time, Marxism-Leninism could not be completely abandoned as it had become an intrinsic part of China's identity and its world view. To steer his country out of the chaos of the previous era, he retained the communist–socialist ideals of establishing an egalitarian society, nevertheless, disseminated all-encompassing reforms to resuscitate the economic base.

He recognised the recklessness of Mao's socialist endeavours in not sufficiently bolstering the economic self-sufficiency of the nation and hence he avowed that like any other country China must "look after its own" and safeguard its own interests, sovereignty, and territorial integrity- particularly in the view of its past century of humiliation.[61] He was deeply perplexed by the development of socialism during Mao's tenure as several questions had already begun to be raised as to whether socialism had actually been successfully engendered in China or not. To reiterate his faith on socialism he persuasively declared:

> "Under the leadership of the Communist Party, China had become a proud and independent nation-state that would no longer be the vassal

of others or submit to anything deleterious to its interests. All that achievement would however be lost if the people forsook socialism and the leadership of the Communist Party, as only socialism can save China, and only socialism can develop China."[62]

This decision also reflected the compulsions of deriving legitimacy from history and avoiding any stance which reflected a severe break from it. Considering the indispensable need for political legitimacy "nationalism" during Deng's era became more of a "political ploy" to gain legitimacy. Nonetheless, Deng Xiaoping contributed immensely to the building of a Chinese identity by enlarging the sphere of people who could be considered by identity as Chinese. Like Sun Yatsen, his conception of the Chinese people included ethnic Chinese all over the world. He believed in their innate sense of nationalism and appealed to them across the world to "love our country and help to develop it."

He embarked upon the mission of the "Four modernisations"[63] to ensure that China would "stand firm forever" in the world,[64] and conceptualised it in three stages. The goal of the first stage in China's economic modernisation was to achieve the doubling of its per capita GNP from US$250 in 1980 to US$500 by 1990, so as to "ensure that people have adequate food and clothing." Stage two reckoned another doubling of per-capita to US$1,000 in the year 2000 by when Deng expected China to have "shaken off poverty and achieved comparative prosperity." The third stage called for a "new starting point" which would conclude by the year 2030 or 2050, which will bring China at par with the moderately developed countries.

Remarkably, the first goal was achieved well in advance of the specified timeframe and China today prides itself on being the third largest economy in the world (slated to become the second very soon in the near future). A critical disjuncture augmented during the times of Deng Xiaoping from the command economy of Mao is in large measures responsible for this image of China. He reemphasised the *ti-yong* dichotomy and renounced the isolation that China had subjected itself to. He asserted that for China's development, it must "persist in opening to the outside world and refrain from blind opposition" to anything that was foreign. He reasoned that "*not everything that developed in capitalist countries was capitalist in nature*" and as spelt out by Marx—science and technology were a part of productive forces and devoid of class character. He began importing science and technology on a large scale and opened several special economic zones but maintained that his policies would be on the basis of "equality and mutual benefit" and will not compromise China's sovereignty at any cost.

He also realigned his faith in the intellectuals whom Mao had derided and considered as unworthy of the "Red" bunch and politically suspect. He believed in the intrinsic nationalism of the Chinese people and requested the intellectuals who had fled to foreign lands during the Cultural Revolution to return to their motherland and contribute to the development of the Chinese nation. He prioritised order and stability in the country for economic growth over the idealism of communist principles.[65] However, his more radical thoughts did not stop him from denouncing "bourgeois liberalism" which vehemently favoured Western democratisation and freedom.

He was aware of the incipient nature of his country's stability and did not want to provide any excuse for the demolishment of the Chinese nation-state. He postulated that rather than imitating the West, China was to have its own brand of "socialist democracy." He envisioned a China, which in the times to come, will be increasingly modernised and its people would have acquired high levels of income, education and capacity for rational thought and decision-making and the Party would have matured enough for the tolerance of popular participation in government.[66]

A retrospective analysis would convince a contemporary observer of the far-sightedness and pragmatism of Deng's views. As the contemporary events unfold it is becoming clearer that certain leverage is being created for the common Chinese people who had earlier witnessed the perils of a totalitarian regime. In many ways Deng's conceptualization of China's identity continues to be the guiding force of nationalism in contemporary China.

Whether Deng actually believed in a goal of achievement of communism for his country or it was a mere charade to avoid destabilisation of his government is difficult to ascertain, but it can be established beyond doubt that his policies created a sense of *belongingness* and *patriotism* which enriched the discourse of development of the Chinese nation. However as he prioritised development over political reform or probably prioritized it for the lack of sufficient time it has left critical lacunae in the political fabric of the nation.

Development refurbished the economic strength of the country but the unintended consequences that followed this rapid scale of modernisation weakened the social fabric of the nation. Relative freedom of thought and behaviour has been coupled with rising inequalities, rising crime rates, peasant and labour unrest, pandemic corruption within the party, government and military and growing ethnic separatist movements in Xinjiang and Tibet. He remains the main architect of China's policies towards its minority nationalities, which by the constitution of 1982[67] were accommodated substantially into the fabric of the nation.

By far, he managed to transform China from a weak and an isolated nation to an economic giant and stabilised the political realm by restraining power struggle within the Party. The post-Deng era did not witness the leadership of a particular individual directing the strategy of the country; rather the Party began to decide as a collective. Deng's successor Jiang Zemin did not enjoy the public stature, which could be associated with the earlier leadership. He reverentially invoked Deng's philosophical understanding to steer his country on the path of nationalist determination, nonetheless, increasingly the focus of political events and nationalist discourse shifted away from the one-man leadership to an eclectic derivation.

Nationalism in the Post-Deng Era: Deconstructing the White Papers

Besides the ideological frameworks provided by these prominent leaders of the country, various institutions and processes also helped in engendering nationalism in the Chinese historical milieu. Most importantly, the vision of the CCP which has been set through the Party Congress documents beginning 1949 and starkly visible after the eighth Party Congress in 1956, demonstrate the ideological leanings of the nation. With the collapse of the Soviet Union and the bi-polar structure, China recognized its own potential in bringing forward a multi-polar world and hence, revived its status as a "thoroughly traditional great power." The 1990s witnessed what many scholars have described as populist nationalism and an anti-imperialist nationalism in China which provided a valuable public space for popular participation outside the country's political institutions.[68]

This rhetoric radicalised the emotional elements in nationalist discourses and constructed nationalist politics as a fulfilment of the nation's otherwise unavailable democratic public life. It was a direct expression of the debates on modernity, post-colonialism and their impact on polity. The phase witnessed a growing quest for a great power status by China, besides creating multilateral power structures. The significant tenets of Chinese nationalism during this phase can be gauged in its aggressive foreign policy measures witnessed from the 1990s to the present times, discerned in the White Papers released by the State Council of PRC. An analysis of these White Papers between 1990 and 2007 reveals the growth of nationalist rhetoric in Chinese foreign and security policy discourse.

During the 1980s the party outlined the new maxim of "China's special characteristics" (*zhong guo tese*) to deal with the process of nation-building (an idea which was reiterated by Hu Yaobang in the 12th Party Congress, concretized in the 13th Congress of the CCP in 1987 and reaffirmed at the 14th Congress in 1992). The party advocated a new culture in its 1986 resolutions drafted by Zhao Ziyang, that is, a culture "that incorporated the best from historical traditions" and "inspired a sense of national pride, self-respect and self-confidence." The Party also stressed upon the need for a scientific worldview and culture:

> "We should work actively to change those undesirable customs that still prevail in the cities and the countryside, to advocate cultured, healthful ways of living ... these reforms should be carried out voluntarily by the masses"[69]

Similar directions were outlined in the White papers from the 1990 onwards where aggressive foreign policy measures were undertaken to achieve national interests. For instance, in the 1991 White paper, the Chinese government highlighted its independent sovereign realm by sending a message to the world community to keep away from the questions of human rights in China given to its "particular history and national conditions." It states:

> "Chinese government and people have spared no effort to safeguard human rights ... and have achieved remarkable results. This has won full confirmation and fair appraisal from all people who have a real understanding of Chinese conditions and who are not prejudiced" (referring to the Western nations). Moreover, the "issue of human rights is an internal sovereignty issue of each country and needs to be judged with regards to its history and national conditions and evaluated away from a preconceived model."

The 1991 White Paper was a milestone in terms of outlining China's nationalistic goals and worldview and thus requires some detailed analysis. It enunciates how the historical themes continue to affect the current policy formulation. To quote from the paper:

> "Without national independence, there would be no guarantee for the people's lives. When imperialist aggression became the major threat to their lives, the Chinese people had to win national independence before they could gain the right to subsistence. After the Opium war of 1840, China, hitherto a big feudal kingdom was gradually turned into a semi-feudal country. The imperialists sold, maltreated and caused the death of numerous Chinese labourers, plunging countless people on old China into an abyss of misery. Under the colonial rule, the Chinese people had their fill of humiliation and there was no personal dignity to speak of. In face of the crumbling state sovereignty and the calamities wrought upon their lives, for over a century the Chinese people fought the foreign aggressors' in an indomitable struggle for national salvation and independence."

Praising the ability of the CCP to manage the early crises, the paper outlines that "the Taiping Heavenly Kingdom movement, Boxers Movement and the Revolution of 1911, which overthrew the Qing Dynasty broke out during this period. These revolutionary movements dealt heavy blow to imperialist influences, but they failed to deliver the nation from semi-colonialism. A fundamental change took place only after the Chinese people, under the leadership of the CCP, overthrew the GMD Party and founded the PRC."

The strong anti-colonial and anti-imperialist tenor is evident in the articulation of the rhetoric that the CCP, soon after its inception in 1921, set a clear goal in its political programme to "overthrow the oppression by international imperialism and achieve the complete independence of the

Chinese nation" and to "overthrow the warlords and unite China into a real democratic republic." The Chinese nation, which makes-up one-fourth of the world's population, it declared, was no longer one that the "aggressors could kill and insult at will. The Chinese have stood up as the masters of their own country; for the first time they have won real human dignity and the respect of the world. National independence has protected the Chinese people from being trodden under the heels of the invaders."

The paper also recognized that despite gaining independence, China was still a developing country with limited national strength. The preservation of national independence and state sovereignty and the freedom from imperialist subjugation were, therefore, the very fundamental conditions for survival and development of the Chinese people. It was an intrinsic wish and demand of the Chinese people and a long-term urgent task of the Chinese government to maintain national stability, concentrate efforts on developing the productive forces, persist in reform and opening to the outside world, strive towards rejuvenating the national economy and boosting national strength.[70]

It further stipulated that all nationalities in China were equal and that all the nation's minority nationalities enjoyed equal democratic rights with the Han people and that China opposed great-nation chauvinism, especially great-Han chauvinism, as well as local nationalism.[71] In the White paper released in 1992, the Chinese government condemned the imperialist instigation of the Tibetan independence and stressed its conception of "one country two systems" to define its approach towards problematic regions.[72] The following quotations reflect China's irredentist behaviour and nationalist fervour with regards to Tibet:

> "By the Tang Dynasty (618-907), the Tibetans and Hans had, through marriage between royal families and meetings leading to alliances, cemented political and kinship ties of unity and political friendship and formed close economic and cultural relations, laying a solid foundation for the ultimate founding of a unified nation."[73]

It further stated that in his inauguration statement of the Republic of China, on 1 January 1912, Sun Yatsen, the provisional first president declared to the whole world "the foundation of the country lies in the people, and the unification of lands inhabited by the Han, Manchu, Mongol, Hui and Tibetan people into one country means the unification of the Han, Manchu, Mongol, Hui and Tibetan races. It is called national unification." The five-colour flag used as the national flag at that time represented the unification of the five main races. In March, the Nanjing-based provisional senate of the Republic of China promulgated the republic's first constitution, the Provisional Constitution of the Republic of China, in which it was clearly stipulated that Tibet was a part of the territory of the People's Republic of China."[74]

It even quoted Indian Prime Minister Jawaharlal Nehru recognizing China's rights over Tibet. In reference to the separatist movement in Tibet it stated the mere fact that installation of the Dalai Lama had to be endorsed by the national government is sufficient proof that Tibet did not possess any independent power during that period. Delineating its attitudes on the Taiwan question in the 1993 White paper, the Chinese government stated that it was completely an "issue of self-determination, national unity and territorial integrity" and the international community should restrain from interfering in the matter as well as abide by its official doctrine of the *"one country two systems"* promulgated by Deng Xiaoping.[75]

In fact the settlement of the Taiwan issue and achievement of national reunification was a sacrosanct mission of the entire Chinese people. But this was largely to be realised through peaceful means. But it did mention the catch, when it stated that peaceful reunification is a set policy of the Chinese government, though any sovereign state is entitled to use any means it deems necessary, including military ones, to uphold its sovereignty and territorial integrity. China did, however, seek international support for this cause by stating that it is confident that it can count on the understanding and support of governments and people of all countries in pursuit of its just cause of safeguarding its state sovereignty and territorial integrity.

The subsequent white papers laid down the tenets of China's peace and development policy inaugurated by Jiang Zemin, which adhered to the goal of nationalist development.

The need for asserting nationalist sentiments further became indelible in the wake of globalization, which brought along an expanded consciousness of the world. The cultural threat perceived by the state (and other groups) through increased individualism and consumerism constituted a significant challenge to it in terms of defining and guarding what it understood to be a "Chinese culture and identity." The achievement of CCP's long harboured intention of developing a socialist state was challenged by a state of constant friction with the values of capitalist system and global culture and deference of action. The state's response thus, came under the aegis of a rejection of the cultural impacts of globalization and a propagation of the "strong society" and a theory of "cultural resistance."

President Jiang Zemin and his advisers resorted to an emphasis on superiority of Chinese culture. The economic liberalization during 1990s witnessed the opening of economy for business but also simultaneous distrust for foreigners and also significant periods of closure.[76] Zheng offers insightful evidences of how, even previously, political crisis resulting from Mao Zedong's policy failures at the ideological level and Deng Xiao Ping's economic decentralization at the political level led to nationalistic response of "new Left" criticisms of modernization as Westernization in the 1980s. The reforms led to a crisis of political identity which had to be countered with specific Chinese conceptualization.[77] The White paper released in 1998, further evolved the self-concept of China's role in the world system of states and thereby became a milestone in the change of the rhetoric to a more confident country willing to accept responsibilities and stakes in the global order. It stated

> "It is the aspiration of the Chinese government and people to lead a peaceful, stable and prosperous world into the new century."[78]

The paper identified "hegemonism" and "power politics" as the main source of threats to world peace and stability; cold war mentality and its influence and the enlargement of military blocs and the strengthening of military alliances as fostering instability in international security. It lamented the old, unfair and irrational international economic order that disregards the interests of developing countries. And commented on the local conflicts caused by ethnic, religious, territorial, natural resources—questions left over by history among countries which remain unsolved—and terrorism, arms proliferation, smuggling and trafficking in narcotics, environmental pollution, waves of refugees which pose renewed threats to international security.

One of the most significant aspect of the contemporary Chinese nationalism became the fixation with issues of sovereignty which flared up massive nationalistic passions as witnessed in several incidents like the emergency landing on China's Hainan island by a damaged American EP-3 reconnaissance plane in 2001 which generated an outcry amongst the Chinese. Similarly, when the US bombed the Chinese embassy in Belgrade (apparently accidentally), the anger felt by Chinese was voiced categorically. And the languishing dispute in the South China Sea region which involves massive stakes for the South-east Asian countries.

While on the one hand, China has voiced its intentions of building a "prosperous and harmonious society" with defence and economy situated in the international environment and "permanent peace", as the two strong pillars of development, on the other hand, it has not let issues of territorial sovereignty be relegated to the background. Instead it continuously endeavours to integrate the efforts of its people and the international community to safeguard its own national interests as highlighted in the White Paper released in 2005.[79]

In continuation of its nationalist visions, the CCP coined the theory of "the Three Represents"[80] (*san ge dai biao*) in 2000 to provide a vision of development for its people, giving due consideration to the forces of globalization and technological revolution. The growing influence of democratic ideas and dissent groups, specially the Falungong, continuously distressed the CCP during this time. However, adjusting with the needs of the time, the 16th party congress headed by Hu Jintao endorsed the rhetoric of harmonious world and peaceful development.

In the most recent scenario, the 2009 White paper again qualifies the intentions of the leadership in China. The prosperity of Tibet under the stewardship of the mainland China is one of the various ways which China has adopted as an axiom to continue to claim its sovereignty over the region. The renewed emphasis is conspicuous in the fact that every alternate year China is churning out a White paper on Tibet. It is managing to realign with Taiwan through economic engagement and its new found indication on leadership of Sun Yatsen seems to be in light of the Taiwan question.

The Party as an Institution Propagating Nationalism

The creation of CCP in 1921 was a result of the May 4th movement, which sought radical changes in the nationalist discourse. Li Dazhao, and Chen Duxiu the founder members of the CCP portrayed China's pain and agony through poems and stories written by Lu Xun and criticised the outdated political institutions of China. While the Nationalist Party had been successful in defining its goal as establishing a "Party nation" and promoted the new government's ideology through a modern national culture, it failed to gain the support of the people for its cause. The CCP on the other hand, carried forward the process of state-building by stirring up enormous support from the rural and urban masses. Franz Schurman and Orville Schell in *Republican China* trace the evolution of the CCP in a tussle with the GMD for the recognition as the pioneer of nationalist ambitions in China.

The differences between the CCP and the GMD were glaring, which was seen in the approach adopted by the leadership of the two parties. The CCP party rhetoric holds that since the very day of its founding, it had been "holding high the banner of democracy and human rights." It encouraged and assisted Sun in reorganizing the GMD, effected the cooperation between the Kuomintang and the Communist Party and launched the Northern Expedition against the reactionary rule of the warlords. It holds Chiang Kai-shek as a betrayer of the democratic revolution and posits that after his exile, the Party united all patriots and democrats and mobilised people in a struggle against civil war, hunger, autocracy and persecution. In the liberated areas, it established "democratic governments which guaranteed the people's democratic rights and resolutely implemented its own democratic programs. Under the Party's leadership, the Chinese people overthrew the GMD reactionaries' dictatorial rule."

Besides these irreconcilable differences between the two parties, the political programme adopted at the first National Congress of the CCP suggested that the early political literature of the CCP had developed a mature understanding of Marxism and espoused the creation of a new society based on communist ideals. While the earlier deliberations in the party congress demonstrated the evolution of the Marxist paradigm as a corollary to this thinking and made determined efforts to oust the imperialist elements,[81] after the establishment of the PRC in 1949, the party began to debate more about the modernisation of the Chinese society. It is imperative to delineate at the outset that comprehending nationalism through considering the institution of the party forces one to engage with the nationalist goals of the post-1949 era. Hence, nationalism has to be viewed through the prism of promoting national interests.

The attempts by the Party at reconstructing the nation soon after the establishment of the PRC can be studied through the writings of contemporary party leaders. One of them being Chen Yun, who articulated the aims and methodology of the party in a series of articles which were later published as his selected works. Surmising on "Building a new People's Customs system" he delved on the challenges before the Party—"it is a major reform to transform a customs system that for a century has been under imperialist control into a system completely under our own control, one appropriate to new democracy ... Cadres new and old, who are working in the customs service must unite in a concerted effort to build a new system that truly belongs to the people."[82]

He also favoured the readjustment of the relations between the public and private sector so that the provisions laid down in the article 26 of the Common Programme could be realized in full measure—"only when all five sectors of the economy are given due consideration and allowed to play their part can we all work together to build a new democracy and then socialism."[83]

At the Eighth Party Congress convened in Beijing in September 1956 the CCP hailed the economic achievements of the first-five year plan (1953-57) under the influence of the de-Stalinization program initiated by the 20th congress of the CPSU which deleted the term Mao Zedong thought from its political report diminishing the cult of Mao.[84]

Nonetheless, the Ninth Party Congress convened in 1969 sent a clear message to the international community that Mao was still in command and proposed Lin Biao as the successor to Mao. The 10th Party Congress revised the constitution of the CCP and reinstated Mao Zedong thought as theoretical basis guiding the future of the country. With the death of Mao, the party embarked on the path of building socialism with Chinese characteristics under the guidance of Deng Xiaoping, who in the process of nation building renounced the belief in communist utopia which had extolled egalitarianism.

The key concept that emerged during the 1980s to deal with the process of nation building was that of "China's special characteristics" (*zhong guo tese*), an idea which was mooted by Hu Yaobang in the 12th Party Congress, as mentioned before. For this purpose the party advocated a new culture in its 1986 resolutions drafted by Zhao Ziyang, that is a culture "that incorporates the best from historical traditions" and "inspires a sense of national pride, self-respect and self-confidence." The Party also stressed upon the need for a scientific worldview and culture:

"We should work actively to change those undesirable customs that still prevail in the cities and the countryside, to advocate cultured, healthful ways of living ... these reforms should be carried out voluntarily by the masses."[85]

One of the salient features of the Deng era was the development of the entrepreneurial class as speaking in Marxist terms—a "class for itself." They had utilised the symbolisms of the leading figures to enhance their business interests and now were accruing the benefits provided by the opening up of the economy. Hence, they assumed the role of interest groups that inhibited the reinvention of Maoist communism. The focus of the party hereafter was on the issues of modernisation, democracy and corruption. The government even crushed the democratic movement led by the students and intellectuals in 1989 in order to "save Chinese socialism." It forced the Chinese leadership to revisit its notions of development and trace back its roots to the Maoist era. However, this was denied on account of the fact that the younger generations had been brought up under relatively free polity and were becoming accustomed to the ways of modern infrastructure and thus would not appreciate the government's stance of market socialism.

The CCP also undertook systematic assessments of the causes for the collapse of other communist regimes around the world to avoid any internal and external challenges to the party. These led to intra-party reforms affecting each sector of state, society and economy.[86] While these introspections created a space for the advent of democracy in China, it was Jiang Zemin who streamlined the significance of the party by allowing the public spaces to continue with limited autonomy and argued China had no option but to be ruled by the CCP.

The CCP reviewed major policy statements to bring them in consonance with the political exigencies. For instance, the environment protection committee reviewed its policies and suggested fourteen laws; the state industrial policy of the 1990s was revisited, anti-corruption drives were taken up and medical aid was furthered. The party also articulated the nation's response to the Western perspectives on world order advocated by Samuel Huntington, when Xu Yunchang wrote an article in *Beijing Review*, that Huntington's thesis reflected a growing uncertainty and a lack of confidence about the future of Western civilization, he advocated that the West and the East should learn and adapt from each other.[87] This articulation was very critical as it demonstrated the nationalist visions and aspirations under the aegis of the party. Many others like Jiang Changbin of the Central Party School, reiterated the need for improved "inner-party democracy" (*dangnei minzhu*) and improving inner party life (*dangnei shenghuo*)—which meant improving consultation at all levels of the party apparatus.[88]

Jiang Zemin further endorsed the privatisation drive aiming at making the Chinese nation an industrialised economy at par with the advanced countries at the 15th Party Congress held in 1997, which was preceded by the development of townships and village enterprises.[89] He nevertheless, did not succumb to the pressures from the democratizing influences of the modernisation drive. Once again he relied on the past to prepare ground for the future in advocating an anti-imperialist genre of patriotism. However, continuing the tradition of the Party, the 16th party Congress in 2002 brought Hu Jintao to the realm of affairs and endorsed the policy lines set by his predecessor. It also took a variety of political initiatives aimed at establishing a "more institutionalised more formalised and more-procedure based system."[90]

Thus, one can discern from the direction of the policy formulated under the CCP's guidance and the rhetoric assumed by the leadership that CCP is visualizing the ascendance of the Chinese nation as "a country to be reckoned with" focusing on its national ethos and interests, thereby provoking a nationalism that is bolstered by state assistance. Several Sinologists concur the nature of politicized nationalism created by the highly moralistic communism advocated by the party was reminiscent of the culturalism of the late nineteenth century.[91] But it is also significantly different in the manner that it is managing to adapt and realign its attempts at political reform to bring in people from various sections of the society. This is most prominent in its recruitment of the entrepreneurial class into the party which was suspended in 1989 but has been reinitiated after 2001.[92]

It has resorted to suppressive measures in the public domain for the purpose of consolidation of territorial gains and has not allowed much dissent to proliferate or sustain. However, with the gradual increase in the impact of the global forces, the CCP cannot afford to retain the honour of being the sole spokesmen for Chinese nationalism as the legitimacy of the CCP itself is under scrutiny, which might make way for democratic ideas to permeate and influence various sections of its society. Various other forces, mostly the common masses through medium like the Internet and media have come to fore voicing their own understanding and beliefs on Chinese nationalism, which is likely to force the CCP to revisit its understanding of what kind of a nation it will like China to become.

PLA as an Agent of Nationalism

The People's Liberation Army (PLA) came to the fore under the auspices of the CCP following the white terror of 1927. It played a crucial role in assisting the CCP to power and moved towards modernisation and gradually came out of its guerrilla warfare tactics. As militaries all over the world remain the biggest tools of nationalism and steel-hardy organisations of the state apparatus, the PLA also exhibited the extreme indoctrination of this phenomenon. Historically, the army protected the communist base areas and eventually seized state power for the party by defeating the nationalist army on the mainland. In effect, the first generation of the Chinese Communist Military leaders became the founders of the PRC after 22 years of military struggle.

It became an enabler of the nationalist discourse by helping the Party in consolidation of the far-flung regions, for instance Tibet, in which the PLA was the sole reflector of state authority. However, under the tutelage of Lin Biao, the PLA underwent a radical transformation in terms of ideological indoctrination and politicisation. Lin Biao abolished the ranking system in the PLA to make it a more egalitarian body reflecting the communist stint. The PLA came to be projected as a model for the entire nation to be revered and followed. The soldiers were assigned many civilian tasks since the time of the Great Leap Forward and its revolutionary characteristics were regularly highlighted in the media and in the official documents of the Party and the State.[93]

It was also the main instrument of Chinese national power projection in the South Korean war and against US imperialism. However, no major efforts were made to modernize the PLA and it remained by far the Chinese army of the "people's war" days or a peasant army. Nevertheless, after 1978, when development became the leading jargon of the country's nationalist goals, the PLA refurbished its support for the Party's programme. At a panel discussion held by the PLA on 13 October, 1992, Yang Baibing, representative to the 14th National Congress of the CCP and the Secretary-General of the Central Military Commission, said that:

> "The whole party, army and people across the country must work together to carry forward the great cause of building socialism with Chinese characteristics. He said the key to achieving this great objective lies in unswervingly upholding the basic line of the party ... the PLA should spare no effort in giving publicity to the idea that only when we have a prosperous country can we have a strong national defence..."[94]

As China went through the phase of transition from a traditional to modern society based on industrialisation, several reforms were launched to transform the PLA from a labour-intensive (*renlimiji*) to a technology-intensive (*jishumiji*) army.[95] China's increasing political ambition and rising international position necessitated the armed forces to be technologically capable to counter the Western military forces. One can discern a paradigmatic shift in the PLA's role after the 15th Party Congress of the CCP, whereby the PLA acquired an unprecedented potential for wielding political influence that was not possible under the earlier leaders. Thus, there was a rupture in the Party–PLA relations that essentially defined the pre-1990s scenario. In November 1995, China brought out a White Paper on "China's Arms Control and Disarmament" wherein it laid stress on the need for peace in the world given the disastrous consequences of the two world wars, but the development of Chinese military and marine capability later during the decade marked a shift from this approach.

China acknowledged that as a major developing country with a long coastline, it was necessary for China to indulge in marine development and protection.[96] To allay negative impressions from the international community, China qualified that its defence was largely defensive in nature and was kept subordinate to and in the service of the nation's economic construction. It wanted to create an image of a responsible stake holder on the international arena. Its National Defence policy paper argued that the task of the armed forces of the PRC was to consolidate national defence, resist aggression, defend the motherland, safeguard the people's peaceful labour, participate in national construction and strive to serve the people.

In its National Defence Paper in 2002, China harped on the discourse of the international situation undergoing profound changes and the development of a well-off society in the changed scenario. Yet, this rhetoric was undermined to address the growing uncertainties of the non-traditional threats to the Chinese nation. The paper outlined the following tasks and goals of China's national defence:[97]

- To consolidate national defence, prevent and resist aggression
- To stop separation and realise complete unification of the motherland
- To stop armed subversion and safeguard social stability
- To accelerate national defence and military modernisation
- To safeguard world peace and oppose aggression and expansion

The PLA by promoting the national interests and goals identified by the political leadership has functioned as one of the most prominent organization proliferating nationalism in China. It is even involved in popularizing and strengthening national defence education with "patriotism at its core."[98] Its role has been even more significant in the realm of shaping the strategic thinking of the Chinese leaders since each of them have traditionally received some training in the military schools.

In 2004, in its National Defence Paper, China again recognised the services provided by the PLA to the building of the Chinese nation. The Fourth Plenary Session of the 16th CPC Central Committee (CCCPC) and the enlarged CPC Conference of the Central Military Commission (CMC), held successively in September 2004, paid a high tribute to Jiang Zemin for his outstanding contributions to national defence and military modernization. China believed that at this time the tendencies of hegemonism and unilateralism had gained ground and the struggles for strategic points, strategic resources and strategic dominance was increasing in the international arena. The Iraq War in 2003 also exerted far-reaching influence on the international and regional security situations.

This led to a further shift in its focus on developing its maritime capabilities than just the PLA. However, the PLA cadres continue to be held in high esteem and their contribution to the China's comprehensive national power is lauded. The 2006 National Defence Paper added a further dimension to the PLA's role in China's national strategy besides the goals outlined earlier. The PLA was to be "dedicated to performing its historical missions for the new stage in the new century, namely, providing an important source of strength for consolidating the ruling position of the CCP, providing a solid security guarantee for sustaining the important period of strategic opportunity for national development, providing a strong strategic support for safeguarding national interests, and playing a major role in maintaining world peace and promoting common development."[99] This was ironically juxtaposed with a parallel downsizing of the PLA by 200,000 troops and a broadening of its activities into the social service schemes, thus literally involving it in the procedure of nation-building.[100]

The National Defence Paper released in 2009, which was a compilation of PLA's work till 2008, reiterated the defensive nature of China's national defence.[101] For the first time, it mentioned the "informationization" as the goal of modernization of its national defence and armed forces. Interestingly, it also mentioned that these guidelines adhered to the strategic concept of people's war. At present, its influence in the political sphere is much more perceptible along with its military function. The scope of its activities on both national and international level is increasing by the day and as a representative body it has been delegated major responsibilities in the task of national unification and sustenance. Besides these two significant institutions several processes like formation of a national literature, use of imagery and cultural propaganda also bolstered nationalism during this period.

Social Processes and Nationalism

Increasingly, the media and literature have become the sites of establishing political or popular discourse in contemporary times. Thus, the processes which generate nationalism in any country are reflected in social events of cultural integration through modern symbols. For instance, the celebration of the National Day,[102] the sentiments attached to the unfurling of a flag, the territorial depiction of their country in government directed maps and an education system which is increasingly being made to bear the burden of rebuilding nationalism and imparting patriotic education.

The earliest attempts at building public consciousness through such symbolism in the Chinese case can be deemed to have been started in September of 1915 with the first issue of New Youth (Xin Qingnian), an influential and quickly imitated magazine. In the first plenary issue of *New Youth*, its editor, Chen Duxiu, later one of the founders of the CCP, published his essay "Call to Youth." In an electrifying polemic, Chen encouraged young people to discard the shackles of Confucianism and the traditional culture to cultivate an attitude opposite to that of Confucianism: independent, scientific, aggressive and progressive.[103]

The New Culture Movement was instigated as a result since the state was strong enough to enforce monopolization of language literature and propaganda sources. Even in regions as far off as Tibet, the only official language to be taught was Chinese. While these attempts were parallel to the nationalist tenor of complete subjugation of the individual to the state, the later attempts revealed an attempt to adjust the nationalist rhetoric to a more open culture.

With the changing scenario of the 1980s, the atmosphere became more favourable to voicing of disparate ideologies. *Renmin Ribao* (*Jenmin Jiabao*), or the *People's Daily*, the most popular newspaper reflected the opinions of the contemporary cleavages. It not only vocalized the Party strand of thinking but also managed to show the internal bickering and tussle among ideological formulations. It worked as the conscience bearer of the nation by reminding from time-to-time the ill effects of imperialism and capitalism and thus reflected a stream of thought which was initially against the endorsement of market forces (*Renmin Ribao*, 19 September 1982). In 1983, Chinese intellectuals began to express concerns over the growing influence of "right ideology."

One of the most predominant way of creating a national consciousness and identity then came through the effective use of propaganda and posters by the leadership. Several of these "propaganda posters" so called because of their propagation by the state, have been collected and compiled by Michael Wolf, a famous photographer (known for his work on cultural identity of China) who discovered the cult-value associated with them. A closer look at these posters evinces how cultural legacy, imagination and pedagogic steering were woven into one single whole to formulate a discourse of nationalism.

The primary purpose of these posters was to create a legend of revolutionary martyrs who would become figurative role models for the current generations. Reflecting an entire generation's fancies, the posters show the unbridled eagerness and zeal of the masses. Anchee Min, a partaker of the revolutionary era who also became a leading figure of the propaganda films created by Jiang Qing (Mao's wife), recollects the ecstasy of the contemporary masses in a prologue given to this collection:

> "I wanted to be the girl in the poster when I was growing up.[104] Every day I dressed up like that girl in a white cotton shirt with a red scarf around my neck, and I braided my hair the same way. I liked the fact that she was surrounded by the revolutionary martyrs, whom I was taught to worship since kindergarten."[105]

With a nostalgic tenor she remembers the sense of loyalty and selflessness cultivated by these posters to entice the youth to join in the nationalist cause.

Another person who witnessed the development of the rhetoric of nationalism and patriotism also reflects on the efficacy of these posters in abetting the didacticism of the contemporary practices. Duo Duo recollects an anecdote from his neighbourhood where a child was inspired by the allegory being imprinted by these posters and shouted at the top of his voice to every passer-by: "I have three arrows that can work miracles. When I shoot the first arrow, our building will turn into a 30-storey scraper. When I shoot the second, skyscrapers will spring up all over China. When I shoot the third, communism would be implemented all over the world." Duo Duo observes that these posters had an undercurrent of folk art hidden underneath them; they had roots in traditional myths, legends, and in the notion of bringing together ancient history, people and nature they became the source from which a new soul of the nation sprang up.

It is easy to trace the element of construction of the "myth and legend" from the anecdotes presented by these people which had been envisaged as the prime-agent of nation-building by scholars like Anderson and Hobsbawm. Besides the obvious purpose of entertainment these posters carried an important edifying function: they were meant to educate the people on the sense of differentiating between the right and the wrong and given the constraint of illiterate people, they spread the political message through visualizing abstract ideas. The original works of art were reproduced in journals and magazines and sometimes also as postage stamps. The larger posters could be seen almost in all public spaces: on the streets, in the railway stations while the smaller ones were distributed through the network of the Xinhua bookshops for mass consumption. The contents pledged "allegiance to the Communist cause, or obedience to chairman Mao," or were engaged in "the glorious task of rebuilding the nation", as specified by Stefan R Landsberger. They also provided testimony to the shifting focus of consideration from the Maoist era to Deng's times. While the earlier posters glorified work and personal sacrifice for the greater well-being and paid scant attention to the private dimensions of people's lives, to rest and recreation, the later posters under Deng Xiaoping shifted their focus to an "arts for art's sake" belief.

Other interesting notions also came to play in the social sphere. Earlier not having Mao's portrait on display indicated an apparent unwillingness to go with the revolutionary flow of the movement, or even counter-revolutionary outlook. But during Deng's era the posters became a part of the larger unregulated art market and the main aim was to design posters which could create public support for the new multi-faceted policies that made up the reform package. More and careful attention was paid to the new affluence that manifested itself in the Chinese society, particularly in the urban areas. Most significantly, people were shown enjoying themselves and actually having fun.

Also, while the earlier genre was replete with posters declaring axioms like—"life is exciting in a mountain village", "a bad element is publicly criticized", "study Marx and Lenin; think clearly", "maintain constant vigilance, destroy the enemy" and "be a good child of the party" et al, the new approach was embodied in posters depicting the four modernizations. One of the most prominent posters belonging to this genre was the one depicting "three children on a rocket soaring towards a woman who was believed in the Chinese mythology to be a fairy named Chang-E who lived on the moon with her rabbit."[106] China's first rocket thus derived its name from a traditional legend, which epitomized the drawing together of myth, legend and modernity for the purpose of welding the nation, which was reflected in this poster designed by an artist, Jin Dingsheng.

The posters of this period made absolute use of allegories, mythological creatures and colourful portrayals to rejuvenate the sparks of nationalism. Celebrating youth and beautiful souls, the new posters claimed "China must achieve great things for humanity," "an army without culture is a dull-witted army and a dull-witted army cannot defeat the enemy" et al. Many of the stories presented in these posters were later co-opted by the Chinese cinema and still form a part of most opera performances in China. Thus, these posters provided a legacy to the nationalist rhetoric by providing a direction to the youth and the older generations. While art developed into an autonomous expressive space, it contributed largely to the corpus of developments which helped in engendering nationalism in China. The nationalist discourse hereafter was voiced by different repositories and had to let go much of its didactic tenor.

These processes were further intensified until the Tiananmen incident, which posited a challenge to the governmental apparatus and the government curtailed the freedom in public spaces. Immediately after the incident *Renmin Ribao/People's Daily*, published an article evoking patriotic themes of China's past humiliation by the foreigners. Thus, despite the presence of alternative space the Party or the state were able to manoeuvre the media for the purposes of nation-building and strengthening. Very large number of articles on tradition and national culture appeared in newspapers like *Guangming Daily* and various journals became a dais for expression of official and non-official opinions. According to one estimate more than 1500 articles were published during the great academic debate on culture in China in 1984-89, several new journals were founded and over twenty centres for cultural study were established.[107]

The PRC school textbooks from the 1990s onwards began to contain government-issued maps that showed three borders for China: the current boundaries; those in 1919; and those in 1840 at the time of the Opium war. All alienations were labelled and students were taught how these respective lands were taken from the Chinese. The goal of "national reunification" began to be deeply embedded into the citizens' psyche as a part of the Communist Party's Patriotic Education campaign. Several ancient scholars were cited to rekindle the patriotic sentiments of the Chinese people, for instance: Zhang Taiyan's works:

> "So long as there are nation-states (guojia), we must uphold nationalism (minzu zhuyi). ... We are concerned not just for our own Han race, but for other victimized nations, whose lands have been conquered, rights usurped, and people enslaved. ... A true nationalist is one who extends his sympathy to others who have suffered from the same (national) excruciation."[108]

A Chinese bestseller in the mid-1990s, *Zhong guo keyi shuo bu* or "China Can Say No" authored by Song, Zhang and Qiao, 1996, created immense fervour and gave rise to a reactionary and emotive nationalism. It criticized a number of pro-democracy activists like physicist Fang Lizhi and journalist Lin Binyan. Describing the disenchantment among Chinese with the US starting during the 1990s especially after it adopted China-containment rhetoric, rejected China's bid for WTO and apparently worked against China's bid for the 2000 Summer Olympics, the book criticised US foreign policy and American individualism. It claimed that America used China as a scapegoat for American problems and derided Japan as a client-state of the US. It led to the growth of a political clique, which is seen as the say-no nationalists in the Chinese political apparatus.

Moreover, the recent Japanese history textbook controversies and China's objection to Japanese Prime Minister Junichiro Koizumi's visit to the Yasukuni shrine demonstrate the growing nationalist sentiments of the Chinese government. These issues shall be dealt in a greater detail in the following chapters. In the recent years, the nationalist tenor is more apparent in the fiscal and development reforms. In 2000, the government unveiled an ambitious plan to develop the poorer western parts of the country, where most ethnic minorities reside. Provinces with predominantly non-Han populations have been given the highest level of subsidies. These strategies are being devised for the purpose of greater assimilation of the social fabric of the nation.

Nationalism and Identity Issues

A question that is indelibly intertwined with the deliberations on nationalism is that of identity. While the earliest forms of association were primarily based on the racial or ethnic lineages, the global era has posited a need for specific delineation of who a Chinese is? What it means to be one? How the Chinese perceive themselves and respond to questions of identity? Generally the word used by the Chinese to describe their self-identity is the *ren min* (the people). This, however, is daubed of political connotations as a concept covering loyal and true citizens in contrast to "counter-revolutionaries." Further, the concept of *Zhonghua minzu* (the nationalities of China) is often used to invoke a sense of unity among the national groups and to counter *da Han zhuyi* (*Great Han-ism or Han chauvinism*) as well as separatism among national minorities.[109]

National identity is normally circumscribed by the boundaries of a nation, whose dimensions tend to coincide with such objective criteria as common language, ethnic or racial origin and political culture. Also, boundaries are determined by the sovereign state carving out a precarious identity by force and guile in a competitive international environment. While several scholars look at the creation of an identity in terms of a relationship of identification between the state and the nation, the identity of the state can be largely construed as a "symbol system known as the national essence, which consists of myths, rituals, ceremonies, and folklore that relate how the nation came to be and what it stands for."[110]

This symbol system or cultural identity is subjected to a historical evolution influenced by the projected aspirations and demands of the citizenry, domestic political history and foreign policy experience. However, a crisis can occur when these boundaries blur, or are challenged at the margin. As Pye puts it "in the process of political development an identity crisis occurs when a community finds that what it accepted as the physical and psychological definitions of its collective self are no longer acceptable under new historic conditions."[111]

It was probably this crisis, which unabashedly stared the Chinese in their face when questions of identity of its minorities and diaspora arose. The diaspora Chinese have found it more difficult to be assimilated into the Chinese polity once they have gone and resided abroad. In fact, during the early twentieth century, most Chinese who went to the US or European countries were declared as traitors and were not allowed to come back to the mainland. It was only after the establishment of the PRC, and more so during the Deng era that these expatriates began to be seen as assets for the country. This was especially evident in the Chinese students who had gone to France for higher studies under various research programmes and they began to be called back to their nation and help with the development process.

While the Western understanding, most recently voiced by Michael Ignatieff, suggests that group identities breed conflict and that the only solvent for the intolerance and hatred of competing chauvinisms is the replacement of group identification by raging individualism, the eastern responses have definitely been more accommodative. The identity question is even starker in the domestic realm where the state is finding it difficult to assimilate ethnic groups differing in origin and history. The Tibet, Taiwan and Xinjiang questions remain the biggest challenge for the nationalist consolidation of the Chinese state precisely for the reasons that they are culturally or racially or historically difficult to assimilate.

"National defence" (*guofang yishi*) as a strategy identified by the Chinese government and understood by the Communist Party as the preservation and maintenance of the PRC's territorial integrity aims at preventing the ethnic minorities in the autonomous regions of Xinjiang and Tibet from seceding or "splitting." Though it is not necessary to delve into these sub-nationalist tendencies in this particular work, but it is important to cite these cases which reflect the struggle within China given identity politics as opposed to a largely Han nationalism.

In brief, as far as the Taiwanese question is concerned, the Chinese government is constantly involved in enticing the Taiwanese entrepreneurs by providing them lucrative packages to create extra-economic linkages. It continuously aids the pro-integration lobby to come to power and initiate the process of national integration. Thus, China's influence is perceptible in the outcome of the Taiwanese election results where it utilizes the economic linkages of the Chinese entrepreneurs to influence the behaviour of the electorate as well as the Party leanings.

While anxiety among many mainland leaders and citizens grows with a push for independence in Taiwan, which is regarded by most of them as a part of the Chinese nation, the Chinese citizens increasingly support the government's efforts in bringing the Taiwanese island under control of the mainland administration. In a survey conducted by Wang Jisi, Director of the Institute of American studies of the Chinese Academy of Social Science, it was deduced that the majority of Chinese Internet users believe that the mainland government has been too soft on the Taiwan issue and were willing to support more aggressive measures by their government.[112]

Similarly, the Tibetan issue remains at the core of nationalist identity formation for China. The riots of April 2008, which demonstrated Tibet's unwillingness to be assimilated completely into the Chinese nation and a craving for support from the international community for its endeavour to establish an autonomous independent kingdom, instigated massive populist reactions from the Mainland Chinese *enmasse*. They perceive it as an attack on the solidarity of their nation and denounce any kind of intervention by any other country.

Moreover, foraying into the ethnic dimensions of the Xinjiang problem, where the Muslim Uyghurs are contending for a separate administrative apparatus,[113] one finds an intense struggle against the Han majority which is seen as accruing all the benefits of development as opposed to the indigenous people. Though the state has implemented the Western Development Campaign and the Strike hard campaigns as its strategy to deal with the Xinjiang problem, to provide a basis for assimilation of the Uyghur minorities, these have failed drastically due to the identity divide. Still the Chinese state persists in its endeavour given its unrelenting faith in the benefits of national integration.[114]

Chinese nationalism thus bears the responsibility of creating a plank for resolution between all these forms of identities. While the return of Hong Kong and Macau had bolstered the sense of nationalist accommodation, the current situations still posit severe challenges to the task of nationalism. Homogenization as a trait of globalization endorsed by Ernest Gellner does not provide substantive avenues of understanding these issues in the Chinese temporality. While territorial entities can be easily assimilated, the separate economic and ethnic systems simply need recognition. Like in the case of Hong Kong and Macao, their previous economic systems could not be completely done away with, which augmented the need for accommodation as a strategy.

Only accommodation can provide the necessary basis for realignment of Chinese identity that today assumes a diverse character. There is an increasing trend of defining the self in congruence with the role allotted to the citizens by the government. The Chinese citizens exhibit a culturally bounded perception of self and national identity whereby they feel a need to conform to the traditional expectations and downplay the differences to display "normality."

This is particularly true in relation to the overseas Chinese today who draw on series of Chinese cultural resources for managing their identities in a largely non-Chinese atmosphere. They perceive Chinese identity as "an invaluable defining feature to hold onto."[115] The Chinese government which is eager to utilize the economic and intellectual resources that the overseas Chinese can provide has promulgated certain administrative and legal concepts for integrating them into the mainstream nationalism. *"Huaqiao"*—Chinese citizens residing abroad and *"huaren"*—Chinese who have assumed foreign nationality, are constantly beckoned to contribute to the cause of Chinese nationalism. The setting up of China towns in the countries of residence and massive saving habits which help in accumulating financial resources for the mother country, exhibit the strong sense of "imagined community" that the overseas Chinese identify with.

A titillating mode of national identity formation among the Chinese today is the influence of the Opera as suggested by Ashley Thorpe, who extrapolates that construction of identity through "performance" has been one of the significant contributions of the Chinese opera culture. Such a representation makes traditional performance "pure" and "unchangeable" and creates a fixed identity that exhibits a perceptible "Chineseness" in different contexts.[116] Further metamorphoses in identity formation have to be construed within the changed parameters of global influences. While the global forces beckon a more rationalized and world-class citizen outlook, a strong nationalism beckons loyalty to the country. Hence these two contending genres of identity formation are also vying for attention from the Chinese citizens. It is within the contestation of these two paradigms of identity formations that the identity issues of the citizens will be further construed.

Contemporary Chinese Nationalism: "The Manifestation of a Pragmatic and Eclectic Discourse"

The debunking of the idea of a homogenous entity in the form of the nation becomes the bedrock for studying the character of nationalism in a multi-ethnic China today. It is also essential to bear in mind that when one deliberates on the issues of history and identity of a nation it is imperative to suggest that at any given point of time the discourse of nationalism was not the "only one." It was one of a set of identities that existed simultaneously in China, however, as a predominant influence. It is remarkable how in the Chinese case this identity has been allowed to subsume all other kind of identities for a long period of time than in case of any other country. The polyphonies and contradictions have been negotiated in much regressive terms to shape a monologue of the nation which still persists.

The need for asserting nationalist sentiments has become indelible in the wake of globalisation, which has brought along an expanded state of consciousness of the world. The cultural challenge perceived by the state (and other groups) through increased individualism and consumerism constitutes a significant challenge to it in terms of defining and guarding what it understood as a "Chinese culture and identity." The CCP's long harboured intention of developing a socialist state faces a severe challenge from constant friction with values of capitalist system and the global culture and deference of action. The state's response thus, has come under the aegis of a rejection of the cultural impacts of globalisation and a propagation of the "strong society" and a theory of "cultural resistance."

Chinese nationalism today is a mix of statist, ethnic, jingoistic and populist, developmental and other categories which have been scrutinized above; it derives a little from each of these sentiments without renouncing any one in particular. Hence it can be comfortably argued that the nationalism extant in China today is primarily "discursive" in nature and "accommodative" in spirit (within the ambit of a nation). It aims at being "eclectic" deriving support from its various nationalities and manifests itself in form of a mature national ideology, which is willing to consider pragmatic solutions for keeping its integrity intact. A shift is perceptible in its rhetoric which was earlier aimed against a foreign aggressor or reprobate nations, to the one that is comfortable and confident of dealing with the other nations and has redirected its efforts to solve internal dissensions and assume a leadership role on the global front. This paradigm of nationalism can be christened as a *"discursive and syncretic nationalism."*

This is a nationalism that has economic development at its core and is being buttressed through the *"media"* constantly; a "nationalism" which fosters an unprecedented revival of national pride and a sense of collective self-actualisation through accommodating differences. This metamorphosed nationalism manages, realigns and curbs the dissentions and contradictory spaces created by the global onslaught while providing for qualified reasonable public spaces. It is manifested through a language that produces a discourse of an institutionalised way of thinking and a social boundary, which is impossible to escape. Moreover it is this syncretism that allows it to mould the multitudes of the daily lives of millions of people into a single undifferentiated identity of being a Chinese.

While the "thread of development" and the stable governance under a one party leadership has provided continuity in discourse throughout the growth of the ideology, this accommodative nationalism has recognized that globalisation as a phenomenon creates more avenues and provides enough spaces for alternative dissent. Thus, the only way to maintain the integrity of the nation will be to assume the responsibility of accommodation wherein the minority nationalities would be allowed to retain certain kinds of autonomy and still owe their allegiance to the Chinese nation. The government has also realized the potential of the public institutions and media in creating favourable or unfavourable mass opinions about the state and hence, it has assumed a moralistic dimension that runs parallel to the national ethos. Thus, an ecumenist trend is also palpable in its latest discourse.

With the basic aim of national integration the formulation of strategies like the "one country two systems, cultural autonomy, privileged rights for regions such as Tibet, Taiwan and Xinjiang" have been devised as strategy for spread of nationalism. It is not the aim of this work to predict the efficacy of this accommodative nationalism, but to delineate the trends, which enunciate the accommodative spirit within the nation while a discursive rhetorical propaganda in its handling of foreign nationalities. Nationalism is being construed as a double-edged sword which is bolstering public opinion in support of the government as well as acting as a tool in the hands of the government.

However, there is no scope for "alternative nationalisms"—which some of the Sinologists comprehend in the resurgence of ethnic or cultural nationalism under the current structures of Chinese self-conceptions. Given the nature of the party state all these ethnic as well as cultural sub-nationalisms are subsumed or accommodated in the larger rhetoric of the state which inspired by the national interests recognizes the need to cull or eliminate any such tendencies that might prove inimical to the national interests of China or loss of its territorial assets. Moreover, the discourse of Chinese nationalism has throughout included the conceptualization of the "ethnie" and it cannot be regarded as a resurgence of this particular trait of it. Hence, one has to relent that there can be no "alternatives to nationalism" only dissentions in form of sub-nationalism. That is not to say that the consequential nationalism is homogenous in nature, the reality is far from it.

With inferences from the recent events the syncretic character and the discursive nature of contemporary Chinese nationalism can be deduced. The irredentist form of nationalism is quite perceptible in response to the international community on their reaction to the Tibetan unrest as a violation of human rights, where China maintains its stance of "no intervention in internal matters." This is strongly supported by the common citizens who have come to accept the terms that the future of their country lies in consolidation of their territorial possessions, which in turn calls for pragmatic solutions. Moreover, the growing confidence of the Chinese economy is shifting the psyche of the nation from that of a victim of foreign aggression to one of an impending superpower. This shift leads to a sophistication and flexibility in the government as well as the public behaviour.

The developmental nationalism of Deng's era is reiterated in the vision of the Party in contemporary times. Hu Jintao, in his address to the Boao Forum for Asia Annual Conference in 2008, advocated the continuing of reform and opening up and advancing win-win cooperation. Drawing upon the traditional lineages he asserted, "Over the past 30 years the Chinese people, acting in a pioneering spirit and making bold innovations, have unswervingly carried out reform...historical changes have taken place in China."[117]

He further deliberated upon the goals of Chinese nationalism and its congruity with the peaceful aspirations from China by the international bodies:

> "China will firmly keep to the path of peaceful development, a strategic decision made by the Chinese government and people...the fundamental interests of the Chinese people and the Common interests of the world's people are in harmony. Peaceful development is the only way leading to the great rejuvenation of the Chinese nation."[118]

Further on Hu demonstrated the furtherance of the nationalist goals of making China a reckonable country by propounding that "China is dedicated to building a harmonious world of lasting peace and common prosperity. We endeavour to make international relations more democratic. We take active part in international cooperation in counter-terrorism, non-proliferation, climate change...we work for a more just and equitable international order."[119]

Hu provoked similar sentiments earlier in the report to the Seventeenth National Congress of the CCP delivered by Hu Jintao on 15 October 2007. The report streamlined the direction of development and challenges being faced by the Chinese nation:

> "the world today is undergoing extensive and profound changes...this brings us unprecedented opportunities as well as unprecedented challenges ... the party must hold the great banner of socialism with Chinese characteristics and lead the people in starting from this new historical point, grasping and making the most of the important period of strategic opportunities, staying realistic and pragmatic, forging ahead with determination, continuing to build a moderately prosperous

society in all respects and accelerate socialist modernization and accomplishing the lofty mission bestowed by the times."[120]

It is perceptible that the Party and the leadership continue to rely upon its legacy to derive legitimacy for contemporary development models, which portray the pinnacle of nationalist determination of growth trajectory. The party statements released by the 17th Party Congress in October 2008, under the leadership of Hu Jintao depict the continuing trend of the Party's influence on the nationalist rhetoric.

This continuation of the Party's rhetoric is further substantiated by public approval hence what comes to be manifested is a "discursive nationalism"—which was to begin with a brainchild of the state government has now assumed a character of popular support through discursive and rhetorical propaganda. It not only provides an identity and solidarity to a society experiencing the disruptive forces associated with rapid development but also provides a way of expression to the cultural ethos of the country.

The public spaces or the public sphere, as coined by Habermas, opens up the arena for contestation between the state-bred nationalism and the populist nationalism. The nationalism born thereby is not the nationalism of the educated elite or the political elite, or the few privileged individuals, it is but the nationalism of any common citizen literate or aware enough to understand and react to the spread of information.[121] Though Christopher Hughes limits this nationalism to the techno-nationals of the twenty-first century China, it is possible to stretch the argument to various other elements in the society who are capable of gathering sources of information and endorse a selective affirmation of day-to-day experiences.

Various tools of mass propaganda assist this process. While on the one hand the Internet has become the largest source of information and provides for the most vociferous vocalization of nationalistic rhetoric,[122] on the other hand, the Chinese cinema and literature are also providing a glimpse into popular nationalist responses. It is this medium which is of late leading to an indigenisation of nationalism in China. One of the most significant repercussions of this "endemicisation" of nationalism is that while earlier the fate of the CCP and Chinese nationalism were intertwined but not inter-dependant, now it is the virtual manifestation of nationalism which is going to determine the future of the Party. Since any policy which might hinder the national interests as perceived by the Chinese citizens will oust the regime from power.

The manifestation of this Internet generated nationalism and the literary influences on nationalism as a part of the interaction between the Chinese public sphere and nationalism needs to be further explored. It is imperative to acknowledge here, that given the historical experience and the sense of collective psyche in the Chinese society, this discursive nationalism not only represents the *raison d'etre* of the Chinese Communist state but also the brimming confidence of its new generation. It is the Party which is seemingly becoming concerned about the boisterous and strident nature of Chinese nationalism while the common people have become its vanguard. Thus, deriving from the various genres of its historical experiences the Chinese nationalism of the twenty-first century exhibits a syncretic and discursive character that is moulded through its interaction with the urban and rural local public spaces.

NOTES

1. The word *minzu zhuyi*, to begin with, was essentially believed to be an adaptation from the Japanese language, which can be attributed to the fact that consolidation of education through print capitalism first occurred in this island country. However, there is a huge debate surrounding the term as this legacy is highly contested by the Chinese and they claim it as an indigenous term and a *sinicized* way of explaining the particularity of Chinese nationalism.
2. Haraprasad Ray, *Chinese Sources of South Asian History in Translation*, Volume I, The Asiatic Society, Kolkata, 2004, pp. 11–44.
3. Franz Michael, *China through the Ages*, Westview Press, USA, 1986, p. 48.
4. Ibid., p.48.
5. Maria Hsia Chang, no. 41, pp. 20–36.
6. David Bonavia, *The Chinese*, Allen Lane, Harper and Row, United States of America, 1980, p. 1.
7. Jacques Garnet: *A History of the Chinese Civilization*, Cambridge University Press, USA, 1982, pp. 364-368.
8. The state monopolized all goods of mass consumption like salt, iron, tea, wines, education and literature as well as many aspects of daily life including dress, music, birth and death.
9. Tan Chung, *China and the Brave New World*, Allied Publishers Private Ltd, New Delhi, 1978, p. 9.
10. It gave foreigners in China immunity from its laws and criminal justice system.
11. White paper on Human Rights in China, Information Office of the State Council, Of the People's Republic of China, November 1991, Beijing, Online URL: *http://english.peopledaily.com.cn/whitepaper/4.html*, Also see *http://www.china.org.cn/e-white/7/7-I.htm*
12. An eminent Chinese politician, one of the "Four Famous Officials" of the late Qing Dynasty who advocated controlled reform.
13. Christopher Hughes, *Chinese Nationalism in the Global Era*, Routledge, New York, 2006, p. 6.
14. An idea that can be regarded as the precursor to the Harmonious World ideology popularised by Hu Jintao in the recent times. It refurbishes the idea that the Chinese endeavours are deeply inspired and rooted in their history.
15. Schurman & Schell (ed.), *Republican China*, Penguin Books, London, 1967, p. 23.
16. Which so pervasively influences the paradigms of international behaviour by China.
17. Chang, Ch. 1, no. 41, p. 74.
18. Li Hongzhang was a Chinese civilian official and a leading statesman of the late Qing Empire. He suppressed several major rebellions and served in important positions of the Imperial Court, once holding the office of the Viceroy of Zhili. Despite his contributions to the modernization of Chinese military he gained notoriety for his role during the Sino–Japanese war.

19. Hu Sheng, *Imperialism and Chinese Politics*, Foreign Language Press, Beijing, 1981, pp. 9–45.
20. Lín Zéxú was a Chinese scholar and official during the Qing Dynasty. Lin's forceful opposition to the trade on moral and social grounds is considered to be the primary catalyst for the First Opium War of 1839–42.
21. Hu Sheng, Ch. 2, no. 19.
22. Sun Yatsen was born and raised in China, educated since the age of 13 in the Western sciences and initially participated in the struggle against the Manchu kingdom from overseas.
23. Liew & Wang (ed.), *Nationalism, Democracy and National Integration in China*, Routledge Curzon, London and New York, 2004, p. 3.
24. Altman & Schiffrin: 'Sun Yatsen and the Japanese: 1914-16,' *Modern Asian Studies*, Vol.6, No.4, (1972), Cambridge University Press, Cambridge, pp. 385–400.
25. Gregor and Chang, 'Nazional Fascismo and the Revolutionary Nationalism of Sun Yatsen,' *The Journal of Asian Studies*, 39(1), Nov 1979, Association for Asian Studies, pp. 21–37.
26. Certain theories have yet again begun to emerge which argue that high demography can be asset to nations in the long term.
27. F Gilbert Chan's review article of Wu Hsiang-hsiang's book *Biography of Mr. Sun Yatsen*, in *The Journal of Asian Studies*, 44(2), February 1985, Association of Asian Studies, pp. 391–92.
28. Sun Yatsen, Chung-shanch'uan-shu quoted from William Theodore de Bary, comp, Sources of Chinese Tradition, Columbia University Press, New York, 1960, pp. 768–71.
29. It is credited to such beliefs of these leaders that led many of the significant scholars of nationalism to argue that nationalism was a bulwark of "inventions of tradition" by the elite for justification of the existence and importance of their respective nations (for instance E J Hobsbawm).
30. Eugene Anschel, *Homer Lea, Sun Yatsen and the Chinese Revolution*, Praeger Publishers, USA, 1984, p. 182.
31. Harrison, Ch. 1, no. 21, p. 169.
32. Eugene Anschel, no. 86.
33. Chang, Ch. 1, no. 41, pp. 115–29.
34. Chiang Kai Shek, *Soviet Russia in China: A Summing-up at Seventy*, Farrar Straus and Company, New York, 1957, p. 3.
35. Chiang Kai Shek, Pei-faCh'eng-kung houtsui-chin-yaoti kung-tso (The most important Tasks after the Northern Expedition) December 18, 1928, quoted from Chaing Kai Shek- Life and Times (1981) by KeijiFuruya, St.John's University, New York, p.271.
36. Lee Hsiao-Feng, "The faces change, the Lies remain," *Taipei Times*, Thursday 26 April 2007, World News Connection, OSC Transcribed Text, Accession Number 243201345.
37. Liew and Wang, Ch. 2, no. 23, p. 4
38. Schurman and Schell, Ch. 2, no. 15, p. 95.
39. Harrison, Ch. 1, no. 21, p. 171.
40. Ibid., p. 172. Though this testimony has not stood the test of times as seen in retrospect the state did utilise popular sentiments to buttress nationalism.
41. An argument that substantiates Benedict Anderson's claim of print capitalism being the foremost tool of nationalist propaganda. Hobsbawm attests the development of a particular stage of 'technological and economic development like printing, mass literacy, mass schooling' et al are a prerequisite for the "social engineering" of nationalism.

42. Sreemati Chakrabarti, *China*, National Book Trust, India, 2007, p. 20.
43. Harrison, Ch. 1, no. 21, p. 211.
44. Chang, Ch. 1, no. 41, p. 82.
45. Chakrabarti, Ch. 2, no. 42, p.23.
46. Liew and Wang, Ch. 2, no. 23.
47. Saich and Yang, The Rise of the Power of the Chinese Communist Party, From Mao's Speech in 'Introducing the Communist' delivered on 4 October 1939, M E Sharpe, p. 907.
48. Mao Zedong, "On New Democracy," in *Selected works of Mao Zedong*, Vol.II, Foreign Language Press, Beijing, 1965, p. 381.
49. Mao Zedong, "On Nation" in *Selected Works of Mao Zedong*, Vol.II, Foreign Language Press, Beijing, 1967, p.196.
50. Mao Zedong, "The Chinese People have stood up" (September 21, 1949) in *Selected Works of Mao Zedong*, Vol, V, Foreign Language Press, Beijing, 1977, p. 17.
51. Ma Jisen, *The Cultural Revolution in the Foreign Ministry of China*, The Chinese University Press, Hong Kong, 2004, pp. 16–40.
52. Mao Zedong, Ch. 2, no. 50, p. 15.
53. *'On Ten Major Relationships'*, Mao in his speech adjudged that socialism like other ideologies was not perfect. Hence he believed that China had to learn from the strong points of all nations, and learn all that is genuinely good in political, economic, scientific and technological fields and in literature and art.
54. Mao Zedong, Ch. 2, no. 50.
55. In his selected works, Mao has put forward his conceptualization of the world order and China's emphatic need for resurgence. The didactic nature of his speeches and enchanting verbiage provided the Chinese masses an inspirational ideology to work with.
56. Chang and Halliday, *Mao, The Unknown Story*, Vintage Books, London, 2007, p. 59–76. To quote—"Approaching twenty-seven, Mao had become a communist—not after an idealistic journey, or driven by passionate belief, but by being at the right place at the right time, and being given a job that was highly congenial to him.
57. Even Liu Shaoqi did not hold a favourable opinion of the rural party cadres and maligned them as "rocks" weighing down on the peasants and wanted to have them removed from their posts.
58. Ibid, p.133. In 1983, after Mao's death, 238,844 people in Jiangxi were counted as 'revolutionary martyrs', i.e. people who had been killed in wars and intraparty purges.
59. Mao Zedong, "You are the models for the Whole Nation," *Selected Works of Mao Zedong*, Vol. V, Foreign Language Press, Beijing, 1977, p. 41.
60. Ibid., "Criticize Han Chauvinism," p. 87.
61. Deng Xiaoping, "We are Confident" and "No one can shake Socialist China" in *Selected Works of Deng Xiaoping, Vol. II*, Foreign Language Press, Beijing, 1982, pp. 316–18.
62. Ibid., "Urgent tasks of China's Third Generation of Collective Leadership," p. 302.
63. That is industrial, agricultural, scientific/technological and military modernizations.
64. Deng Xiaoping, Ch. 2, no. 61, "We Shall Speed up Reform," p. 235.
65. Deng Xiaoping, Ch. 2, no. 61, "The overriding need is for stability," p. 227.
66. Chang, Ch. 1, no. 41, p. 165.
67. Though Mao had provided the basic framework for dealing with minority issue in the first constitution framed in 1954, he had acquired some notoriety amongst the minority dominant regions by the nature of aggressive intervention. Hence, it remained up to the future CCP leadership to normalise relations with these regions.

68. Ben Xu, *Chinese Populist Nationalism: Its Intellectual Politics and Moral Dilemma*, Representations 76, University of California Press, Berkeley, 2000, pp. 20–40.
69. Resolution of the Central Committee of the Communist Party of China, *Beijing Review*, 1986.
70. Human Rights in China, The Right to Subsistence- The foremost Human Right the Chinese People Long Fight for, Information Office of the State Council of The People's Republic of China, Online URL: *http://www.china.org.cn/e-white/7/index.htm*
71. Ibid., The Chinese people have gained Extensive Political rights.
72. White Paper on Tibet, Information Office of the State Council of The People's Republic of China, September 1992, Beijing, China, Online URL: *http://www.china.org.cn/e-white/tibet/9-1.htm*
73. Ibid.
74. Ibid.
75. White Paper on Taiwan, Taiwan Affairs Office & Information Office State Council, The People's Republic of China, August 1993, Beijing, Online URL: *http://www.china.org.cn/e-white/taiwan/index.htm*
76. Tony Saich, *Governance and Politics of China*, Palgrave, New York, 2001.
77. Zheng Yongnian, *Discovering Chinese Nationalism in China: modernization, identity and International Realations*, Cambridge University Press, Cambridge, 1999.
78. White Paper on China's National Defense, Information Office of the State Council of the People's Republic of China July 1998, Beijing, Online URL: *http://english.peopledaily.com.cn/whitepaper/2.html*
79. White Paper on the Peaceful Development Road, Information Office of the State Council of the People's Republic of China, Beijing, December 2005, Online URL: *http://www.china.org.cn/english/2005/Dec/152669.htm*
80. Which were: the party should represent the advanced productive forces in society; the party should represent advanced modern culture; the party should represent the interest of the vast majority of the people.
81. Saich and Yang, Ch. 2, no. 47, and Liu Shaoqi's Report on the revision of the Party's constitution, 14 May 1945, pp. 1244–54.
82. *Selected Works of Chen Yun* (1949–1956): Vol. II, Foreign Language Press, Beijing, p. 36.
83. Ibid., p.106. This collection of Chen Yun articles deals mostly with the economic situation of China and the efforts made by the CCP to overcome the difficulties faced thereof.
84. Political Report of the 8th Party Congress delivered by Liu Shaoqi, 27th September 1956, Document CCP Central Committee, September- April 1956, Vol. I, Union Research Institute Hong Kong, 1971, p.32. Also quoted in Ravindra Sharma, *China from Marxism to Modernisation, Post-Revolution Documentary history of the CCP (1956-2002)*, Manak Publications Private Limited, New Delhi, 2003, p. 45.
85. 'Resolution of the Central Committee of the Communist Party of China on the guiding principles for building a socialist society with an advanced culture and ideology', *Beijing Review*, 29(3), 6 October 1986.
86. David Shambaugh, *China's Communist Party, Atrophy and Adaptation*, Woodrow Wilson Center Press, Washington D.C., 2008, p. 2.
87. Ravindra Sharma, *China from Marxism to Modernisation, Post-Revolution Documentary history of the CCP* (1956–2002), Manak Publications Private Limited, New Delhi, 2003, p. 101.
88. Shambaugh, Ch. 2, no. 86, p. 81.
89. Li Peng called them a great innovation by the Chinese farmers: Li Peng's report, delivered at the fourth session of the Eight National People's Congress, held on March 5, 1996, *Beijing Review*, 8, 1996, pp. I–XII.

90. Sharma, Ch. 2, no. 87.
91. Harrison, Ch. 1, no. 21, p. 226.
92. Andrew G Walder, "The Party elite and China's Trajectory of Change," *China: An International Journal* 2(2), September 2004, pp. 189–209.
93. Chakrabarti, Ch. 2, no. 42, p. 40.
94. Sharma, no. 143, Text of Report, Yang Baibing, Chi Haotian and PLA delegates discuss Defence and development, The 14th Congress of the CCP, p. 629.
95. Li Xiaobing, *A History of Modern Chinese Army*, The University Press of Kentucky, USA, 2007, p. 2.
96. Information Office of the State Council of the People's Republic of China, July 1998, Beijing, Online URL: *http://www.china.org.cn/e-white/6/index.htm*
97. White Paper on China's National Defence in 2002, Information Office of the State Council of the PRC, December 2002, Online URL: *http://www.gov.cn/english/official/2005-07/28/content_177780.htm*
98. Ibid.
99. China's National Defence in 2006, Information Office of the State Council of the People's Republic of China, December 2006, Beijing, Online URL: *http://www.china.org.cn/english/features/book/194485.htm*
100. Between 2004 and 2006 the engineering troops of the Army, Navy and Air Force took part in more than 430 key construction projects for transportation, hydropower, communication and energy infrastructure. The PLA assisted in building new socialist villages in the countryside, and provided regular assistance to poor farmers in more than 19,000 villages. It helped build over 48,000 small public projects such as water-saving irrigation projects, drinking water projects for both, people and livestock, roads, and hydropower projects, bringing immediate benefits to nearly 800,000 people. In addition, it helped build or enlarge 211 primary and secondary schools, enabling 142,000 school dropouts to return to class. PLA troops stationed in China's western region took part in such ecological engineering projects as the construction of shelterbelts and the improvement of small drainage areas. They planted 210 million trees and sown grass on more than 13 million sq m of land. PLA hospitals established regular assistance relations with more than 400 county or township hospitals in the western region. They helped train key members of the medical staff, made rounds of visits offering free medical consultation and treatment, and donated medical equipment and medicine. The PLA and PAPF dispatched over 340,000 troops to take part in more than 2,800 emergency rescue and disaster-relief operations, involving more than 40,000 vehicles, flew more than 2,000 sorties (including the use of helicopters), evacuated over 3.4 million people and prevented economic losses of several billion yuan. At the end of 2006, the PLA donated 230 million yuan and over 930,000 cotton-padded clothes and quilts to disaster- and poverty-stricken areas.
101. White Paper on China's National Defense in 2008, Information Office of the State Council of the People's Republic of China, January 2009, Beijing, Online URL: *http://www.gov.cn/english/official/2009-01/20/content_1210227.htm*
102. While addressing the First Plenary Session of the Chinese People's Political Consultative Conference, Mao Zedong inaugurated the enactment of the Organic Law of the central People's Political Consultative Conference, and the Common Programme, and decided on Peking as the capital of the PRC, adopted a flag with the five stars on a field of red as the national flag of the PRC and the March of the Volunteers as the present national anthem, adopted the Christian era as the chronological system of the PRC, and elected the National Committee of the Chinese People's Political Consultative Conference and the Central People's Government Council of the PRC.

103. Sandra Eminov, Folklore and Nationalism in Modern China, *The Journal of the Folklore Institute*, 12(2/3), pp. 257–77.
104. The poster is of a young girl who is holding a book named 'The story of Lei Feng' and the caption reads- Du ge Ming ghuxuange Ming ren dang ge Ming jie ban ren.
105. Cited from the Collection of posters on China by Stefan R Landsberger, Online URL *http://www.iisg.nl/landsberger/*. Also see no.162.
106. *Chinese Propaganda posters, From The collection of Michael Wolf*, with essays by Anchee Min, Duo Duo and Stefan R. Landsberger, Taschen, London, 2003, p. 253.
107. Soren Clausen, "Party Policy and 'National Culture': Towards a State-Directed Cultural Nationalism in China?" in Kjeld Erik Brodsgaard and David Strand (ed.), *Reconstructing Twentieth Century China, State Control, Civil Society, and National identity*, Clarendon Press, Oxford, 1998, p. 262.
108. Rebecca Karl, *Situating the world, Chinese nationalism at the turn of the twentieth century*, Duke University Press, Durham and London, 2002, p. 151.
109. Clausen, Ch. 2, no. 107, p. 274.
110. Dittmer and Kim (ed.), Ch. 1, no. 12, pp. 14–30.
111. Pye cited in Dittmer and Kim (ed.) *China's Quest for National Identity*, Cornell University Press, Ithaca and London, 1993, p. 7.
112. Liew and Wang (ed.), *Nationalism, Democracy and National integration in China*, Routledge Curzon, London and New York, 2004, p. 12.
113. This resulted from the various experiences of the people in this region who feel disadvantaged as the linguistically advantaged Han population take over most of the jobs. Secondly, Xinjiang has been the site of Chinese nuclear testing programme, provoking concern that the fallout has caused health problems among the local population.
114. The government has adopted both repressive and developmental measures to bring this region under control. The crackdown on 'separatism' in Xinjiang in the early 1999, with the official announcement of 21 executions of those accused of involvement in 'counter-revolutionary rebellion, stands juxtaposed with the 4.7 billion Yuan investment that Xinjiang draws every year from the Chinese government.
115. Christiane Hargiz, Danielle Juteau, Danielle Juteau Lee, Irina Schmitt (eds.), *The social construction of Diversity: Recasting the Master narrative of Industrial nations*, Berghahn Books, New York, USA, 2003, p. 98.
116. Ashley Thorpe, "*Operatic China: Staging Chinese identity Across the Pacific*," (review article), *Asian Theatre Journal*, 25(2), Fall 2008, pp. 387–90.
117. Hu Jintao, Address to the Boao Forum, *China Daily*, 13 April 2008, Online URL: *http://www.chinadaily.com.cn/china/2008-04/13/content_6612499.htm*
118. Ibid.
119. Ibid.
120. Hu Jintao, 'Hold High the Banner of Socialism with Chinese Characteristics and Strive for new Victories in Building a Moderately Prosperous Society in all Respects, 2007, Online URL: *http://news.xinhuanet.com/english/2007-10/24.*
121. The Chinese government dubs them as the 'netizens' or the 'cyber men' mostly comprising the youth and middle-aged politically aware people.
122. Francoise Mengin (ed.), *Cyber China: Reshaping National Identities in the age of information'*, Palgrave Macmillan, New York, USA, 2004.

3

Nationalism in the Cultural Sphere

Nationalism as a phenomenon is best perceptible in the public sphere of a nation. Most often the Chinese public space is seen as constrained and exclusive though the process of regulation is not smoothly achieved. Several recent developments highlight the role of public sphere in the construction and spread of the political discourse of the nation. These developments are not completely new, rather they bear precedents in multiple narratives present in the public realm, however how credibly can be a matter of debate. The understanding on public spaces in China is very limited and questions have been raised time and again whether China really has an independent public sphere which allows free articulation of opinions, devoid of political undercurrents.

The traditional understanding of the public sphere as visualised by philosopher and sociologist, Jurgen Habermas, in the socio-political set up of an eighteenth century bourgeois France, has become a standard reference for most explorations on the subject. The electronic and print media, as well as the literary sphere, in form of institutions and processes are two such arenas which help to enhance the understanding about Chinese nationalism. The realm of public discourse also overlaps with the civil society discourse in China. A whole range of literature, poetry, drama and folklore provide the corpus within which the nationalist visions of the state are authenticated and the same processes arc instrumental in enhancing the public discourse by non-state actors as well. Thus, the resultant mulitiplicity of discourse indicates the broader trends and visions of the state and the citizens and their aspirations about what their nation ought to be.

Conceptualising the Realm of the "Public"

Habermas in conjecturing one of the first theoretical frameworks for "public sphere" propounded that the public sphere functions as a site for the production and circulation of discourses that are in principle critical of the state and mediate between the "private sphere" and the "sphere of public authority." In this paradigm, the private sphere comprises a civil society while the sphere of public authority deals with the state, realm of the police and the ruling class.[1] He believed that through the medium of public opinion, public sphere brings the state in touch with the needs of society.

He did not envision the public sphere to be an arena of market relations but rather one of discursive relations and distinguished it from the official economy. The public sphere is construed to act as a theatre for debating and deliberating rather than for buying and selling. These distinctions between "state apparatuses, economic markets and democratic associations" are according to him essential to democratic theory which is the pivotal point of his conceptualisation.[2] The idea of participatory democracy and public opinion as a political tool remain at the core of his argument. Democratic governance rests on the capacity of and opportunity for citizens to engage in an enlightened debate and should be achieved by that very means. A critical essence of the public sphere was thus the concept of "neutralisation of power" which results from the opportunity for everyone to come on an equal platform to deliberate on issues of common concern or interest.

The capacity of the citizens to act as an active and reasoning public is primarily determined by the circulation of information through the print medium, which according to Habermas affects the political, cultural, economic and technological developments of the period under consideration. It is the emergence of the critical sphere that plays a significant role in the development of an active reasoning public as against a collection of subjects. The bourgeois public sphere construed by him is comprised of private people coming together as "public" and the public sphere is slated to wrest the culture and its interpretation from authority structures corrupted by public power.

Inherent to this understanding is a belief that as art and literature are commoditised, they assume intrinsic worth and cease to function as strategic tools of the old powers and become accessible to all. This culture during his times (the seventeenth and eighteenth centuries), became manifest in the salons, coffee houses and literary societies which brought about erasure of status and secured a place for a person as an "individual." The public sphere rose in the broader strata of the "bourgeoisie as an expansion and at the same time completion of the intimate sphere of the conjugal family."[3] Moving away from the public realm of "mere representation" under the feudal structures, the eighteenth century public sphere provided legitimacy to the ideology of "private autonomy."

Trade and finance capitalism were central in providing the springboard for transformation of public realms in Habermas' observations on Britain,

France and Germany. However, in Kant's articulation the self-image of a critical public sphere was that of "subordination of politics to morality" paving a bridge between the civil and political realms.[4] Pure reasoning free of manipulation and coercion were deemed to be the tenets of this public sphere. Thinking of one's self as a public member and not a private individual became the virtue of the new man of the eighteenth century in Habermas' understanding.[5]

By conceptualising the term "Public Sphere" (*Öffentlichkeit*), Habermas not only enlisted the broader configurations of the phenomenon in the European context but also provided a framework of analysis of similar socio-political processes elsewhere. Drawing comparisons with the Chinese polity, it is possible to suggest that he fails to underline the convergence of private and public interests and the possibilities of open-ended deliberations that can be kept in abeyance, or to manoeuvre through nationalist moorings, which has become an endemic feature of the Chinese polity in the twentieth century. He established an inextricable link between liberal democracy and public sphere but in the Chinese case where democracy is not yet a functioning reality, the public sphere has managed to make an appearance without its democratic essentials.

In this regard, one of the most significant dimensions that needs to be taken into cognisance while delineating the trends of development in public spaces in China is the inextricable nature of state and society as sociological entities and thus, reducing the extreme differentiation present in Habermas' frame of analysis. Moreover, though Habermas conceptualised the fractionalisation of power from the hands of the bourgeois elite, in the Chinese contemporary scenario it is the educated and informed elite which in a sense can be compared with the bourgeoisie, which is providing the leadership by seizing power from the state in favour of individual and professional interest. The culmination of mass opinions into a full-fledged public sphere idealised by Habermas have begun and China is approaching the idea with its own different perspectives and proclivities or more appropriately with "Chinese characteristics."

So, how has this public sphere come about in China? What has been the nature of its growth? Is it considered a tool of manipulation by the state or does it function as an independent entity. How has it contributed to the development of the discourse on nationalism? And what is going to be its likely role in the future? The following sections attempt to answer these questions.

Chinese Public Sphere and Construction of the Nation

The conceptualisation of public sphere is definitely not new to twentieth century China, though the perspectives on understanding what "public" means are certainly different from the Western notions. Kant's concept of "publicity" which was essential to Habermas's *oeuvre* was known to the Chinese people as *"gongkai,"* which derives from their age-old concept of the "public" (*gong*).[6] The Confucian classics distinguished between the "self" (*zi*) and "public" (*gong*), which was interpreted as an opposition between selfishness (*ziside; zixin*) and selflessness (*wuzi; wuzixindi*).[7] While the self-centric view of an individual was disparaged in the Chinese moral order, the Western traditions deriving from individual predilections supported both the notions of "public" and "private" in political behaviour. On the contrary, Chinese conceptions heavily influenced by Confucian ethics envisaged the primacy of public interest over an individual's interests since they were welded around the idea of "greatest benefit of all citizens through the realisation of nationalistic goals." These ethics strongly encouraged the construction of a nationalistic rhetoric.[8]

Even during ancient times, alternative paradigms of thought existed in the form of Taoism, Buddhism and the Secret Societies. The *xinzheng* reforms before the 1911 revolution and the May 4th Movement also reflected the need for alternative discourses in the public realm. Support for internationalism against the statist proliferation of nationalist doctrine prominent during the early 1900s was yet another instance of deviation which flowered on account of availability of public space. However, the two ideologies were counter-posed in a manner that nationalism often overshadowed the discourse of internationalism.

The pull between nationalism and internationalism was further shaped by conceptualisations of several individuals and societies like Cai Yuanpei,[9] who espoused the idea of cosmopolitanism (*shijie zhuyi*).[10] Given his non-jingoistic and non-conformist behaviour he remained rather an overshadowed leader in Chinese history, though he was a contemporary of Sun Yatsen and involved in the political realm quite actively. He was opposed to the "narrow minded patriotism" of the contemporary period and argued for the revival of the Chinese traditional doctrine of Great Equality (*da tong*).[11]

He was one of the first intellectuals to draft the idea of harmony (*zhong he*) based on the concept of mean (*zhong yong*).[12] He wanted to keep education and politics independent of each other and opposed extreme conservatism and even tried to form a Chinese league for the protection of civil rights in 1932 with Song Qingling, (Sun Yatsen's widow) to show his opposition to Chiang Kai-shek's dictatorship which he thought had reached the stage of "corruption" repressing freedom of speech, press, association and assembly.[13]

Similarly, the Science Society of China, the first comprehensive scientific association, which was organised by a group of Chinese students at Cornell University in the US in 1914, strove to create a civil society and shore up public sphere in China. Criticizing the government in its paper *kexue* (science) monthly, it created a space for articulation and proliferation of opposite views. However, besides its highly professional profile, it maintained the rhetoric of scientific nationalism which substantiated the imprint of nationalism on the minds of common masses and created its legitimacy beyond the emblematic realms of state.[14] It visualised science and technology as primary tools of making China a strong nation. It can be argued that the reason why a critical public sphere as stipulated by Habermas could not reach fruition in China was because it came to be strongly managed through the indoctrination of the ideology of nationalism after Sun Yatsen's period. The monopolization of the public discourse by nationalists was even more evident during Mao's guidance.

Emphasising the significance of the public realm, Mao conceded in his speech at the Yenan Forum on Literature and Art in 1942, that "in the Chinese people's struggle for liberation there were various fronts, among them were the "fronts of the pen and of the gun,"—the cultural and military fronts and that literature and art had become a successful part of the cultural front since the May 4th Movement.[15] He insisted on the need for a "cultural army," which would be absolutely indispensable for uniting the Chinese ranks and defeating the enemy.[16] He was determined to make sure that the literature and art being produced in China should fit well into the whole revolutionary machine as a component part and then operate as powerful weapons for uniting and educating the people for attacking and destroying the enemy. The only problem which he could visualise as an impediment to this vision was the language and dialect barrier for which he gave specific instructions that "the vernacular should be best understood since the audience for these texts was to be the workers, peasants, soldiers and the revolutionary rural cadres of the countryside along with the city-dwellers." Moreover, the Party stand was to be strictly adhered to:

> "if our writers and artists who come from the intelligentsia want their works to be well received by the masses, they must change and remould their thinking and their feelings. Without such a change, without such remoulding, they can do nothing well and will be misfits."[17]

Mao further criticised the relationship between the bourgeois literature and exploitation. Though scholars like Liang Shih-chiu[18] believed in the capability of literature to transcend classes, Mao considered them to be upholding bourgeois art and literature and opposing proletarian art and culture. In 1951, when Mao drew up the movement for counter-revolutionaries, all kinds of non-government establishments and intellectual work suffered heavy repression. He demanded that everyone follow the Party line irrespective of their personal opinion. In his instructions added to the draft resolution of the Third National Conference on Public Security he declared "unified action, strict examination of the lists of persons to be arrested or executed, attention to tactics in different phases of the struggle, widespread propaganda and education (through conferences, cadre meetings, forums and mass rallies)" was to be undertaken for the purpose of suppressing counter-revolutionaries.[19]

The debate on what the Chinese nation should stand for and how it should be perceived by others grew more severe with the debate on the movie *The Life of Wu Shun*. Mao vehemently criticised the production of this film as it portrayed an immoral image of China internationally.

"How can we tolerate praising it to the masses, especially when such praise flaunts the revolutionary banner of "serving the people" and when the failure of revolutionary peasant struggles is used as a foil to accentuate the praise? To approve or tolerate such praise is to approve or tolerate abuse of the revolutionary struggles of the peasants, abuse of Chinese history, abuse of the Chinese nation and to regard such reactionary propaganda as justified. The appearance of the film The life of Wu Shun, and particularly the spate of praise lavished on Wu Shun and the film, show how ideologically confused our country's cultural circles have become!"[20]

These objections from Mao were carried out in the *People's Daily* reflecting the urgency attached to the task of recognizing national heroes and "model" workers/role models in the field of education, literature and art. The subsequent discourse also reflected the necessity to plunge opposition from Taiwan, which was constantly observing and reacting to affairs from the mainland. The struggle was reflected in Mao's criticism of Liang Shu-ming who was dubbed as man of "high integrity" by the "reactionary" Press[21] in Hong Kong and Taiwanese broadcasts for his role in the peace negotiations with the GMD. Liang Shu-ming's ideas on China's problems as a problem of cultural maladjustment and the need for a colourless, transparent government were also brushed aside by Mao as completely irrational and biased. All form of dissent was curtailed under the banner of forming a positive image of the nation and China's national interests.

Rather a parallel propaganda was adopted by the CCP under the leadership of Mao to propagate what it considered as national literature and culture. Mao classified individuals based on "genuine patriotism, sham patriotism and half-genuine and half-sham and vacillating patriotism."[22] The first category comprised those who had broken their ties with imperialism and the "Taiwan gang," the second category patriots were those capable of putting up a fine mask of allegiance to the country but felt differently inside, the third were those switching their allegiance with the change in contemporary trends.[23]

At the same time, Mao himself acknowledged the significance of ideological struggle, as without confrontation of ideas no clarity and thoroughness could be attained. He often used anecdotes from historical texts to serve his ideas in the present. For instance, to criticize the counter-revolutionaries he cited "we should not be like the bogus foreign devil in *The True Story of Ah Q*, who bars Ah Q from revolution, nor should we ape Wang

Lun the scholar in White in *Water Margin*, who also bars other people from revolution and ends up losing his life."[24]

He also started the practice of commemorating previous leaders of the nationalist struggle. In his speech commemorating Sun Yatsen on 12 November 1956, Mao envisaged China's role as a major international player by the year 2001. In the field of international relations he wanted the Chinese people to have rid themselves of great-nation chauvinism (a vision which still remains unfulfilled) and become a powerful industrial socialist country.[25] He even seems to have laid down the tradition of not being too critical of their predecessors, which is discernible in the CCP's behaviour till date.

The CCP on its views of public opinion used two terms: *yulun*, which referred to the leadership views, as reflected in official media and the *renmin qun zhong de yijian* which reflected the opinions of the masses.[26] The acknowledgement of opinions from the masses at large provided the leadership a certain legitimacy which buttressed the functioning of state apparatuses. Even Mao acknowledged the dichotomy of the public and private in his conceptualization of "On the Correct Handling of Contradictions Among the people"[27] but he prioritized the interest of the party thereby curbing individual freedom. The Chinese belief on the "public" elicited a moralistic tenor which provided a consolidated framework for governing the polity. However, given the nationalistic pressures, the published news was a mere reiteration of authoritative judgments rather than articulation of unbiased facts.

The mass media largely began to function as a part of the propaganda system (*xitong*) which included the Ministry of culture; the Ministry of Broadcasting, television, movies, the Bureau of information and publication; the Academy of social sciences, the Xinhua news agency; the official central newspaper (*People's Daily*); and the official journal (*Qiushi*). This was a direct consequence of the fact that the Party organ newspaper editors came to be appointed by the Organization Department as per the decisions of the Standing Committee of the Party committee and most prominently the managing editor and the editor-in-chief became members of the Party committee. All newspapers on the national level had to accommodate members from the Politburo or Secretariat, who were in turn assigned supervisory responsibilities especially that of ideological supervision of the citizens.

The debate became more heated when the CCP as the vanguard of nationalism began to curtail literary freedom. Prominent amongst these cases was that of Wang Guowei, who in his reading of Chinese novels and other literary conceptualizations constructed the first of critical theories in China.[28] His interpretations on the novel *On a Dream of the Red Chamber* and talks on poetry—*Shihua* or *Cihua*[29] were exemplary and path-breaking by the standards of those times. However, the restrictions on intellectual space and hindrances to express his views freely pushed him to a stage of intellectual frustration and his consequential demise attributed to a suicide marked a serious taint on the image of the Chinese state. His predicament was only one such instance of the detrimental influence that the state held over the literary circles.

Control on the literary sphere was also evident in a letter dated 16 October 1954 addressed to the "comrades of the Political Bureau of the Central Committee of the CCP and other comrades concerned" which archives the reactions of the CCP on two articles refuting Yu Ping-Po as an authority on *The Dream of the Red Chambers*.[30] The letter confessed that a petition for a public debate and carrying on the criticism had been denied on the basis of "the article being written by two nobodies" and declaring that "the party paper was not a platform for free debate." The case was similar to the films *Inside story of the Ching Court* and *The Life of Wu Hsun* when they were shown. *Inside story of the Ching Court* was a reactionary film which vilified the *Yi Ho Tuan* Movement (Boxer Rebellion) of 1900 and preached capitulation to imperialism. The letter states that this film of national betrayal was extolled by Liu Shoaqi as one of "patriotism."[31]

The consecutive period also witnessed a reassertion of state control in the public sphere through various organs. Political prisoners became common due to non-availability of expressive space. Nevertheless, it is yet to be actually determined whether these were serious cases of anti-party alliance or were fabricated by the state for the purpose of curbing all forms of dissent. First among these was the incident of the Kao Kang and Jao Shu-shih alliance, both of whom were severely criticised and condemned by the CCP for their actions. Zhang Zhixin, a dissident during the Cultural Revolution who became famous for criticising the idolisation of Mao Zedong and the ultra-left was imprisoned for six years (1969 to 1975) and tortured, then executed, for having opposing views while being a member of the CCP.[32] A second party member who expressed agreement with Zhang was sentenced to eighteen years of rigorous punishments.

But the above-cited instances do not imply that opposition did not survive in the Chinese public sphere at all. The publication of the Reference News (*Cankao Xiaoxi*) and the criticisms aimed at elitist, bureaucratic and intellectual circles exposed the bifurcated conceptualisation of the CCP's programme. The Reference News contained mostly international news as well as fragments of Hong Kong and Taiwan news that could not be published in newspapers for sale to the general public. As a result, a continuous struggle between the "mass base" and the "private-elitist base" existed during the latter half of the twentieth century.

However, Deng Xiaoping, after assuming command, tried to usher in political transparency. Compared to Mao's communitarian and centralising opinion[33]—*yiyuantang*—a one-voice hall, Deng strove for formalisation and secularisation. He tried to remould the centralized proclivities of the party into a collective leadership model. The new government under his guidance publicly "condemned the imposition of a single political doctrine over all spheres of activity as fetishism."[34] While clandestine intrigues defined the nature of political developments during the previous decades, the formalisation or openness of the post-reform era witnessed the genesis of civil society organisations. Massive spurt in circulation of newspapers and enlargement of the field of coverage of issues showed the relaxation of controls over the mass media organisations. The political atmosphere had not however completely developed yet for the growth of an informed and organized public sphere and the incipient democratisation led to a movement questioning the legitimacy of the state.

The critical disjuncture witnessed after the opening up of the 1978 reforms which unleashed the emancipatory effects of globalization creating leverages for development of "art for art's sake" and scope for individual recognition was shortlived. Massive encumbrance of public opinion was legitimized by the Chinese state after the Tiananmen Square incident as a part of its nationalist endeavour. In contemporary times this contest has yet again begun adducing the mechanisms of Internet and literary media for the sake of proliferation of this ideology and this is equally contested in the blogosphere by the citizens. Nevertheless, a synoptic assessment of the Tiananmen incident on the growth or restrain of the Chinese public sphere becomes imperative before further scrutiny.

Tiananmen and the Inhibition of Public Space

The management of spontaneous political activism by the state in consonance with its legitimizing needs was evident in its handling of the Tiananmen Square incident of April to June 1989 and so was the failure of general masses to extort space for democratic movements. While many people uphold it as a glorious chapter in Chinese endeavours towards democratization, the movement failed to destabilize the power structures of the government which were refurbished through state intervention. Nonetheless, the movement evinced one of the most effective demonstrations of use of public display for establishing a public culture. The movement was not a complete success but it was a strong indication of the will of the people and reminded the state of the fundamental principle of democracy: "all of state's power belongs to the people, and the power of the ruling party and government is not intrinsic, but flows from the people."[35] The incident made effective use of big and small character posters, declarations and announcements and public speeches by the people to draw the attention of the state, while the state demonstrated its ability to enforce its commands through military apparatus.

The Tiananmen incident brought to fore the discrepancy between the professed ideology and the practice. While the constitution of the PRC "guaranteed" rights to freedom of assembly and debate, the state had never allowed the realization of these rights in praxis. The opening up of 1978 brought Western influences through the technical personnel who returned home after training from Western universities. This created an imbalance in the societal life which was unaccustomed to initiative and incentive. In the mid-1980s Deng and other anxious government leaders for instance Hu Yaobang and Zhao Ziyang tried to isolate China from this influence by launching mass campaigns against "spiritual pollution" and "bourgeois liberalization"[36] but could not succeed. The rising level of corruption and inflation infuriated the masses who resorted to mass demonstrations in an attempt to induce the government with a sense of responsibility.

The slogans of "Down with Corruption! Long live Democracy! Long live Freedom!"[37] were raised by the students and other intellectuals involved in the street demonstrations. Instigated by the passing away of Hu Yaobang, the students petitioned seven demands to the standing committee of the National People's Congress. The demands called for the government to:[38]

(a) revaluate Hu Yaobang and his achievements;
(b) renounce the (1987) anti-Bourgeois Liberalization campaign and the (1983) anti-spiritual campaign;
(c) allow citizens to publish non-official newspapers and end censorship of the press;
(d) reveal the salaries and other wealth of party and government leaders and their families;
(e) rescind the Beijing municipal government's "Ten Provisional Articles regulating public marches and demonstrations;
(f) increase state expenditures for higher education; and
(g) provide objective news coverage of the students' demonstrations.

However, the government response to these demands was tepid. The party also wanted to forestall the process of democratization to an uncertain future which was succinctly expressed by Premier Li Peng[39] in March 1989—"the process of democratization in China must be in accordance with national conditions; we cannot move too quickly." Following this remark signature campaigns for the release of political prisoners were carried out; especially notable was the case of Wei Jingsheng.[40] Several letters requesting the adherence to norms of equality, fraternity, human rights and liberty in the wake of the 200th anniversary of French Revolution, were addressed to Deng Xiaoping and other members of Standing Committee of the National People's Congress. Criticizing the privileges of the bureaucracy, the common masses posted big character posters disparaging the concessions being given to them. Several poems and allegorical representations were publicized through the medium of the big character posters to bring out the social realities which were in antagonism to the social aspirations and polemic of the party.[41]

It could be observed that most public resentment surfaced during the movement against corrupt practices of the bureaucrats and the party members who continued to siphon off funds and amassed huge amount of wealth which was otherwise allocated for public welfare.[42] The public ridicule of violation of party discipline and the law at large, which stemmed from the capitalistic spin-offs and was in many senses against the ethic of the socialist endorsements of the country, became possible as a result of capitalization of the critical spaces provided by the post-reform atmosphere. The incident not only challenged the authority of the party but also beckoned them to reconcile the aims of the development with the aspirations of the common people. However, the party fell short of delivering on the expectations of the students, intellectuals or workers and rather under the discourse of the national interests claimed—"These people have come under the influence and encouragement of Yugoslavian, Polish, Hungarian and Russian elements who agitate for liberalization, who urge them to rise up and create turmoil. Their goal is to overthrow the leadership of the Communist Party. They will cause the country and the Chinese people to have no future. We must take measures and act quickly, without losing any time."[43]

On the other hand Chen Yun[44] blamed certain party members especially Zhao Ziyang for "failure to do public opinion, ideological and theoretical work properly", claiming that "entire ideological front was occupied by the bourgeoisie and nothing proletarian was left."[45] Many deliberations were convened in the Politburo to denounce the signature gathering campaigns and assertions made by people like Fang Lizhi.[46] The State Council's Education Commission was assigned the task of supervising college campuses to remove inflammatory wall posters and stall protest movements.[47] By and large the protests were dubbed as "extremely small segments of opportunists" plotting civil unrest attempting to rally the public behind themselves. In an editorial in the Xinhua News "Uphold the flag to clearly oppose any turmoil", supported the official version of turmoil and disturbance rather than supporting the initiatives of the youth.[48]

The most palpable repercussion of the student protests for the public sphere was the formation of several federations and organisations which were hitherto non-existent. The civil society groups which provide a stable base for the enlargement of public sphere had begun to take shape in the backdrop of turmoil and reform. Several student newspapers were published through procurement of mimeograph machines. For instance the Beijing University students assisted by students from other schools inaugurated the publication of the *News Herald* (*xinwendao bao*), which became possible due to the massive support enjoyed by the students among the masses at large.[49]

Another outcome was the debunking of the myth of the monolithic ideology of the CCP, wherein a bifurcated power struggle ensued between the anti-protest wallops and Zhao Ziyang's faction which did not want to oppose the students with any violent means. The freedom of speech available to the mass media during the early days of the struggle was also effectively utilized to expose the *realpolitik* of the party. *The Science and Technology Daily* and *The Herald* published several articles at the cost of earning the ire of the state as they subverted its interests. Qin Benli, the seventy-year-old editor-in-chief of *The Herald* was dismissed for expression of independent thoughts.[50] The above-cited incidents further strengthened the nationalist discourse as all the victims of state oppression came to be venerated as national heroes.

As the public sphere evolved into a more mature space for voicing of dissent, simultaneously more instances of stirrings and critical assessment by citizens came to fore in the major cities of China like Beijing. The countryside however, continued to lurk in unawareness and political apathy. Also, the tussle between the state and non-state actors was more palpable in the northern and coastal cities of China, while the other regions continued to depict nonchalance. Thus, the geographical spread was uneven and the scale of protests declined as one moved into the inner regions away from the coast. The management of the reports of the mass media continued as per the directions of the state bodies and an accurate estimate of the dead and wounded was difficult to make. Much of the political leverage that was relented by the state to the citizen's post-Mao and pre-Tiananmen was curtailed in the aftermath of the Tiananmen incident. Even the author of the documentary series River Elegy (*He Shang*)[51] was arrested and many others had to flee from the PRC.

The incident was an eye-opener to peasants, workers, journalists and other non-governmental petitioners of democracy and freedom as they realised that protesting against the government provided little respite. The resort to martial law in countering a peaceful demonstration not only depicted the insecurities of the state but also its unwillingness to part with power. The contradiction in terms was even starker as nationalism was yet again brought to the rescue of the state. Li Peng, in his speech to the special meeting of Central and Beijing Municipal party government and army cadres on 19 May 1989, declared

> "As our party and the government have stated many times, the intention of the great majority of the students are good and honest; the students are patriotic; they hope to advance democracy and fight corruption in the government...but irresponsibly resorting to methods such as marches, demonstrations, class boycotts... have harmed social stability."[52]

Fascinatingly, the state was not the sole claimant to the interests of the nation. In an emergency declaration from the people of the capital to the people of the nation, the citizens rallied others to the cry of: "The capital is in danger! China is in danger! The nation is in danger! The republic is in mortal danger!"[53] As a result, the classes preferring status quo beckoned mass support for prompting patriotic sentiments which would aid the work of the official structures. This was despite the demand of the students for revocation of the article published in the People's Daily and reassessment of the student movement as a patriotic one rather than as unrests.[54]

The Tiananmen incident was one such attempt at the realisation of public spaces by the common masses through a bottom-up approach, however; it was followed by the reasserting of state control over media and the public sphere. It brought to fore the inadequacies of institutionalised political forums in the 1980s which could moderate and channelise conflicts in a more structured manner.[55] The subsequent organisational and institutional endeavours in the field of reiterating opinions en masse were channelised through the prisms of the state. The only tenet of public sphere which was apparent according to the Habermasian paradigm was the growing awareness of the educated elite or students who took upon the role of voicing the society's concerns. One of thc outstanding examples was the channelisation of popular mood by Cui Jian in his music albums in the 1980s which were based on traditional folk themes and peasant songs. His claim to fame lay in his song *"Nothing to My Name"* and his first album—*"Rock and Roll on the New Long March"* which became a rage during the Tiananmen protests. But this also led to a ban on his career post-Tiananmen.[56]

Nevertheless, the protests transformed Tiananmen Square from a state-oriented sacrosanct space to a setting for popular discourse which would be often referred to in future. Second, the international media attention gathered by the incident created a stake for international intervention which began to be witnessed during late 1990s, early twenty-first century. The internationalisation of culture, wrought initially by capitalist expansion and Western imperialism, set the backdrop for other Chinese protests.[57] The traditional unity of the state and society as foundation of the Leninist democracy was challenged in both theory and practice through the multidimensional process of intellectual, socio-organisational and cultural change.[58] In fact the movement defined the interests of the state as antagonistic to that of the citizens and beckoned future efforts to take into cognisance this dichotomy.

The emergence of public sphere hereafter was characterised and moulded by the evolution of civil society organisations and a democratizing movement which aimed to bring the state in close association with the needs of the people. While mass participation formed a critical part of the Chinese political set up during previous times, it was however, elicited more in conformation to the needs of the state hereafter. Thus the most significant aspect of the twentieth-century Chinese public sphere was its malleability by the state. This began to slowly change after the Tiananmen Square incident though a thread of continuity remained. Even though the assertion of public space was aimed at establishing a balance between the needs of the state and the needs of the people, the public sphere became, what Edward Shils dubbed, "a creature of the state as much of the society."[59] That is to say, it mirrored the *inherent contradictions* existing in contemporary China.

Besides creating an image of Hu Yaobang as a leader and liberal political aspirant, the Tiananmen incident marked a critical opening up of the public sphere. The legacy of the incident is today perceptible in the anxieties of the state, which fears similar massive protests occurring in near future and hence accommodates antagonistic views more readily to avoid large scale demonstrations. The nationalist dictum of the state has however prevented the realisation of this liberty to a full extent. Even as the students and other community groups celebrated the 20th anniversary of the incident on 15 April, 2009, the state resorted to clamp down on dissident forces.[60] While the state is considering several revisionist approaches of dealing with these dissidents it has not yet been able to gauge the effectiveness of such strategies and hence is increasingly reverting to repressive measures. A "strict surveillance" combined with "reasonable distance" remains its agenda for the time being. But the political juggling over which the state has a preliminary advantage, in no way hinders the available space to those who seek the nation beyond the defined parameters of the state.

Yet, before foraying into the realm of the civil societies and organised dissent in post-Tiananmen China, it is imperative to highlight the Chinese socio-political exigencies within the larger framework of discourse and theory. Traditionally, the most significant aspect of the development of civil societies and public sphere is the existence of an arena of independent associational activity, free from state interference. As Gordon White remarked, the "civil society" paradigm owes much of its power to its utility in the interpretation of the "generalised contestation between state and society."[61] However, in the Chinese case as mentioned before, the state held and continues to hold predominant control over the society and hence the understanding of public sphere has to come through the limited space available for the masses to negotiate with the state. Democratic centralism, as pointed out by Franz Schurmann, as a practical ideology of the state has become embodied in the organisational structure of the Chinese society.

The analysis has to be further situated within the disjuncture between the state's dictums of representing the "development trend of advanced productive forces, the orientation of advanced culture and the fundamental interests of the overwhelming majority of the people in China"[62] on the one hand and its "praxis" on the other hand. The aim of the strategy to create certain public forums adopted by the party was to bring into its fold the new classes that had become prominent during the opening up of the economy, most importantly—the entrepreneur class and the state did not necessarily envision a responsibility of creating liberal spaces for the people at large. Fortunately, for these entrepreneurs, who had experienced a stunted growth of opportunities during the Maoist era, it came as a golden opportunity to capitalise on the socio-economic gains from the liberalisation drive and foray into zones which were earlier inaccessible.

The public sphere that emerged from such attempts of developing autonomous spaces away from the scrutiny of the state created a situation where both the state and the market began contending for control. An atmosphere of "counting on non-interference while risking punishment"[63] in case the state decided to intervene became customary. Also, given the changing global economic scenario the state found it difficult to maintain its hold and was forced to adopt "managing dissent" as its new stratagem. Further, nationalism or national interests per se began to delineate the mechanisms of contraption or expansion of these tenuous spaces. The following sections try to grasp which sections of the Chinese society are involved in these discursive practices and how do the literary mechanisms further institutionalise nationalism.

State and the Public Spaces: Accommodation or Manipulation?

The twenty-first century has ushered in new vistas of technological advancements which provide a platform for public assertion and debate bringing the state under direct public scrutiny. The twenty-first century Chinese public sphere, in addition to being a propagandist plinth, has also become a portal for re-engineering public sanction. However, it remains to be seen how reasonable the creation of alternative spaces has been and whether the influence of its interaction with nationalism has been beneficial or detrimental to its growth.

Right from the early 1990s critical themes have emerged in literary and philosophical depictions and the artistic representations of various social and political issues whereby enterprising individuals built up a *salon culture* (a manifestation of the fondness of the *nouveau-riche* for luxurious living, a class which came into being as an unintended consequence of the opening up process of 1978). To begin with, this representation outside the paraphernalia of the state was construed by the state as politically antagonistic and as a threat to its stability. Hence, a negotiation was initiated to uphold the principles of state ideology. These representations started creating horizontal pilferages for individual gains albeit giving due consideration to the state's sensitivities. Tracking the genesis of the new artistic organisations in one of his studies, Lu Peng observed that in order to curb and control the activities of the unofficial art circles, the state tried to reinforce its ideological hegemony over mass culture by enlarging acceptability of its professed motto or approach on the public sphere.[64]

The state's response was aimed at contravening the de-legitimising tendencies of liberal artistic representations as substantiated by Sheldon Lu who believes that by virtue of being iconoclastic, unofficial arts made a political gesture regardless of contents, thereby earning the state's indignation. Most of the contemporary art was interpreted by the state to be representing political dissidence. For instance a controversial avant-garde exhibition at the *Zhongguo Meishuguan* (National Art Gallery) preceded the 1989 student demonstrations.[65] Though the National Art Gallery was allowed to reopen following the incident, it was forbidden to showcase controversial forms of art such as installations or videos. The unofficial artists nevertheless, circumvented the state's arrangements and found clientele-based relationships to access the market.

Although it was difficult to work outside the paraphernalia of the state, the artists and other entrepreneurs indefatigably aspired to create their own space and to make best possible use of economic opportunities for artistic recognition. Performance artists created their own sphere in artist villages for organising events. They even engaged in certain kinds of "guerilla tactics"[66] to secure places for performances not known to the authorities. Time and again, artists staged events in suburbs or small inland cities, where the authorities held an estranged attitude to contemporary art. These artists were also able to muster support from the press which helped contemporary art in finding its roots. For instance, *the Beijing Youth Daily* organized officially sanctioned exhibitions featuring unrecognised artists to provide them a launching pad. In many cases where closures had been ordered by the state the artists appealed to the masses directly to put pressure on the government to forestall the closures.

It was also around this period that investigative journalism as a tool of making the state accountable began to assert its presence. Newspapers like the *Nanfang Zhoumo* (Southern Weekend) and media for foreigners like *the Beijing Scene* became portals for individual artistic and sometimes radical presentations. Contemporary art Internet sites began to appear around the year 2000, and several art villages were set up in small townships like the Dashanzi.[67] Needless to say, the state continued to be at unease with the growing cyber culture and the evolving genre of online news delivery. Though initially it did not restrict the display of information on online portals like the *Sina, Sohu, Netease* etc, however, within a span of three to four years the government began to regulate the content of the news on these sites.

The press and broadcast media had served, through much of the 1990s, as an arena of contestation between management of public information and debate and generation of consensus and promotion of consumer culture. Though the CCP remained largely the "owner, manager and practitioner"[68] in the media sector and developed the CANet and the CERNET as well as the CHINAPAC to demonstrate its resolute control over media organs, which was justified in the name of preservation of the nation's cultural legacy, a parallel stream of determinative discourse began to flow in the public sphere. On the one hand, the media was largely posited to effectively disseminate the CCP's policy initiatives and to serve as its "eyes and ears"[69] which bore the imprints of its feudalistic past and tendencies of public mass-displays. On the other hand, the "constant tussle" between the state and the society in the backdrop of liberating spaces created by globalisation remained at the core of interaction between the state and its public sphere.

Driven by an urgent need to manage this tussle and to prune political dissent, the state began to cultivate a discourse propelling mass support for its ambitions. The political exigencies called for the state to reach a level of ease with its social elements and even win them over, as exhorted by James Madison:

> "If it be true that all governments rest on opinion, it is no less true that the strength of opinion in each individual, and its practical influence on his conduct, depend much on the number which he supposes to have entertained the same opinion. The reason of man, like man himself, is timid and cautious when left alone, and acquires firmness and confidence in proportion to the number with which it is associated. When the examples which fortify opinion are ancient as well as numerous, they are known to have a double effect. In a nation of philosophers, this consideration ought to be disregarded. A reverence for the laws would be sufficiently inculcated by the voice of an enlightened reason. But a nation of philosophers is as little to be expected as the philosophical race of kings wished for by Plato. And in every other nation, the most rational government will not find it a superfluous advantage to have the prejudices of the community on its side."[70]

The state began accommodating non-state actors palpable in the Chinese public sphere in the array of NGOs comprising both social organisations (SOs) and non-governmental and non-commercial enterprises (NGNCEs), which endeavoured to work relatively autonomous of the state. One of the most remarkable features of these NGOs was that they did not always function in opposition to the state; rather they began to assist the government in several socio-economic and cultural tasks. That is, they were able to find common grounds which served the best interests of common people. In addition, many times these organisations addressed social issues neglected by the government[71] which worked to the benefit of the state as it was able to capitalise on the goodwill for these organisations in times of need, thereby, forming a relationship of mutual dependence with these organisations.

While on one level these organisations began to work as auxiliary agencies bringing the society in a close engagement with the state. On the other hand they formed the basis for a consensus building which became crucial for understanding the nexus between the Chinese art and society. The consensus built hereby was later transposed into a popular nationalist base supplementing government decision making. The flexibility and adaptability of the party and government in adjusting their policies to the comfort of these organisations is evidenced in their reformulation of traditional institutions such as trade and professional associations and the new campaigns launched for societalisation of social welfare (*shehui fuli shehuihua*) and community construction.[72]

Of more than 4,00,000 NGOs (registered) striving in China today most have been instrumental in centre-staging various public issues. One of the main rationales behind the promotion of these NGOs by the government as well as popular masses is their malleability through control either by state or popular perceptions. Further as the government recognises that these organisations provide social and professional services in times of need. The massive mobilization witnessed during the SARS crisis or in the wake of the Beijing Olympics capitalized much on the resource base provided by these organisations.[73]

The government also realises that these institutions provide a pulpit for state rebuilding activities, thus, enhancing the image of the state. As a result, it was made mandatory for all registered NGOs to have sponsoring government agencies, commonly referred to as "mothers-in-law," to oversee their activities.[74] This provision has led to evasion of any direct clash of interest between the government and these organisations. So far, the NGOs have preferred to stay in the background and have adopted a far less confrontational approach to the government. In fact they have adopted "negotiation" as a tool for meeting their ends, hence establishing a completely different identity for themselves than that of the NGOs in the West. The *raison d'être* for this arrangement is the institutionalisation of dissent and the state's interest in formation of a nationalist ideology. The "dual management system"[75] (*Shuangchong guanli tizhi*) allows fulfilment of state objectives without hindering the purpose of social cause that remains at the core of their establishment. National interests dole out a common plank for both these entities, thereby reducing tension and furthering national ethos.

This is not to say that these organisations are devoid of autonomy. A two-way process characterizes the nature of their existence and debate and deliberation in the Chinese public sphere. The official statistics show that more than 85,000 protests occurred between 2005 and 2008 over issues such as corruption, public health, the environment and land use[76] which were taken up of by these NGOs. In 2005 there were around 74000 protests, while in 2006 around 87000 and 1,20000 protests in 2007 and around 1,40,000 protests in 2008.[77] (Of these only one, the 2005 anti-Japanese protests was considered nationalist by nature) Many scholars believe that emerging as alternative paradigms, these NGOs have become increasingly powerful instruments of opinion-making which the Chinese people utilise in public affairs and form a collectively engaged and active citizenry.[78] The notion of the public sphere is increasingly shifting from the *gong kai* ideology to the *gong min she hui* representing a new image of the Chinese people who take responsibility for the public good and behave accordingly. Given the organisational capacity of these NGOs the people have been successfully enabled to fulfil this role.

The idea of "constructive interaction" between the state and society is providing for a system of checks and balances and a transition to the rule of law in the Chinese political realm.[79] This idea was clearly visualised in the New Chinese Regulations on Foundations which replaced the "Regulations on the Management of Foundations" (*Jijinhui Guanli Tiaoli*) of 1988. These regulations delineated the specific roles and functions of both Chinese as well as foreign NGOs operating in China. They evinced some degree of political compromise by the government in allocating privileges to the NGOs. One of the most prominent compromise for these organisations was made under the *Measures on Open Environmental Information*[80] (for Trial Implementation) of 2008 which brought a level of transparency in the government mechanisms allowing for right to information to the common citizens.

Nevertheless, this development should not be hailed as a tremendous success as the regulations pertained to environmental issues alone and depicted in a more blatant manner the reservations of the government in allowing greater transparency among other crucial segments of economic and political engagements. Moreover, the registration process for these entities facilitated the state's attempts at eliminating those organisations that the CCP discerned as threats to itself. The fundamental principle underlying the state's NGO policy was not to empower the people vis-à-vis institutional structures as asserted in China's constitution but to offer restricted vocal space and defend its own interests. Most of these NGOs continue to be threatened by the state and prefer to be apolitical and avoid getting entangled in political frays.

The citizens on the other hand were able to exploit this space to their advantage as witnessed in several instances of mass pressurising. For instance, the Chinese state was forced to adopt an accommodative approach with regards to intensive campaigns led by a state TV anchor for the closure of a Starbucks coffee house inside the palatial compounds of the Forbidden City.[81] In yet another incident, social activism through Internet led to revocation of Liu Yong, a businessman who deluded several state officials, local party bosses and policemen in 2003. A vociferous mobilisation by the common people forced the Supreme People's Court to turn over its ruling and convict him for the charges levelled against him.[82]

In a campaign on several Chinese websites such as sina.com, sohu.com and also on certain foreign sites like boxun.com about "what kind of communist is Mr. Chen Hua?," an anonymous author who claimed to be a veteran Xinhua journalist exposed the authoritativeness of the Chinese political authorities by bringing out corrupt practices of state officials.[83] In uncovering the range of factors mediating between the official state policy and the blogosphere, he quoted Chen Hua, Deputy Director of the Internet news Management Department of Beijing Internet Propaganda Management office, as claiming "The Netizens freedom of expression is given by me (Chen Hua) I give them as much as I please."[84] Displeased by the stance of such undisciplined and authoritative behaviour of the Deputy Director, the citizens reprimanded that it was against the spirit of the nation to ostentatiously claim such authoritative powers.

They even seized the tools of the government, more particularly the Internet, for controlling the government itself. It can be discerned from such instances that regulatory mechanisms instilled by the government can often be subverted and utilised by the citizens against the authorities themselves. Several incidents exhibited the minutest levels of scrutiny that the citizens were making in an attempt to defend their rights.[85] The scale of mobilization was also effectively gaining government attention for this purpose.

However, these instances are too few to be established as a trend. The ambiguity is palpable in the government's stance which leaves one to question the level of propaganda involved in opening up of the media. Since the state allows these firms and organisations to evolve as independent identities there is a level of bargaining involved which provides for the propagandist tenor of some of these organisations. In the garb of accommodation the state ensures "institutionalized dissent." While the nature of autonomous organisations in China is shaped mostly by the political culture and the mixed influences of international media, Western perspectives as well as traditional Chinese mores, the grip of the state exerts paramount influence.[86] In a society transiting from an authoritarian structure to a consensus-based polity, the two-way tussle is not devoid of manipulation.

The biggest impediment to the establishment of an autonomous public sphere has been the regulation through propaganda departments that is intrinsic to the Chinese political behaviour. In brief, the State Administration of Radio, Film and Television (SARFT), the General Administration of Press and Publication, the Publicity Department, the State Council Information Office and the Xinhua are the state apparatuses which influence the nature of the public sphere. The propaganda department or the "publicity department"[87] of the CCP currently under the flagship of Liu Yunshan, Deputy Minister of the Central Propaganda Department, enforces media censorship and control and aids and assists other media organisations such as SARFT, and General Administration of Press and Publication.[88]

It is also apparent that journalists and editors not adhering to the state instructions and leaking news to foreign media are often accused of divulging state secrets. At the same time, the growth of a non-state sponsored civil sphere has been associated in the Chinese political deliberations with the expectations of strengthening democracy. The contemporary Chinese public sphere has to be thus, studied under the dimensions of debate about the relationship between state and society.

Several instances of state intervention have surfaced during the recent years. A Hong Kong newspaper—*Ming Pao* reported the banning of a book detailing the stance of a Hubei-based teacher Yao Lifa, who had been running for many years for the post of delegate to a grassroots People's Congress as an independent candidate and who had been dubbed "forerunner of popular elections", by the Propaganda Department of the Central Committee of the CCP as giving vulnerable information about the nitty-gritty's of the Chinese elections. Written by a China Central Television (CCTV) journalist Zhu Ling, who hosts the CCTV programme "Today's Legal Talk" (*Jinri Shuofa*), the book "I Oppose—The Legend of a People's Congress Delegate's Participation in Politics", garnered tremendous unanticipated attention despite the low-profile publication and self-censorship by the publisher, Hainan Publishing House, who had already removed a large number of incisive criticisms contained in the book and had withheld the names of most of the officials.[89]

The ban reflected the insecurities of the state and its unwillingness to share crucial information with the public at large. The debate however managed to garner enough attention for the author who through the medium of press was able to put her point across to the masses. The state had clearly stated that the contents of the book ran counter to the wishes of the central authorities and touched upon the source of the authority of the ruling stratum, thus, the work touched upon domestic strategic issues. Such revelation would have been detrimental to the state's image and hence the state could not allow the publication. These efforts of the state were yet again projected from the prism of nationalism as the state employed the ideology to substantiate the nature of its reactions.

Similarly, in an effort to regulate the content of TV programmes the SARFT announced a drive to crack down on "vulgar" TV reality shows.[90] Wang Taihua, general director of the SARFT declared "Reality TV was booming in China and the move was part of the efforts to "clean up TV screens" of the bad influence that was spreading in the society rapidly."[91] Other measures included tighter supervision of legal and entertainment programmes, censoring programme design and carrying out real-time monitoring. The state was particularly alarmed as the reality shows were being emulated even by religious organisations. For instance, Shaolin Temple teamed up with the Shenzhen Television Station to stage a Shaolin Kongfu star contest. Even ascetic Buddhists were not able to resist the lure of the market.

This phenomenon posited startling concerns for the state as the availability of public space not only provided scope for portrayal of novel issues by the rising entrepreneurial class and the youth but also became a portal for depiction of repressed thoughts among various sections of the rigid strata of society. The Buddhist monks who to a large extent worked in sync with the state's arrangements[92] were also circumventing the regulations of the state in order to accrue capitalist gains. The fundamental pillars of state-building were thus, threatened by the avalanche of opportunities that the spread of information brought along with it.

In yet another instance, a freelance writer Li Hong from Zhejiang province was brought to trial by Ningbo Intermediate People's Court for subversion of state power. Li was employed with the "Aegean Sea" website which was one of the portals expressing bold views regardless of official censorship. He was convicted and detained for expression of support for a human rights activist Gao Zhicheng.[93] The government once again expressed its intolerance in facing dissenting voices.

Media censorship was equally influencing the information flow on the Internet. In an observation made by a Paris based organisation *Reporters Sans Frontieres* (RSF), a wave of online free expression violations was registered. The report alleged that while Internet was developing at a breakneck speed in China, there was no let up by the government in its censorship measures:

> "Both in Beijing and the provinces, the authorities still crack down on those who discuss sensitive political issues online. We are particularly shocked at the report of Guo Feixiong being tortured in prison. China continues to be an authoritative state that sees the internet as something to be censored and controlled. This must be resisted."[94]

Meanwhile, the instructions of the state were very clear as spelt out in the Official Regulations which held that the state takes over the responsibility of spreading only such information which aids in the moral and intellectual development of its citizens and censors anything politically incendiary. Section 5 of the Computer Information Network and Internet Security, Protection, and Management Regulations approved by the State Council on December 11, 1997, states the following: No unit or individual may use the Internet to create, replicate, retrieve or transmit the following kinds of information:[95]

1. Inciting to resist or breaking the Constitution or laws or the implementation of administrative regulations,
2. Inciting to overthrow the government or the socialist system,
3. Inciting division of the country, harming national unification,
4. Inciting hatred or discrimination among nationalities or harming the unity of the nationalities,
5. Making falsehoods or distorting the truth, spreading rumors, destroying the order of society,
6. Promoting feudal superstitions, sexually suggestive material, gambling, violence, murder,
7. Terrorism or inciting others to criminal activity; openly insulting other people or distorting the truth to slander people,
8. Injuring the reputation of state organs,

and other activities against the Constitution, laws or administrative regulations.

Several websites covering corruption charges have been removed and contents manoeuvred through Internet policing. Among various other instances, the police in Xiamen, the south-eastern province of Fujian, censored www.lixinde.com, a website founded in 2003 that published news about corruption cases and monitored the activities of local authorities. In a case of repetitive censoring, the *Zhongguo Guoqing Zixun* (Polls) website faced its 13th closure within a span of one year.[96] Hunan Changde Public Security Bureau threatened the owner of the website Lu Guanghui with dire consequences if his website refused to change its course of action. Lu believed the problem stemmed from an online survey conducted earlier that involved political democracy and the one-man one-vote election system.[97] Not confident of how to deal with this dilemma of access or denial, the state has resorted to a method of applauding workers who prove themselves proficient at protecting state secrets. The Ministry of Personnel and the National Administration for the Protection of State Secrets constantly works towards bestowing awards and recognition on those cited for meritorious work in the field of protecting state secrets.[98]

The above-cited case also propelled the government to dole out a new set of regulations on the assessment of government employees, especially extending certain powers to the common masses to evaluate high-ranking civil servants.[99] While the earlier measures of censorship were deemed to be prohibitive in nature, these provisions on the contrary, extended a scrutinising role to the people. Since the traditional media tended to work within the normative fold of Government reforms, the freelance web investigations began to fulfil the watchdog role of press. These freelance investigators exposed the unbridled corruption and loopholes built into government mechanisms. Notwithstanding the severe government restrictions, many Internet websites continued to burst intra-governmental scams consistently. The government reaction under the chargeship of Beijing News Management Office was also equally repressive. Even more, recent crackdowns on allegedly vulgar content and screening of popular themes have become a cause of hardship for many websites in China, particularly Beijing. The netizens relentlessly continue to force government to take notice and remove corrupt officials through the "Human-Flesh Search engines."

Such outright incidents between the state and the common masses have put the government on guard. The state realised the need for change in its behaviour from that of forcing public opinion to be in congruity with state architecture to a stance of accommodation. Yet, this accommodation was functionalised with a covert aim to manipulate the citizen's moral consciousness through a system of rewards which was strategised as "supervision by public opinion."[100] With this aim, the state began retracting from the public space at provincial levels. Simultaneously, the state developed new tools of reigning in opposition, notably; the strategy of "Supervision by Public Opinion Award" in honouring central and provincial press reporters who exposed social evils was instrumental in achieving government aims. It not only helped the government to maintain the law and order but also pruning disturbing elements.

The provincial governments also capitalised on this policy which soon gained popularity. Cai Wu (the director of the State Council Information Office) publically claimed that the SCIO and foreign media were in a "constructive, cooperative partnership." The provincial government at Chenzhou in Hunan province continued to shower praise on Chenzhou which the provincial leaders declared was not treating reporters as "devils" but as straight-faced supervisors and the government looked upon criticism by the media as a force pushing it towards "better management." Cai Wu further asserted that "this was certainly a great leap forward on part of the city when compared with some other jurisdictions in which reporters on assignment were "shadowed at all times" by local officials. Chenzhou was worthy of praise."[101]

This policy nevertheless began to draw a lot of criticism from the Central government as soon as it realised the flipside. Instead of creating democratic spaces which would guarantee proper working of the media, the local governments begun creating alternative support-bases detached from the national interest of the nation. In other words, they were resorting to an otherwise avoidable publicity stunt in trying to propagate a right image of their county or province. The phenomenon of "proper reporting" in Chinese localities was being superficially institutionalised.

Noam Chomsky had noted this fact as "propaganda is to democracy what violence is to totalitarianism."[102] But, in the Chinese case both seem to have become intertwined given China's partial totalitarian regime and quasi-democratic set up. From the tussle between the state and the society and the incomprehensiveness of the state on the amount of freedom to be relegated to its nascent public sphere, one can visualize the emergence of a temporality where leverages are being created for an individual to formulate informed opinions. Being in a state of transition and given its consistent struggle for legitimacy the Chinese state continues to have an overbearing influence over the public sphere and hence the public realm is not devoid of state interference.

Nation and the Blogosphere

Habermas visualised the bourgeois public sphere in the "world of letters"[103] which he thought would become a precursor to a more direct political public sphere. In contemporary Chinese dynamics, this role has been extracted by the "world of the videos and blogs", which pre-emptively take up political issues and help in circulation of opinions from the various segments of the society. The media and the Internet therefore have become the most prominent platforms where the contest on discourse of the nation occurs. It should however, not be presumed that this contestation occurs necessarily within a divergent-dichotomous framework between the state and the people.

The contestation largely is a spectacle of a claim-game wherein both the contenders employ historical precedents to salvage their notions of *national honour* and *interests*. While the statist nationalism is swathed of the ideological discourse providing shape to the nationalist rhetoric, the citizen's perceptions associate nationalism with their country-love and duty. The contest manifests itself in the public sphere in an inexorable state of building a "national character" and "identity." The rapid growth of netizens/cyborgs and their espousal of the tenets of popular nationalism in China's rapidly modernising and globalising society provide a yardstick for measuring the dynamics of this interaction.

From the party perspective, China as a country was to become a global information and technological power by 2010 with more than 420 million Internet users (26th Statistical Survey report on the Internet Development in China, June 2010).[104] This dream seems to have been partially realised but since the influences exerted by technology have immense effect on transforming identities, living styles and the perceptions of the people, the state remains in a constant state of vigil about their capacity to erode state authority. While the fifteenth party Congress laid the foundations of "digitally empowered development" in 1997 (15th Party Congress documents),[105] the emergence of netizens in to a group in itself is becoming an apparent phenomenon. As the Internet expansion and proliferation of knowledge continues fresh avenues for dissent would further emerge.

The task of the government thus becomes even more cumbersome as it negotiates and re-negotiates with its citizens on the formulation of a discourse that accommodates the needs of the state and the society. Under the guidelines set via the "three represents" strategy of Jiang Zemin and the subsequent endorsement of "harmonious world" strategy of development by Hu Jintao, the state has moved away from the characteristic rigidity of the communist system and has shown remarkable flexibility in engendering institutional and systematic readjustment to globalization. The Chinese government has embraced the sophisticated technological know-how to aid day-to-day procedures and at the same time it continues to spend considerable resources in attempting to tame the Internet via its Internet police. The citizens, more appropriately, the 'netizens' have succeeded in abating these restrictions by their innovative ways of circumventing legal procedures.[106]

State and the Press

The present discourse of nationalism has thus been refigured under the larger perspective of the government vis-à-vis the role of the press in building the state's image. In 2009, President Hu Jintao opined on an Internet portal—

> "Currently, with the worldwide increase in the frequency of all kinds of ideological and cultural exchange, mixture, and conflict, the pattern of "the West is strong, China is weak" in international public opinion has not fundamentally changed. This undoubtedly seriously restricts the projection of the nation's soft power. Changing this pattern of public opinion by allowing our media to follow in the entire nation's coordinated rise, from our point of view, is an extremely urgent task"[107]

He further exhorted that since economic rise alone would not be sufficient for gaining international respect, China needs to pay more and more attention to international public opinion. Believing that opening up was the only way out the government has made several concessions to the domestic as well as foreign media to enhance its image as an accommodative polity. Simultaneously, the government also set itself the target to aid the rise of media which was to become a pillar of the nation's progress in future.

The party also expressed similar views:

> "Powerful nations must have a developed media. Only upon possessing a developed media will we be able to take the initiative in setting agendas. Only upon possessing a developed media will we be able to use the voice of the people to persuade the world and use culture to do the same. A developed media is a nation's greatest business card and the degree, to which it develops, in reality, reflects the state of a nation's freedom and prosperity. If a nation wants to be truly powerful, it should cherish its media as it would cherish its own eyes, and it should, to the greatest extent possible, create conditions to facilitate the rise of the media."[108]

The party also endorses the President's views while stating that the "domestic media's explosion of power would not only win professional respect and glory for the media itself, but in the end, it will also win respect and glory for the entire nation." The party insists that the strength or weakness of the media is an important indicator for measuring the strength or weakness of a nation's soft power.

Irrevocably, the fate of the media has been intertwined with the fate of the nation which makes obvious the utilization of propaganda as a part of its media culture. For the government, the media becomes a part of its contrivance to achieve its overall nationalistic goals. The allegorical substantiation generated for the masses becomes an effective medium of control than direct suppression of dissent or propaganda. The belief in the media's capacity to buttress national image formation is also then used to justify the continued restraint on the content of the media as the leadership believes that any information causing harm to its national image needs to be censored.

Several leaders including Li Changchun, a member of the Standing Committee of the Politburo of the CCP Central Committee have lauded the role of the press and underlined its responsibility in shaping the domestic and international image. For instance while congratulating the *People's Daily* website on 14 January 2007 on its 10th anniversary, he opined that

> "People's Daily Online has played a core role in influencing the public's opinions and reporting China to the outside world in the past decade. With the rapid development of information technologies, the internet has left greater impact on the people's ideas and social life, and thus become an important tool of impressing the public and improving China's image in the world. The People's Daily should stick to its tenet of being authoritative, popular and credible, further enhance its influence both at home and abroad, and contribute more to a better press for China's progress towards a harmonious society and peaceful development."[109]

This confirms that the state has identified the Internet and the media as a tool for propagating the nationalist goals wherein a strong media is being visualised as a significant corner stone of China's peaceful rise.[110] In 2010, the Chinese government issued a White paper on "Internet in China" showcasing the rising significance of public opinion in policy formation.[111] The move was triggered by the realization of the ability of the Internet to provide a platform to common masses to voice their perceptions on matters affecting social stability and legitimacy of the government. It states:

> "China takes Internet development as a significant opportunity to boost its reform and opening-up policies and modernization drive. The government has worked out a series of policies for Internet development, defining the phased priorities to boost IT application across the country. In 1993 the State Economic Informationization Joint Meeting was initiated to lead the construction of a national network of public economic information. In 1997, the Ninth Five-Year Plan for State Informationization and the Long-range Objective of the Year 2010 was formulated, which listed the Internet as part of the state information infrastructure, and set the goal of pushing forward national economic informationization by vigorous development of the Internet industry... The Internet also helps promote the development of the culture industry. Online gaming, animation, music and videos are emerging rapidly, greatly multiplying the overall strength of the Chinese culture industry."[112]

Also, a huge amount of literature is now flourishing which does not necessarily restrict itself to the views endorsed or prescribed by the state. Such developments have led to growing anxiety within the Chinese state in maintaining and shaping the public discourse and simultaneous metamorphosis of the public spaces. Therefore, the Chinese government claims in the White Paper that it "encourages and supports the development of Internet news communication undertakings, provides the public with a full range of news, and at the same time guarantees the citizens' freedom of speech on the Internet as well as the public's right to know, to participate, to be heard and to oversee in accordance with the law."[113]

Besides these attempts by the government, there are several levels at which the opinions of the state and the masses differ and also several issues where their interests coincide. Unable to resist the moral tenor citizens have begun to appreciate the role of the government in restricting and abolishing "online obscenity" through its continuous crackdown on Internet content, especially porn.[114] Consideration of the moral and psychological sentiments of the people at large has provided the government a legitimacy which it reinvents and exhibits at times of need. Some of the citizens are neglecting the propagandist tenor of the media which has also been legitimised in the backdrop of the continuous foreign criticism about the CCP's stance on the new national culture, which is seen as a national humiliation by the Chinese citizens.

There is yet another faction amongst the citizens, which believes in effectively challenging the state government and its claim that it is the best representative of China's national interests. Anguished citizens and overseas Chinese are successfully deconstructing the intentions behind the CCP propaganda. Tracing the roots of denial from the Maoist tradition of deriding traditional Chinese culture and distorting Chinese civilization they have embarked on a trajectory of a novel discourse on nation-building. This contest is starkly palpable on the Strong Nation Forum (SNF),[115] a portal on the *People's Daily* website, which raises issues about the national identity and foreign affairs. The SNF during the Seventeenth Party Congress opened a special column for the "direct, simultaneous broadcasts and comments" on the conference and initiated a heated discussion among the netizens on a host of "hot spot" issues enumerated in the report to the Party Congress. In the aftermath, the PD mobile Phone Online Strong Nation Forum hosted a large-scale joint-dialogue, at which netizens submitted close to 200 questions. For its role as providing a window to the much closed backstage of the Party, it has been acclaimed as the "most notable Chinese Forum."

Falun Gong and its Version of Nationalism

Dissident groups like the Falun Gong and several overseas Chinese attempt to present a more open image of China as a part of their non-state driven discourse. They have capitalised the Western media's collaboration with Chinese enterprises to put across their stance to the larger audience of the world. The New Tang Dynasty Television (NTDTV) a non-profit Chinese language television broadcaster based in New York City is one such organisation which has been instrumental in helping dissident groups since its launch in 2001. Though the station's mission, according to the official website, is to foster mutual understanding between Chinese and Western societies and "promote multiculturalism, peace and compassion," the Chinese government perceives it as a threat to its cultural legitimacy. This is largely due to the fact that it is a part of a media enclave founded by and affiliated with Falun Gong practitioners along with *The Epoch Times* and *Sound of Hope Radio Station.* Since it is explicitly known to sympathize with the plight of Falun Gong, and critical of the CCP, the PRC has been incessantly trying to convince the indigenous satellite operators to stop carrying NTDTV broadcasts. In many instances matters have reached a point of collision, like in January 2005 when NTDTV aired the video versions of the Nine Commentaries on the Communist Party,[116] an editorial condemning the Party.

The advertisements and programmes carried over by this media channel displays an over-riding anti-China tenor thus earning spite from the state which alleged that these channels were "spreading anti-China propaganda." The issue flared an intense debate internationally on issues of the freedom of press and media, while China continued to press for its complete ban, once again under the rubric of its national interests. It was finally successful in getting the channel ousted from the NSS-6 Asia satellite transmission and Eutelsat, a France-based satellite provider. The nationalist elements within the Chinese diaspora also supported the government. The Chinese students of New York University's Chinese Culture Club protested and issued a public letter condemning NTDTV holding a dance competition in the university, accusing it of spreading anti-Chinese propaganda in June 2007 while the NTDTV claimed the protests were instigated by the PRC's sub-organisations. The Eutelsat-NTDTV censorship controversy which brought China in direct confrontation with France also revolved around similar issues. A similar story has yet again played out in 2010, when the Chinese authorities refused to allow Google to work freely within the Chinese territory.[117] This move also gathered huge support from the Chinese audiences since the state declared that it would not allow the monopolization of the Chinese media by a single entity like Google. This was also intended at the same time, to provide better opportunities for the Chinese media entrepreneurs to take advantage of the technology boom.

From the nationalist paradigm, the above-cited incidents reveal the compulsions begotten from the transitory nature of the Chinese state. The Chinese government is under constant pressure to manage its national image which propels it to act as a supervisory entity of the media. In a larger perspective, the vacillation of the Chinese stance results from a dual pressure created on it by national as well as international considerations simultaneously. The development of the country necessitates a free press which can provide accurate statistics related to economic developments abroad, while national interests beckon regulation of the secessionist tendencies generated by the scope provided by the freedom of expression and speech. Also, the entrepreneurial segments, journalists and academics have consistently appealed to the media in both China and the United States to provide accurate, timely and credible financial news for the market and investors in several conferences held from time to time over the last decade.[118]

These are concerns that weigh upon the Chinese government which has tried to make necessary accommodations for foreign media and entrepreneurs who vie for acquiring stakes and contributing in the Chinese knowledge industry. The Phoenix Satellite television exhibits the government response whereby it allowed the global media scion Rupert Murdoch to own 45 per cent stake in the Phoenix Satellite Television. What is even more interesting is that not only are the economic considerations bringing changes within the Chinese media but also the global giants are being forced to keep in account the interests of the state. Before delineating the main concerns of the Chinese government with regards to its national movement, a glance on the Falun Gong movement can provide a preview of the bottom-up tussle in the public sphere and the approaches adopted by different segments in the contemporary Chinese circle.

Falun Gong (FLG) is largely believed to be a non-state entity working to subvert the government's claim to power as the nationalist sentinel. It is a movement of followers who through practising discipline by five sets of meditation exercises and the principles of truthfulness, compassion and forbearance stress upon the "cultivation of virtue and character." Founded by Li Hongzhi in 1992 in northeast China as a spiritual discipline, it has been largely perceived by the Chinese state as a religious dissident movement. In 1998, the Chinese government published a figure of 70 million practitioners in China, while clearwisdom.net/minghui.org, a Falun Gong website claimed 100 million practitioners in more than 80 countries.[119] The existence of the movement became a concern for the government when on 25 April 1999, over 10,000 FLG followers in Beijing grabbed the headlines of the international news media by "laying siege" to the Communist leadership compound, *Zhongnanhai*, and staging a sit-in to complain about the persecution of FLG followers in Tianjin and demanded official recognition of its status as a respectable body. The leadership was unnerved by such a development which its public security services had failed to gauge.[120] Henceforth, the movement came to be derided in China as an "evil cult":

> "Falun Gong is an evil cult and political organization bent on conducting activities against China and sabotaging China-U.S. relations... It has a lot of groups under it, and it's very clear they all oppose the Chinese government."[121]

Hitherto the efforts of the organisation had been to make the government listen to their demands via peaceful protests. However, with the state clamping down so severely, they launched a broadcasting movement including a radio-station, a newspaper in 10 languages in addition to a film-production company, a performing-arts school, dozens of websites and a Chinese cultural show which played around the world, thus, building one of the most significant overseas dissident movement (See Annexure II).

The reason why it continues to be a matter of concern for the CCP is its reliance on the civilisational history in search of a true Chinese identity and providing voice to the anti-CCP segments on a global scale. This true Chinese identity is to be created through the cultivation of traditional Chinese practices among its citizens which would enable them to reach higher levels of self-actualisation thereby becoming ideal citizens. These ancient practices include the *Qigong* and the virtuous citizens practising this exercise would become the *Budhha-Fas*.[122] Dong Xiang, a follower of this movement based in China who hosts two weekly talk shows for the NTDTV, through the assistance of new-age technologies, expressed his desire of engendering democracy in China through this movement. The NTDTV President Zhong Lee shared similar views while delineating that "at the beginning, a big part was to speak as the voice of Falun Gong, but media can also play a big role pushing democracy in China."

The Chinese officials have however, asserted that the growing influence of the movement through the use of media propaganda substantiates its reservations regarding the movement as not simply being a spiritual movement but ideologically driven. For establishing a parallel system of governance through positing a role of speaking for the labourers and the common masses as opposed to the coteries of the state, the movement has attracted large scale of condemnation and repressal by the state. Though the movement provides for one of the large scale movements showcasing dissent, thus stewarding a legitimacy crisis for a one-party state, it is however best kept in mind that movements like these equally resort to the building of propaganda to inhibit the state apparatus. This proves that the "manufacturing of consent," a phrase popularised by Chomsky, is not only a state's endeavour but also a process resorted to by the dissenting elements which use alternative spaces present in the public sphere to entice the masses.

Falun Gong as a movement contesting the state has been effectively utilising the mass media and unregulated spaces to achieve its goals. Moreover, the movement draws upon the legacy of the Tiananmen Square incident to substantiate its claims of creating a better nation to live within. Similar proclivities are tangible in the discourse between the government and the people with regards to Tibet and Taiwan, which remain the most prominent challenges to the Chinese nationalist integration. While the state tries to manage the literary and mass media to bolster integration of these two regions, the regions consistently try to subvert the state through the same medium.

However, focusing on the domestic discourse in China, the perceptibility of China as an *image conscious nation* has furthered a rapprochement between the state's intentions and the public sentiments through the medium of the cyberspace. While the Maoist legacy of being a "land of contradictions" continues to be the norm in terms of higher and lower economic groups, in the discursive realm there seem to be an emerging monologue spearheaded by overtly jingoistic claims of the Chinese citizens which is expressed through composition of songs, jingles and poems based on the themes of popular discontent or which are the site for contestation between the international and the national sphere.

For instance, instigated by Jack Cafferty's remarks on the nature of Chinese people during the recent Tibet riots, the netizens composed the song "Don't be too CNN"[123] and condemned the Western media for spouting "anti-Chinese" opinions. China's Foreign Ministry spokeswoman Jiang Yu and Liu Jianchao, director-general of the foreign ministry's information department, separately showed their anger and stated the fact that the Chinese government was very angry over the incident. The ministry demanded that CNN "take back the vile remarks," and issue a "sincere apology" to the Chinese government and people.[124]

Yet another instance of public display of opinions was the Chinese government's decision to oppose Japan's bid to the UNSC which was influenced by the netizens. A Chinese journalist working for CCTV described that an Internet petition opposing Japan's bid for a permanent seat on the UN Security Council obtained over 40 million signatures. He said:

> "Public opinion may have played a decisive role in determining the state media reporting, not the other way round. After the reactions on the Internet the government changed, so we had to change...before this era the government could act unilaterally. Now something happens on the internet, the government has to change policy."[125]

The Chinese citizens on the Internet blogs in Hong Kong like the *Hong Kong Discussion forum*, *One forum*, *Yahoo blog* and *Xocat II* forum exhibited a similar tendency, when a series of anti-Japanese demonstrations broke out in China. A rather interesting phenomenon has been the emergence of the angry youth (*fenqing*), which has taken upon itself the mantle of demonstrating the Western bias against their country through creating websites like the anti-CNN.com. This cyber nationalism was equally vigilant and active during the 2008 Beijing Olympics and the Sichuan earthquake in 2009 which witnessed massive support from the citizens all over China and reiteration of the empathetic rhetoric on rebuilding of the nation.

In this context, Liu Handing a journalist with the *China Youth Daily*, the first independently operated central Government news media portal, investigated the emergence of two extremist groups on the Internet, the

Chinese left (with a pro-Chinese stance) and right (with an anti-Chinese stance).[126] However, Liu argued that both these groups were acting out of anger and hence were causing more harm to the nation and its people. Similarly, nationalistic impulses were also embedded in the Chinese people's responses to the way Chinese cinema was being perceived in the international market. For instance the movie Kung Fu Panda became a matter of controversy given the Chinese resistance to Western cooptation of Chinese traditions to earn profit. Performance artist Zhao Bandi, who uses pandas in his own work, led the protest against this Dreamworks Animation film by calling for a ban against the movie by the SARFT for "uglifying the image of the panda and harming Chinese feelings."[127] However, it served as an eye opener to the Chinese film industry and the resentment seemed misdirected as the prime question that arose was "why was such a movie not made in China itself?"

It raised a pertinent question of how far the tightened governmental controls actually served the cultural goals of the state. The portrayal of cultural resurgence depicting Chinese traditions, mythology and architecture would have in essence bolstered the cultural aspect of nationalism which is deemed so vital to any national movement. As a consequence of such incidents, the state is being forced to become conscious of its norms of restrictions levied on the quality of cinema being produced today.

There is also a continuous trend of anti-Japanese sentiments which are voiced in the institutions like the "Crazy English" spearheaded by Li Yang.[128] Li Yang is believed to be propagating what the government has alleged to be "huckster nationalism." The frenzied crowds and his exhortations tap a malignant strain of populism that reminds one of the Cultural Revolution of the 1960s. Nationalist stirrings are also observed in the world of journalism where projects like China Media Project foray into conferences dealing with the rise of new nationalism in China (*xin guojia zhuyi*). Liu Jiaying and David Bandurski observe "as a younger generation emerges in China with a sense of entitlement and national pride, they are increasingly battling against more liberal voices in China's media that push for social and political reform."[129]

The above cited trends have led to an apprehension amongst the international community of an explosive kind of nationalism and questions regarding the implantation of democratic apparatus in China have taken a backseat. There is recognition among the international community that given the populist temperament of Chinese nationalism democratic spaces might lead it to get out of bounds and traverse into a more xenophobic kind. Besides, China's quest for a great power status along with the discourse of peaceful and harmonious world is also being seen as responsible for the complicated behaviour of the Chinese people.

Several earlier instances like the May 1998 anti-Chinese riots in Indonesia, the NATO bombing of the Chinese embassy in former Yugoslavia in May 1999, the collision between a US spy plane and a Chinese fighter jet over

Hainan in April 2001 and former Japanese Prime Minister Junichiro Koizumi's visit to the Yasukuni Shrine which became the source of public resentment in China had kept the nationalist pulse spinning. And the recent events build on that nationalism to resuscitate the contention between the state and the masses in claiming and furthering their own visions of the Chinese nation.

The state response to media like Google and Youtube in the aftermath of the Tibetan protests in 2008 became a huge source of inconvenience for the netizens. However, they complied with the decisions of the state believing it to be in the nation's interests at large and perhaps also because there were hardly any effective alternative mechanisms available. The state's unwillingness to let the commotion of dissent tumble its cherished dreams relegated the sphere of public opinion and deliberation to the margins of political debate. Even now, the state remains circumspect of its citizens and ever ready to clamp down most severely on these institutions when it perceives a threat to its legitimacy. The Internet and media then become a part of its larger scheme to create a hysterical and warmongering public which unquestioningly adheres to the dictates of the state.

Sovereignty and the Media Tussle: The Case of Tibet and Taiwan

The tussle becomes more starkly palpable in issues dealing with sovereign territorial integrity. For instance, when in the backdrop of the Global Forum on New Democracies, Chen Shuibian, the then President of Republic of China/Taiwan declared in the press that "both the time and conditions are ripe for Taiwan to give birth to a new constitution that is well-timed, properly designed, and usable for the country" and "we will have regrets tomorrow if we do not do it today," the Chinese government reacted brusquely to the above proposition. A *Hong Kong Editorial* called for firmly curbing "de jure Taiwanese independence."[130] The editor of *Wen Wei Po* website cautioned the citizens from "dancing to the rhythm" set by Chen Shuibian and called for an unreserved endorsement of "Hu Jintao's four point-proposal" and further strive for the prospect of a peaceful reunification across the straits with greatest sincerity and efforts.

The "Taiwan independence" elements regarded the year 2007 as a "heaven-sent chance" to split Taiwan from China and to reverse their disadvantageous position in the elections as the elections were due in 2008 in China and it was set to stage the Olympics. The Beijing government responded by asserting that "the mainland will resolutely defend its national sovereignty and territorial integration, and will safeguard its core national interests."[131] An extremely pragmatic stance was taken by the government when the matters in the press directly appealed to the public (Taiwanese citizens) who were asked to recognise the disastrous consequences caused by a quick independence and were pleaded to join hands with the PRC in checking such an enterprise regardless of their party affiliations and irrespective of whether they belonged to the blue or the green camp. Direct exchanges between the mainlanders and the ROC citizens were initiated in addition to the policy statements made to the ruling party.

Following the Taiwanese example, the Tibetan episode during and after 2008 was manifested earliest on the blogosphere. The issue attracted immediate and overwhelming response, both indigenously as well as at the global level. More so, the Chinese government identified Tibet as a "sensitive area."[132] While the government justified its clamp down in terms of the riots being a secessionist effort against the state by a "clique of independence supporters mainly stewarded by the Dalai Lama," the distress was succinctly visible among common Tibetan people who held the government in low esteem and as an irresponsible and brutal regime. The immediate cause of the mass demonstrations was assumed to be the expulsion of foreign journalists and restrictions put on media operations like the Radio Free Asia in Tibet.

The Tibetan episode demonstrated that the state does not withhold the use of force and violence when questions of territorial integrity arise. The Tibetan unrest also demonstrated the opportunistic behaviour of the common Tibetan masses who thought the games to be an opportunity for exercising their rights of peaceful protest to attract international attention for their cause. Nevertheless it proved fatal as the government resorted to military aid and launched an "in-depth propaganda and education in ethnic solidarity campaign" within the Tibet Autonomous Region (TAR). Besides using the Internet as a tool to proliferate their nationalistic goals, the educational medium also attracted government's attention. (See Annexure III)

The mantra's of China's patriotic education in Tibet was quoted as being:

> 'I denounce the Dalai clique, I will not keep any portraits of the Dalai Lama, I have no desire to become a part of the Dalai clique, I will not engage in any splittist activity, the attempt to separate nationalities of China will not succeed, I owe my loyalty to the Chinese Communist Party, and I acknowledge the gratitude of the Chinese Communist Party'[133]

Another education campaign aimed at criticising the graduates of some 20 years back presently working with the Central Tibetan Administration was carried out on 12 April 2008 and several Tibetan Communist Party members and government employees were issued ultimatums to recall their children studying in exile.[134]

This brings one to the question of the kind of education system prevalent in China today and how far it affects the cultivation of patriotism as a virtue from a tender age to help build the "right-kind" of citizens for future-China. And is instilling patriotism through education a right approach of the CCP government? As mentioned earlier, the literary domain witnesses one of the fiercest competitions between the state and the non-state sectors and brings out the momentum of state intervention. The subsequent paragraphs discuss the entanglement of the government's discourse with education. However, before jettisoning onto the sphere of education as an institution engendering nationalism, a concluding remark on the interaction between media and nationalism is indispensable.

An apparent flipside to this Internet-generated nationalism is the elitist proclivities that stem from its limited receptivity. While the educated youth and intelligentsia increasingly use it for countering detrimental state initiatives, the larger corpus of peasants and workers remain without a voice of their own. Though China does evince an increasing awareness and usage of the Internet in its rural areas, however, the low level of political consciousness remains an impediment to its concrete usage. The so-called generation "Y" nationalists comprise mostly students who utilize the forums provided by college campuses and street plays and more commonly resort to Internet activism to further their patriotic beliefs. Though they are acquainted with the difference between state-led positions and the nationalism of a benign category stemming from local opinions, they do not help substantially in proliferation of this nuance to the common public. Instead they use the Internet to voice their political opinions more in terms of video games featuring conquests and wars, mostly against the Japanese, and signature gathering campaigns as in case of their inhibition against Japanese accession to a seat in the UNSC.

The current efforts by the government to juxtapose the role of media with the image of the nation will perceptibly lead to a further news management system which might be promoted as a national strategy and as being closely linked to the fate of the nation. Nonetheless, its simultaneous aim to create a brand new national image of China as connected with modern civilization will continue to provide space for the development of a public sphere away from the direct gaze of the state. Allowing cyber-protests or protests developing from the ability of the intellectuals to "recognise their responsibility" is placing the Internet in a significant position of guiding political and public participation in the future.[135] In sum, it is possible to argue that the nationalistic underpinnings are more often than not, a legacy of state censorship, Internet policing and selective reporting and are under a process of continuous evolution being shaped by the discourse emerging in the public sphere.

Institutive Nationalism and the Literary Sphere

The principle aim of education besides developing informed citizens lies in the overall development of cognitive abilities of an individual which aids him/her later in life to be able to differentiate between fact and narrative and build social and intellectual capability to contribute to the society at large.

However, in the recent times education has come to serve a different purpose, especially in the Chinese state. From the time a person is born various institutions leave their impact on his/her development. The Chinese educational system finds itself amid such a plethora of ideological cords which vie for an individual's attention persuading the legitimacy of its immediate geo-political zones. In such an environment, the anxieties of the state become time and again transposed to the textbook controversies and the kind of history that the state expects its citizens to know and endorse; thus, determining the roots from where it derives the current form of nationalist responses.

It would no doubt trigger an inkling amongst the general populace as to why this race for ideological indoctrination through education? Or why history writing holds such enormous significance when it comes to state behaviour? While terms like arms race and star wars might be quite commonplace for them, the state's approach towards the use of history/ education is subtle enough to escape common observation. The massive casting powers of education as an institution have been identified by the government (in many parts of the world at some time or the other)[136] as instruments which can reiterate the ideology of the state and reaffirm its legitimacy and are now at the nub of how one and all understand their nation and relate to its identity. The education system thereby becomes not only a tool of contemporary propaganda but also a legitimising tool in the scrutiny of the state for the posterity. This linkage between education and indoctrination is explicitly evident in the Chinese statutory Laws.

The Education Law of the PRC adopted at the third session of the eight NPC on 18 March 1995 states in Article 5 "education in China shall serve the construction of socialist modernisation, be combined with production and labour and satisfy the needs of training constructors and successors with all round development of morality, intelligence and physique for the socialist cause." (See Annexure IV)

Moreover, it states education shall be carried out in the spirit of inheriting and expanding the fine historical and cultural traditions of the Chinese nation and assimilating all the fine achievements of the civilization progress of human beings. From these clauses, it can be discerned that the Chinese state construes the role of education as being concomitant with its nationalist discourse; it is expected to serve as a tool for the construction of a socialist nation. As far as the minority nationalities are concerned, Article 10 of the law states that the state shall help all minority nationality regions develop educational undertakings in light of the characteristics and requirements of different minority nationalities. This is perhaps an attempt at using the dual strategy of handling indigenous elements through accommodation meanwhile keeping the international sarcasm at bay. The liberty to develop regional languages or culture is also, however, limited albeit it might lead to the formation of a distinct individual identity away from the parameters of the state.

Besides the education Law, a series of documents issued in the 1980s "A Few Opinions on Further Strengthening Primary and Secondary School Moral Education," "State Education Commission Office Opinion on further Developing Patriotic Education Activities in Primary and Secondary Schools" and "Outline of the Implementation of Patriotic Education,"[137] depict the stance of the state on the role of education. Most recently, the guidelines issued in "Implementation Outlines to Carry Forward and Cultivate the National Spirit in Primary and Secondary Schools" in 2004 by the CPC Central Committee Propaganda Department and the Ministry of Education are demonstrative of this tenor.

Just as the blogosphere, the educational sphere manifests both the pros and cons of the state's legitimizing behaviour. Bringing in the moral dimension the education law instructs the Radio and TV station education programmes to be designed in terms of promoting the improvement of students in aspects of ideology, morale, cultural and scientific capacity. The state also intervenes at various levels in the process of information dispersal at both indigenous and international levels. This propensity was recently perceptible both in case of Taiwan as well as Japan, wherein the Chinese government vehemently opposed any changes in the textbook structures that were essentially detrimental to its national interests.

Commenting on the Taiwanese authorities' move to revise high school history textbooks remarkably and increase content on "China's reunification and Taiwan independence" Li Weiyi, spokesman of mainland China's State Council Taiwan Affairs Office (TAO) and director of the TAO Information Bureau, criticized Taiwan authorities' "de-Sinicization" effort that aimed at transforming Taiwan's education programmes into "Taiwan independence" education programmes. Reiterating the "One China" policy he surmised that Taiwan was an inalienable part of China and no changes in the textbooks could lead to whipping of public support for any secession.[138]

Comparably, the attempts by the Japanese government to bring about changes in its history textbooks met with similar repudiation. The long drawn skirmish culminated in the Chinese government reiterating its objection to distortion of facts regarding the Sino-Japanese war and the passages on forced suicides during the Second World War in 2005.[139] While the Otawara City Board of Education figured out the correction of history by rephrasing the correct understanding of Japan's history in terms of its "pride and love," the Chinese sentiments were said to be wounded by the translation of Nanjing Massacre into an "incident" and the denial of acceptance of the Japanese actions as "aggression."[140] Deriving from the above incident the Chinese beliefs in propagating moral, ideological education were furthered and this resulted in its intervention in the narrative on race and ethnicity conceptions being formulated even as far as Malaysia.[141]

On the other hand, responding to the above-cited allegations, the Japanese government disparaged the Chinese approach of instilling anti-Japanese propaganda amongst students to trigger nationalistic responses. The then Japanese Foreign Minister, Nobutaka Machimura even requested the Chinese government to "modify" the displays at its memorials on the war of resistance against Japanese aggression which were spread through the major cities of China especially Beijing.[142] The Chinese denied any active element of anti-Japanese propagation in Chinese historical education. A professor with Japan Studies Institute of Nankai University was quoted as saying "every country in the world is advocating and encouraging the youngsters to learn its own history to foster patriotism, not as a weapon against other nations."[143] He further exhorted that the Chinese accounts of the war events were much more objective and impartial as compared to the Japanese versions which bore the imprints of tampering and censoring historical facts since 1982.

Nonetheless, despite the dismissive claims by the Chinese government there has been an active management of memory and rhetoric through symposiums and directions listed out for the myriad cornucopia of research and deliberation seen in the literary sphere. Prior to the scuttle between the two governments, the Propaganda Department of the Central Committee of the CCP, the Party School of the CCP Central Committee, the Party Literature Research Centre of the CCP Central Committee, the Party History Research Centre of the CCP Central Committee, the Ministry of Education, the Chinese Academy of Social Sciences, and the PLA General Political Department jointly held the "Academic Seminar Marking the 60th Anniversary of the Victory in the Chinese People's War of Resistance Against Japan and the Victory in the World War Against Fascism" in Beijing.[144] This seminar was meant to be a grand meeting for conducting exchanges between China's academic circles and reviewing the research results of the Chinese People's War of Resistance against Japan and the World War against Fascism. It also aimed at providing powerful spiritual impetus for building a fully well-off society (*xiao kang she hui*).

The seminar reminisced the War of Resistance against Japan as the first total victory in China's national liberation war against foreign aggression in modern times, thereby marking it as a major turning point for the Chinese nation in moving from decline towards rejuvenation and enhanced its significance in 'vigorously carrying forward and cultivating the Chinese national spirit'. It was applauded for bringing about the great rejuvenation of the Chinese nation under new conditions. Terming it as the most heroic achievement of the United Front and an event that saved the nation from doom, the posterity was beckoned to learn from such instances and develop a sense of self-sacrifice and extreme loyalty for the nation.

A glance at the Compulsory Education Law[145] exposes the aims and methodologies of the government in perpetuating an ideology based education. First, the law makes provision for standardisation of the contents of teaching and management of curricula for organically integrating moral, intellectual, physical and aesthetic education, and further training students in abilities of independent thinking and innovation. Second, it necessitates an ideological training for the teachers to ensure accomplishment of the state's agenda of proliferating patriotic education.

In an interesting study done by Yu Haibo, (a researcher with the National Academy of Education Administration) of the formation of Naxi students' ethnic identity in Yunnan province, she brings out the intricacies of education being used as an instrument for nation-building. In an increasingly globalised scenario the Chinese government aims at developing amongst its citizens the "correct outlook on the world" and "a body of citizens willing to uphold China's glories and honour"[146] thereby, perpetuating an institution which mechanically systemizes the patriotic fervour into a nationalistic ideology. In another case, several demonstrations took place in Xinjiang when certain books published made racial remarks in concern with Kazaks and Uyghurs.[147] The teleology of textbook writing for school curriculum in China then also becomes influenced by the purposes of state. Worth mentioning is an observation made by E.H. Carr (1961) about the processes involved within discourse formation—"it is more important to acknowledge the purposes behind the writing of history than concentrating on the mere representation of facts." And in this case, it is evident from the above-cited instances that the educational paraphernalia in China very much displays signs of institutionalizing predetermined agendas.

The government has also launched several drives to capitalize on the tide of mass opinion through the medium of awareness campaigns. In a mass-education programme held to mark the sixtieth anniversary of the formation of the PRC attired under the axiom of "Is contemporary China patriotic?" Liu Yunshan, the head of the Central Propaganda Department summarized the significance of the campaign as "an important part of the socialist core value system of the building of a strong gravitational force and an important task to stimulate patriotic enthusiasm, inspiring the national spirit and uniting people's power in order to win victories in the all-round well-off society to provide a powerful driving force."[148]

The above statement symbolizes not only the intentions of the government in using the educational system for rejuvenating the national sentiments but also the mounting efforts that the state makes to regulate the inherently patriotic feelings to build a well-organised movement of a nation-community. Where does one then find the alternative voices of the educational culture in the national rhetoric of China? For a very long time, this task has been spearheaded by the overseas Chinese. The scholars who attempted to voice their perceptions being critical of the state were forced to move out and find shelter outside of China.

However, of late not only the expatriates but also the mainland residents are engaging with themes which are not strictly under direct control of the state. *"Unhappy China/China is not happy"* a recently released book calling for social change provides one such instance. *"Unhappy China—The Great Time, Grand Vision and Our Challenges,"* co-authored by Song Qiang, Song Xiaojun, Wang Xiaodong, Liu Yang and Huang Jisu intended to "spur, stimulate and wake up" the intellectuals and called for a radical change in China's foreign policy and re-establishing the world order. The book has been regarded as a follow-up to the 1996 bestseller *"China can say no"*, which had earlier signalled the awakening of nationalism among Chinese intellectuals. The book derides the unwarranted Western criticism on China and brings out the frustration that the common intellectuals have to live with while attempting to break free of both governmental as well as international suppression.

However, the book failed to garner much public support. Though the book has been shaped in rhetoric to rejuvenate the national pride without the involvement of government mechanisms, it has been popularly dubbed as demeaning the nation's identity for not postulating any pragmatic solutions in the near future. Nonetheless, the most significant contribution of the book can be placed within the larger ambit of creation of spaces for the rise of "grassroots intellectuals."[149] And the book marks a significant signboard within the nationalist discourse of China as being one of the major contributions to the alternative stream of thought. As the state continues its sojourn of constructing a socialist spiritual civilization through moral enhancement of its citizens and identifying the students and minor citizens as its foundation for furthering a disciplined and nationalistic generation of pedagogy,[150] literary critics and intellectuals endure to carve out a literary sphere breaking through the norms of the state. While both construe nationalism in their own ways, they tend to coincide in matters of pride and national rejuvenation whereby the non-state actors avoid attracting any inhibitory actions by the state.

The perception of the common masses is at times difficult to scrutinize due to lack of sufficient variables. The situating of the nationalist discourse within the ambit of the educational apparatus is nevertheless, a precarious requisite. As forewarned by Noam Chomsky "... it is the systematic expression of the way our institutions function and will continue to function unless impeded by an aroused public that comes to understand their nature and their true history- exactly what our educational institutions must prevent if they are to fulfil their function, namely, to serve power and prestige."[151] Hence, it becomes the responsibility of the common reader to separate factual analysis from discourse. Though the state is responsible for good governance and image creation of a country on the international front, such a blinkered vision of inculcating and nurturing nationalistic generations might prove in the long-term an anomaly of development. Such a limited scope for expression and an attempt by the citizens to adhere to the state norms has often resulted in insensitivity towards ethnic minorities.

Nation in the Imagination of an Apolitical Generation

It is a mighty paradox that while most of nationalist sentiments are voiced as opposed to "Japanese" aggression, Japan remains one of the most cherished destinations amongst the Chinese youth who aspire to learn from Japan's technological and industrial developments and to join their universities for higher studies.[152] It is also an enigma to the common perception that the youth dressed in the most popular Western outfits can still talk about Chinese traditional cultural legacy which is to be cherished as comfortably as about contemporary forms of cultural expressions. Taking under due consideration these contradictions, one is to ask how does this 'contradiction in essence' survives in the geo-political environment of the Chinese public sphere? Why does the rising consumerism engendered by globalisation not inhibit the protectionist proclivities of social behaviour? How do the new age Chinese citizens or the Generation Y manage these contradictions?

An analysis of the notions of this new generation would bring to fore the pragmatism of the young generation in dealing with the sentiments of nationalism as compared to the obstinate commitment to idealism of the earlier people and the state. This generation is not only influenced by the state's moralistic tenor of acculturation towards nationalism but also in effect influences the state by drawing its attention to developmental issues. On the one hand, they are the ones who endorse the symbolisms of state directives in the most impromptu ways while on the other hand, their reactions turn jingoistic enough for the state to dub them as their foremost concern.[153] These middle class urbanites, who vacillate between the power-mongering state authorities and the peasants and rural workers, are placed at a precarious moment in the turn of events where their role is being defined by the availability/non-availability of free space for expression.

In a survey conducted by me amongst a select group of Chinese citizens mostly students and university professors in Beijing and Shanghai on "Chinese Nationalism,"[154] 53 per cent agreed that it was the students and the younger generation of intellectuals which was the most nationalistic segment of the Chinese society.[155] The response to China's rise was however mixed as some of them envisaged it to be a believer of multi-polar world while others uninhibitedly declared that they would want to see China as the next Global Superpower. A unanimous opinion surfaced on the support to Chinese government on its approach towards Tibet amongst the group set surveyed. On the question of Taiwan's merger with China, almost 38 per cent believed that there was a 50 per cent possibility of the merger, while another 30 per cent were absolutely certain that the merger was unavoidable, while the rest of the people seemed uncertain about the probability of the merger.

On the question whether nationalism was more perceptible in the cities or the villages, more than 60 per cent claimed that it was an urban phenomenon. While more than 70 per cent of them felt that the Western countries were unjustifiably critical of China's approach to issues. This indicates to a very huge domestic support base for the government who will be willing to stand by it in face of external reprobation. In terms of their consumerist ethos, a miniscule of 11 per cent preferred to buy only China-made goods, while the majority population opined that aesthetic value and reliable brands form world-over could be the major determinants in their approach to buy goods. They also highlighted the aspects that were most appreciated by the Chinese citizens; prominent among these were rapid economic development, high standard of living, its fine traditional culture, its hardworking and value-oriented people and even the capacity of the country to help its citizens instantly in times of need. Asked if they would want change something about their country, a majority of them conceded that they would work towards reducing the urban-rural gap within China, help in proliferating democracy while abetting the development of a more transparent media at the same time.

In context of the growing demonstrations taking place in China against foreign companies working from its soil, the questionnaire also posited the issue whether any of them had been personally involved with such demonstrations to which there was yet again a unanimous vote in the negative. On the role of the Internet and the government's meddling with the working of this medium, they confided that the government control could be overlooked to a large extent.

An essential part of their growing up remains impeded by the consciousness of living in an ambience of political brainwashing. Realising the limits of their intellectual development they are more akin to question the half-truths presented by the party. The reason why such ambiguities mark the public realm of these youth is due to the changing notions of nation and nationalism in their understanding. Despite living in an age of globalized citizenship, it is the homophilic preferences that outweigh global identities. While rising consumerism paves way for foreign companies to enter the Chinese markets, at the first instance of a threat to the survival of indigenous corporations, these youth become aware of their identities and loyalties towards their own country. Most of their reactions are elicited by the very norms of a nation-state apparatus that recognises the state as the supreme sovereign authority.

Being an apolitical class thus only signifies the youth's proclivity of staying away from a direct involvement in the political affairs of the party and is not an indication of a waning interest in all political issues. While their immediate lives revolve around the more immediate concerns of bread and butter in an increasingly competitive world, their roots seem well defined by their efforts in the direction of creating a national culture worth taking pride in. It should however, be borne in mind that besides the youth the other segments in the society also actively engage in the cultivation of the memory called nation. The aged people for instance have been seen collecting in the Beijing Central Park every now and then to commemorate the folklore traditions of the Maoist and post-Maoist eras thereby, bringing in a new facet to this phenomenon.[156] However, due to constraint of time and space the folklorist traditions have been kept out of the scope of the present research.[157]

In addition to the mass perceptions built through education and the TV media culture, another arena where substantive struggle between the state agenda and individual artistic freedom as well as the dissident and supervisory role of the media comes into play and helps in redefining nationalism is the world of Chinese cinema. With directors like Zhang Yimou exploring previously uncharted waters (though not being critical of the state in the strict sense of the term), it is becoming difficult for the state to maintain a secure hold on what is being produced and for which kind of audience. In one of his self-acclaimed best movie, "Not One Less" (*yi ge dou bu neng shao*) (1999) Zhang portrayed the positive impact of the interaction of media with the rural hinterlands where the state control is relatively loose and autonomy in many senses is synonymous with indifference.

The movie is one of such a genre of depictions which is increasingly trying to bridge the gap between the state and the society. The watchdog role played by such cinema is less critical of the state and rather prompts the state to collaborate with the welfare mechanisms which ought to be the responsibility of the state. The movie also sheds light on the intriguing relationship between the state and the educational system at large. The state recruitment policy of picking the best athletes from far of regions and training them under state supervision is highlighted through the instance of a student of Wei's school who is picked up by the state recruitment organizers. Moreover, the nationalist tendencies are evident in the manner of how the students are taught to handle the flag and the national song, which provide testimony to the didactic overtones of rural existence.

However, the state response to such cinema is not entirely accommodative. Though the movie received several international acclaims and was lauded for the portrayal of the "real China" it failed to gain any recognition from the Chinese film industry. A sense of deprivation and the collapse of China's social infrastructure permeate the film thus, depicting the inadequacies of the state apparatus. The Asian economic miracle, of which China is regarded as a principal powerhouse is shown to have completely by-passed the countryside which the film poignantly documents. The reactions by the state, whose suspicions were aroused due to the power-eroding potentialities of such depictions, were at most silent and not accommodative. The state also became circumspect of the intentions of the international media which acclaimed such works of Chinese origin. The reluctant acceptance of the portrayal of such movies by the state censor board has rather come in the wake of the international pressure and the attempt at gaining international acceptance for the Chinese nation and its overall image. Thus, it can be viewed under the larger perspective of the state apparatus and its willingness to take cognizance of the international public opinion.

Cinema also provides a space for representing the discourse of the state and the masses in contemporary Chinese public sphere. It is within the ambit of this interaction that one can situate the discourse of nationalism. The pace of constant development of public space in contemporary China would henceforth depend on the level of economic independence that the societal elements are able to solicit from the state, coupled with evasion of state authority for engendering increased social freedom. The opportunities for this endeavour seem plausible given the budding intention of the state for legitimizing its behaviour both on the domestic and international front.

With the pace of interconnectedness increasing, mostly through circumvention of established norms, only an interactive–constructive approach[158] can pave a way for the state's dilemmas. And though the public sphere exhibits the immaturity of a reticent sophomore it is definitely going to be a corpus of multiplicity and dissent in the coming future. And though the state would conceive of a much controlled exhibition of nationalism to contain the revolutionary potential endemic to the ideology, the populist sentiments might de-stabilize its much-espoused dreams. And given the state's reluctance in engendering democratic institutions, China is only sought to become a consultative democracy and not an electoral democracy.[159] The management of the public fervour thus, will continue to happen under the rhetoric of nationalism which espouses accommodation on the national front and a peaceful rise on the international front.

Thus, both the Internet and literary sphere exhibit a preponderant influence of nationalism. And consequentially shape the outcome of the discourse. However, instead of building an apparatus of nationalist demagoguery, the Chinese state also has to accommodate the free will of the citizens to choose and formulate their conceptions of nationalism and whether they wish to buttress the state's conception or beg to differ. A monolithic understanding of nationalism also needs to be avoided since the cultural sphere is largely dominated by the voice of elites rather than giving space to poor peasants and workers. At the same time, a streamlined and blinkered vision of the state's nationalist agendas amongst the youth is likely to produce a hyper-nationalist generation which would be difficult for the government to manage and hence needs to be reconsidered by the state as well.

Notes

1. Jurgen Habermas (German (1962) English Translation (1989), *The Structural Transformation of the Public sphere: An enquiry into a Category of Bourgeois society*, The MIT Press, Cambridge, Massachusetts, pp. 29–30.
2. Ibid., pp. 109–42.
3. Ibid., p. 27 & 50.
4. Luke Goode, *Jurgen Habermas, Democracy and the Public Sphere*, Pluto Press, London, 2005, p. 12.
5. Ibid., pp. 104–106.
6. Lowell Dittmer, *China under Reform: Politics in Asia and the Pacific: Interdisciplinary perspectives*, Westview Press, San Francisco, 1994, p. 110. Also see, Prasenjit Duara, *Culture, Power and the State: North China villages*, 1900–42, Stanford University Press, Stanford, 1998 and The Public Sphere in Modern China, Modern China, 16(3), July 1990, pp. 309–29.
7. Darryn Mitussis, 'Public Sphere in Republican China,' 2008, Online URL: *http://www.digitalguanxi.com*
8. Dittmer, Ch. 3, no. 6.
9. He received modern educational training from universities in the west. Owing to his background in both traditional Chinese and modern education, he served for a long time as the first Minister of Education in the Republic, and Chancellor of National Beijing University (*Beida*). He was also until his death, the founder and president of Academia Sinica, the biggest research institute of pre-1949 China. He was also influential in politics as the Provisional Republic's Minister of Education in January 1912.
10. Tu- Ki Min *Men and Ideas in Modern Chinese History*, Seoul National University Press, South Korea, p. 4.
11. Ibid., p. 5.
12. Ibid., p. 6, cited from Zhou Tiandu Cai Yuanpei Zhuan, *A Biography of Cai Yuanpei.*
13. Ibid.
14. Wang Zuoyue, "Saving China Through Science: The Science Society of China, Scientific Nationalism, and Civil Society in Republican China," *Osiris*, 2 (17), *Science and Civil Society*, The university of Chicago Press, pp. 291–322.
15. The students of Beijing University were the first to show determined opposition to the scheme of Japan enjoying privileges over Shandong province as a result of spoils of the First World War. The Northern warlord government arrested more than thirty students in an effort to suppress opposition. In protests the students of Beijing University went on Strike and large numbers of students in other parts of the country responded. The workers and merchants joined the movement subsequently. Thus, beginning as a movement mainly of intellectuals it rapidly grew into a national patriotic movement embracing the proletariat, the urban petty bourgeoisie and the bourgeoisie.
16. Mao Zedong, 'Talks at the Yenan Forum on Literature and Art,' *On Literature and Art*, English Edition by Rahul Foundation, Lucknow, 2008 (originally published by Foreign Language Press, Beijing in 1967), p. 11.
17. Ibid., p. 16.
18. He was a member of the counter-revolutionary National Socialist Party who propagated reactionary American bourgeois ideas on literature and art.
19. Mao Zedong, 'The Party's Mass Line Must Be Followed in Suppressing Counter Revolutionaries,' *Selected Works of Mao Zedong*, Vol. V, Foreign Language Press, Beijing, p. 50.

20. Ibid., 'Pay Serious Attention to the Discussion of the Film *The Life of Wu Shun*, p. 57. Wu Shun was born in Tangyi, Shandong Province, and lived towards the end of Qing Dynasty when China was undergoing an era of great struggle against foreign aggressors and domestic reactionary feudal rulers. He did not lift a finger against the feudal economic base or its superstructure; on the contrary he strove fanatically to spread feudal culture through the so-called "tuition-free schools" and, in order to gain a position for this purpose, he fawned on the reactionary feudal leaders of successive regimes.
21. Maurice Meisner, *Mao's China and After* 3rd Edition,The Free Press, New York, pp. 58–60. Reactionary elements refer to those who believe in status quo ante.
22. Mao Zedong, Ch. 3, no. 19, pp. 122–29.
23. Ibid., pp. 122–29.
24. Ibid.
25. Ibid., 'In Commemoration of Dr. Sun Yatsen', p. 330.
26. Dittmer, Ch. 3, no. 6, pp. 126–30.
27. Mao Zedong, 'On Contradictions', *Selected Works of Mao Zedong*, Vol. II, Foreign Language Press, Beijing, 1967, pp. 11–34.
28. Tong and Zhou (2002), Criticism and society: The birth of Modern Critical Subject in China, *Boundary*, 29:1, Duke University Press, Spring 2002, pp. 153–76.
29. Ibid., p.156. Also see Xu Yi, Yanzhou Shihua, in Zhongguo lidai shihuaxuan (Anthology of Chinese Shihua), ed by Wang Dapeng, Zhang Dakun et al, Changsha, Yuelu Shushe, 1985, 2:402.
30. Mao Zedong, 'On Contradictions', *Selected Works of Mao Zedong*, Vol. II, Foreign Language Press, Beijing, 1967, pp. 40–55.
31. Ibid.
32. Zeng Linlin, 2004, Online URL: *http://www.hrichina.org/public/PDFs/CRF.4.2004/DeathRow4.2004.pdf*
33. Mao in his Talks at the Yenan Forum on literature and art", Volume 3, Selected Works, opined "there is in fact no such thing as art for art's sake, art that stands above classes, art that is detached from or independent of politics. Proletarian literature and art are a part of the whole proletarian revolutionary cause." Deng tried to move away from this model and visualized giving space for personal artistic expression attributable to the artists.
34. Dittmer, Ch. 3, no. 6, p. 125.
35. Han Minzhu (ed.), *Cries for Democracy: Writings and speeches from the 1989 Chinese Democracy Movement*, Princeton University Press, New Jersey, 1990, p. vii.
36. Ibid., p. xv.
37. Ibid., pp. 6–8.
38. Ibid., p. 10.
39. Li Peng, born on 20 October 1928 was the Premier of China between 1987 and 1998, the Chairman of the Standing Committee of the National People's Congress of the PRC from 1998 to 2003 and was second ranking in the Communist Party of China behind Jiang Zemin on the Politburo Standing Committee until 2002. Concerned about maintaining social and political stability, Li backed the use of force to quash the Tiananmen Square protests of 1989, and due to this, to the protesters Li became one of the least popular Chinese leaders following the protests.
40. Wei Jingsheng born May 20, 1950 is an activist in the Chinese democracy movement, most prominent for authoring the document *Fifth Modernization* on the Democracy Wall in Beijing in 1978. Wei Jingsheng was arrested on 29 March 1979 for "Passing military secrets", and was condemned to 15 years of prison. He had also published

a letter under his name in March 1979 denouncing the inhuman conditions of the Chinese Qincheng Prison, where the 10th Panchen Lama was imprisoned. However, a major part of Wei's essay came from other anonymous authors with personal experiences involving Qincheng.

41. Han Minzhu, Ch. 3, no. 35, p. 42.
42. Ibid.
43. Deng Xiaoping responded to the student's demonstrations in the cited manner on April 24, 1989 in remarks to the party leaders, similar sentiments were also voiced by the *People's Daily* editorial on April 26.
44. One of the most influential leaders of the PRC during the 1980s and 90s and one of the top leaders of the CCP.
45. Lowell Dittmer, "China in 1988: The continuing dilemma of Socialist Reform," in *Asian Survey*, 29, pp. 1–29.
46. Fang Lizhi born on 12 February 1936 was a professor of astrophysics and Vice President of the University of Science and Technology of China whose liberal ideas inspired the pro-democracy student movement of 1986-87 and, finally, the Tiananmen Square protests of 1989. Because of his involvement in the pro-democracy movement, he was expelled from the CCP in January 1987.
47. Lowell Dittmer, Ch. 3, no. 45, p. 145.
48. Most oppose unrest unequivocally, *People's Daily editorial*, Online URL: *http://news.xinhuanet.com/ziliao/2005-02/23/content_2609426.htm*
49. Han Minzhu, Ch. 3, no. 35.
50. Nicholas D Kristof, 'Qin Benli, 73, Dissident Chinese Newspaper Editor,' *The New York Times*, 16 April 1981, Online URL: *http://www.nytimes.com/1991/04/16/obituaries/qin-benli-73-dissident-chinese-newspaper-editor.html*
51. Written by Su Xiaokang, the son of a member of the Communist elite who had grown up in a Marxist household and then been sent to a village in Henan during the Cultural Revolution, this expressed a widespread frustration with the futility of an inward-looking obsession with a past civilisation symbolised by the yellow earth of the loess plateau and by the entrapment represented by the Great Wall. Yet such a production was nationalistic, too, in the way that its call to turn towards the blue ocean and absorb the spirit of science and democracy was aimed at achieving a rejuvenation of the nation. While images of the West were presented as the model for China's future, the West also was portrayed as made up of hostile powers that had attacked, exploited and humiliated China.
52. Andrew Nathan, The Tiananmen Papers, Foreign Affairs, January-February 2001, Online URL: *http://www.wellesley.edu/Polisci/wj/China/Tiananmen/tampapers.html*
53. Craig Calhoun, "Tiananmen, Television and the public sphere, Internationalisation of culture and the Beijing spring of 1989," *Public Culture*, 2(1).
54. Li Peng holds dialogue with Students, 18 May 1989, FBIS, pp. 14–21, Online URL: *http://www.tsquare.tv/chronology/May18mtg.html*
55. Tony Saich, 'The rise and fall of the Beijing People's movement', in Jonathan Unger (ed), *The Pro-democracy protests in China: Reports from the provinces*, M. E. Sharpe, USA, p. 31.
56. Matthew Corbin Clark, Birth of a Beijing Music Scene," *PBS Frontline*, 13 February 2003, Online URL: *http://www.pbs.org/wgbh/pages/frontline/shows/red/sonic/*
57. Calhoun, no. 231.
58. Yijian Ding (2001), *Chinese Democracy after Tiananmen*, UBC Press, Vancouver, p. 3.
59. Calhoun, Ch. 3, no. 53, p. 33.
60. Marianne Barriaux, 'China Dissidents Detained, Harassed on Anniversary of Hu Yaobang's Death,' AFP, Wednesday, 15 April 2009, World News Connection Reports.

61. Gordon White, 'Civil Society, democratization and development; Clearing the analytical ground,' *Democratization*, 1(2), 1994, pp. 375–90.
62. See Jiang Zemin's speech of 'The three represents,' 25 June 2001, Online URL: *http://news.xinhuanet.com/english/20010625/422678.htm*
63. Taru Salmenkari, "Implementing and avoiding control: contemporary art and the Chinese state," *China: An International Journal*, 2(2), 2004, pp. 235–61.
64. Lu Peng, *90's Art China*, Changsha Hunan Fine Arts Publishing House, p. 416.
65. Ibid., p. 243.
66. Lu Peng, Ch. 3, no. 64, pp. 242–48.
67. Salmenkari, Ch. 3, no. 63, p. 57.
68. Ibid., p. 58.
69. Xiaoling Zhang, Seeking effective public space: Chinese media at the local level, *China: An International Journal* 5(1), March 2007, pp. 55–77.
70. Method of Guarding Against the Encroachments of Any One Department of Government by Appealing to the People Through a Convention, *The Federalist Papers*, Independent Journal 49, 2 February 1788, Online URL: *http://www.constitution.org/fed/federa49.htm*
71. Quisha Ma, *Non-governmental Organisations in Contemporary China: Paving the way to Civil Society*, Routledge, US and Canada, 2006, p. 47.
72. Ibid., p. 48.
73. Pallavi Aiyar, *Smokes and Mirrors, An experience of China*, Fourth Estate, Harper Collins Publishers, India, 2008, p.16.
74. China's NGOs independent actors or government puppets, [Internet accessed 24 March 2009] *http://www.wilsoncenter.org/index.cfm?fuseaction=events.event_summary&event_id=182907*
75. Lu Yiyi, 'The autonomy of Chinese NGOs: A new perspective', *China: An International Journal*, 5(2), September 2007, pp. 173–203.
76. Richard N. Haass, 'Rules of Olympic Gamesmanship', *China Daily*, Online URL: *http://www.chinadaily.com.cn/cndy/2008-07/22/content_6865408.htm*
77. Andrew Mertha, Society in the State: China's Nondemocratic Political Pluralization, Online URL: *http://falcon.arts.cornell.edu/am847/pdf/Microsoft%20Word%20-%20Society_in_the_State%5B1%5D.pdf*
78. Quisha Ma, Ch. 3, no. 71, p. 2.
79. Brantly Womack quoted in Ibid., p. 30.
80. Ma Jun, Right to Information: A historic moment, *China Dialogue*, 1 May 2008, Online URL: *http://www.chinadialogue.net/article/show/single/en/1962*
81. Aiyar, Ch. 3, no. 73, *op cit*. India. Also see, China's CCTV anchorman reignites debate over Forbidden City Starbucks, Text of report in English by Xinhua (New China News Agency) 16 January 2007, BBC Monitoring Services Reports.
82. Johan Lagerkvist, 'The rise of online public opinion in the People's Republic of China,' *China: An International Journal*, 1, March 2005 pp. 119–30.
83. Liu Yong executed today: 2003, 22 December 2008, Executed Today.com, Online URL: *http://www.executedtoday.com/2008/12/22/2003-liu-yong-for-corruption/*
84. 'Internet Censorship Official targeted by Chinese Netizens', [Internet accessed] URL: *http://chinadigitaltimes.net/2009/01/internet-censor-official-targeted-by-chinese-netizens*
85. In another instance, a photograph of an official from the land bureau of Nanjing, the capital of Jiangsu province came under scrutiny in December after it began circulating on the Internet. Netizens pointed out that Zhou Jiugeng's imported a watch worth of US$ 25,000 was of quality far exceeding an official's salary. He was consequently, dismissed.
86. Quisha Ma, Ch. 3, no. 71, p. 64.

87. The publicity department of the Central Committee of the CCP is an internal division and therefore is not formally considered to be part of the government of the PRC. Nonetheless, it is the most important of all the organisations in the propaganda system.
88. Anne Marie Brady, *Marketing Dictatorship: Propaganda and thought work in Contemporary China*, Rowman & Littlefield, Lanham, 2008, pp. 13–17.
89. China bans CCTV journalist's book on grassroots election – *Hong Kong Daily*, 7 January 2007, BBC Monitoring Services Reports. The protagonist of the book, Yao, 48, was a native of Qianjiang city in Hubei Province. Since 1987, he had volunteered to run in successive Qianjiang city people's congress elections and was at last elected in 1998. In 2003, he was named "one of the 25 rural reformers with the most inspirational ideas for reform" by the Chinese Academy of Social Sciences. At the invitation of the US State Department, he visited the United States in 2004 to observe the elections being held there. He again ran in the people's congress election in 2006 but lost the election.
90. China to crack down on "vulgar" TV reality shows, 12 January 2007, BBC Monitoring News Services Reports. Excerpt from report in English by Xinhua.
91. China moves to clean up TV screens, China Daily, 12 January 2007, Online URL: *http://www.chinadaily.com.cn/china/2007-01/12/content_782593.htm*
92. Aiyar, Ch. 3, no. 73, pp. 179–200. (Especially Chapter- 9, Opiate of the masses).
93. Court charges writer with "subversion of state power,"13 January 2007, Text of report by Hong Kong newspaper, *Apple Daily's* (*Ping Kuo Jih Pao*) website on 13 January 2007, BBC Monitoring Services Reports.
94. China: Watchdog notes "wave of violations" of online free expression Text of press release by Paris-based organization Reporters Sans Frontiers, BBC Monitoring Services Reports.
95. Computer Information Network and Internet Security, Protection and Management Regulations, Online URL: *http://www.cnd.org/CND-China/CND-China.98/CND-China.98-02-05.html For further information see Annexure VI*
96. 'Authorities close website, Online URL: *http://www.rsf.org/article.php3?id_article=18462*
97. China: Dissident website reportedly faces another closure, Text of report by Hong Kong newspaper Apple Daily (*Ping Kuo Jih Pao*) website on 13 January 2007.
98. 'China awards ten institutions, five individuals for protecting state secrets,' *Xinhua*, Beijing, 10 January 2004, BBC Monitoring Services Reports.
99. 'Public to have say in assessment of China's government employees,' 13 January 2007, *Xinhua*, BBC Monitoring Services Reports.
100. Chinese commentary on "peculiar" media award; urges protecting "proper reporting", *Xinhua*, 12 January 2007, BBC Monitoring Services Reports.
101. Yang Xiaoin, 'Supervision by Public opinion: what it needs are rights, not awards', BBC Monitoring Services Reports.
102. Noam Chomsky, *The Chomsky Reader*, edited by James Peck, Pantheon books, New York, 1987, p. 136.
103. Whereby the circulation of thoughts and information was envisioned to take place through manual circulation of letters.
104. With an increase of 36 million compared to the end of 2009, the popularity rate of Internet has climbed up to 31.8 per cent, with an increase of 2.9 per cent compared to the end of 2009. The size of rural Internet users had reached 84.6 million, increasing by 31.9 million from 2007, with the growth rate surpassing 60 per cent, far exceeding that of urban Internet users. Statistical Reports on the Internet Development in China, 26th Survey Report, 15 July 2010, Accessed on 28 July 2010, Online URL: *http://www.cnnic.cn/uploadfiles/pdf/2010/8/24/93145.pdf*

105. Saich and Yang, Ch. 2, no. 47.
106. Aiyar, Ch. 3, no. 73, p. 56.
107. 'Waiting for the Rise of the Media to change 'the west is strong, I am weak', translated by Xiao Shu, *Southern Weekly*, Online URL: *http://chinaelections.org/NewsInfo.asp?NewsID=130121*
108. Net Support to Nation's goals, China Daily, 27 June 2008, Online URL: *http://www.chinadaily.com.cn/opinion/2008-06/27/content_6800267.htm*
109. Li Changchun congratulates 10th Anniversary of the People's Daily Website, 14 January 2007, Xinhua, BBC Monitoring Reports, 2007.
110. China to show only "ethically inspiring TV Series" in prime time, Xinhua, 22 January 2007, BBC Monitoring Reports.
111. China issues White Paper on Internet, 8 June 2010, Online URL: *http://www.china.org.cn/china/2010-06/08/content_20206978.htm*
112. The Internet in China, Information Office of the State Council of the People's Republic of China, 8 June 2010, Beijing, Promoting the Extensive Use of the Internet, Part II, Accessed on 15 July 2010, Online URL: *http://www.china.org.cn/government/whitepaper/2010-06/08/content_20208003.htm*
113. Ibid., Guaranteeing Citizen's Freedom of Speech on the Internet, Part III.
114. China's Internet Watchdog Reports soaring online racketeering, declining porn, 16 January 2007, Xinhua, BBC Monitoring Reports.
115. People's Daily Online, Online URL: bbs.people.com.cn/ *http://www.peopleforum.cn/*
116. To view the cinematic representation of the anti-China propaganda of the commentary log on to *http://www.youtube.com/watch?v=EbGa1yCaUoc*
117. Ben Worthen, "Researcher Says Up to 100 Victims in Google Attack" 26 February 2010, *Wall Street Journal*, Online URL: *http://online.wsj.com/article/SB10001424052748704625004575090111817090670.html?mod=googlenews_wsj*
118. 'Sino-US media conference ends in Beijing', BBC Monitoring Services Reports, 21 November 2002.
119. Reports of various persecutions and mistreatments of the Falun Gong practitioners within China, *http://www.clearwisdom.net/emh/articles/2009/3/9/105411.html*
120. Zhang Yongnian, *Globalisation and State transformation in China*, Cambridge University Press, Cambridge, 2004.
121. Chinese official position regarding Falun Gong as stated by Wang Baodong, a spokesman for the Chinese Embassy in Washington, BBC Monitoring Reports, 2007.
122. Li Hongzhi, *Zhuan Falun*, (English version), The Universe Publishing Company, New York, 1999, pp. 343–85.
123. Hung Chin-fu, "Chinese Netizens see both sides," *Taipei Times*, 27 April 2008, World News Connection reports, Online URL: *http://www.international.ucla.edu/article.asp?parentid=91400*
124. Ibid.
125. Parker Emily, "The Internet and Chinese Nationalism," Internet and Democracy, 1 April 2008, *Wall Street Journal*, Online URL: *http://blogs.law.harvard.edu/idblog/2008/04/01/the-internet-and-chinese-nationalism/*
126. "Extreme nationalists versus nihilists in China," *China Digital Times*, 6 November 2008, Online URL: *http://chinadigitaltimes.net/2008/11/extreme-nationalists-versus-nihilists-in-china/*
127. Wu Nan, 'The panda as the provocateur', China Digital Times, 14 July 2009, Online URL: *http://chinadigitaltimes.net/2008/07/wu-nan-the-panda-as-provocateur/*
128. Li Yang is the founder of this private education agency where English phrases are antiquated and the Japanese pronunciation of the English is a matter of mockery and humour.

129. 'New nationalism adds to the list of pressures facing China's media', China Digital Times, 18 October 2008, Online URL: *http://chinadigitaltimes.net/2008/10/%E2%80%9Cnew-nationalism%E2%80%9D-adds-to-the-list-of-pressures-facing-china%E2%80%99s-media/*
130. *Hong Kong Editorial* calls for "de jure Taiwan Independence" 27 January 2007, BBC Monitoring reports 2007.
131. Ibid.
132. National Uprising of Tibet 2008 (2008): Tibetan Parliamentary and Policy Research Centre, New Delhi, pp.10–22.
133. Ibid., p. 30.
134. Ibid., p. 32. Earlier in 1994 a policy was instituted demanding that Tibetan parents recall their children from India lest they be demoted or expelled from their jobs, and their children lose their rights to residence permits if they did not return to Tibet in a specified time frame.
135. Hung Chin-fu, "Chinese Netizens See Both Sides," *Taipei Times*, 27 April 2008, World News Connection Reports.
136. Hobsbawm and Ranger (1983) identified the role of institutionalized emblems and ritualized practices of the school in symbolically uniting the people into a community of co-nationals.
137. Yu Haibo, 'Naxi Students' National Identity Construction and Schooling: A case study of Lijiang No.1 Senior Secondary School,' *China: An International Journal*, 7(1), March 2009, pp. 161–175.
138. Chinese Experts criticize Taiwan New Textbooks for promoting "independence", *Wen Wei Po*, 30 January 2007, BBC Monitoring Services.
139. Japan's Controversial choice of a number of Secondary School Textbooks, Online URL: *http://news.bbc.co.uk/.../simp/hi/newsid_4670000/newsid_4679000/4679013.stm*
140. Hiroko Tabuchi, Japan orders history books to change passages on forced World War II suicides, Associated Press, 30 March 2007, Online URL: *http://www.signonsandiego.com/news/world/20070330-0757-japan-forcedsuicides.html*
141. Modifications to the New Version of the Textbook Controversy in Malaysia certainly Chinese Contribution to the content, *Xinhua*, 1 February 2007, BBC Monitoring Reports.
142. PRC Scholar Denies Machimura's Charge of 'Anti-Japanese' Education in China, *Xinhua*, 16 March 2005, BBC Monitoring Reports.
143. Scholar: No Anti-Japanese Education in China,17 March 2005, *Xinhua*, Online URL: *http://www.china.org.cn/english/culture/123040.htm*
144. Hu Zhenmin, "RMRB on Carrying Forward Anti-Aggression Spirit, Realizing Rejuvenation of the PRC," *Renmin Ribao*, 9 September 2005, BBC Monitoring Reports.
145. Education Law of the PRC, Adopted at the third session of the eighth National People's Congress on March 18, 1995, promulgated by Order No.45 of the President of the People's Republic of China on March 18, 1995 and effective as of 1 September 1995, Online URL: *http://www.moe.edu.cn/english/laws_e.htm, Also see Annexure IV.*
146. Yu Haibo, Ch. 3, no. 137.
147. Ibid., p. 93.
148. Is Contemporary China Patriotic? What should we do? 15 April 2009, People's Daily, URL: *http://www.people.com.cn*
149. Fu Qi and Li Huizi, 'Book rallying for social Change Fails to Inspire the Masses,' *Xinhua*, 25 March 2009, Online URL: *http://news.xinhuanet.com/english/2009-03/25/content_11072198.htm*
150. Chen Yanru, 'Notes on an agenda for Moral Education,' *China Daily*, 19 June 2008, Online URL: *http://www.chinadaily.com.cn/cndy/2008-06/19/content_6775483.htm*

151. Chomsky, Ch. 3, no. 102, p.126.
152. Based on personal observations of the author while interacting with several Chinese university students (2008 & 2010).
153. See *http://www.youtube.com/watch?v=po5ZtkGzC0I*
154. The author wants to clarify at the outset that since the survey sample was mostly based on students and university crowd along with some entrepreneurs, it does not reflect the total picture, however it is significant indicator of how China's educated groups perceive their own population and national image as well as strategy and spanned through all age groups beginning 16 to 65 years of age.
155. Internet Survey conducted by the Author on Chinese Nationalism, Web URL: *https://spreadsheets.google.com/embeddedform?key=rQnPXjC3O7BDQ6EZrrtEkJw*
156. Based on personal observations of the author.
157. For further reading on the Chinese pop-culture and music redefining the Chinese state-society relations see 'Popular culture, social change, and political reaction in post-reform China' by L Movius (1998).
158. Quisha Ma, Ch. 3, no. 71.
159. Szu-chien Hsu, 'The Domestic origin of China's Rise and its International Impact', in Hsin-Huang Michael Hsiao and Cheng-yi Lin (ed.)*Rise of China*, Routledge, Francis & Taylor, London & New York, 2008, p. 61.

4

Cinematic Representations and the Chinese Nation

Cinema is becoming the largest and most comprehensive tool of analysis in the contemporary socio-political discourse on nationalism. Being a publicly accessible archive and publicly experienced in several degrees of impact, it aids in the homogenisation of "national culture." It also enables the contemporary analysts in re-imagining the construction of identities through formulation of discursive practices. It is one of the most pervasive tools when public endorsements of certain phenomena are considered. The Chinese cinema[1] (*zhonghua dianying*) conveys the changing nature of state role and the acuities of nationalism in contemporary praxis. Moving away from the unabashedly propagandist tone of Maoist era, the contemporary films are far more successful in providing a glimpse into the multitudinous character of identity formation in a constantly evolving socio-polity and also of its historical lineage. The most noteworthy outcome of this transmutation is the intricately and intrinsically built narrative which unlike earlier is not explicit in justifying a party line but rather allows the viewer to understand, discern and own up his/her perception of the movie as a product of individual cognitive derivation. Chinese cinema is today the third largest film industry in terms of the number of feature films produced annually.[2]

The rise of the "fifth generation"[3] filmmakers augured by the release of movies like the *Yellow Earth* in 1985 has glutted the market with increasingly iconoclastic, adventurous and enterprising portrayals of what they believe to be their nation. Prominent among these have been the film representations by Chen Kaige, Zhang Yimou, Tian Zhuangzhuang, Hou Hsiao-hsien, Edward Yang (Yang Dechang) and Stanley Kwan. A study of the work of such auteurs will be helpful in making a two-dimensional foray into the archive of films. First, cinematic representations act as a part of the corpus of historical sources—narratives which trace continuities and ruptures across issues of form, representational formats and narrative structures. Second, they are contextualised in terms of spectatorial sites and distributive constraints. Though most of these present a relation between the urban temporal sites and the masses, it is the rural for which they act as the single most influential medium of construing the nature of the state through the public eye.

It should not be assumed that the "new age cinema" or contemporary cinema represents the rolling-back of the Chinese state. On the contrary, the relations between ownership and production determine the nature of state influence if not the themes of depiction. The contemporary cinema in no way escapes the yoke of presenting the current aspirations of the people and the leadership; thereby it is significantly guided by national interests. It is in essence precisely the interaction of the state management with the popular aspirations of the masses that sets the tone of reflections that are made accessible to the world at large.

Also, cinema or what can be termed as the unconventional educator, has become a process facilitating national integration sometimes deliberately and many a times unintentionally. The redefinition of the nation in these productions occurs primarily as a revisionist attempt of providing multitudinous historical depictions of the way the Chinese nation came to be built historically and is being shaped currently. Better distinguished as *guopian/zhongguo dianying*,[4] the national cinema is no more restricted to a communitarian vision as professed by Yingchi Chu[5] rather is construed through its increasing tendency of presenting the "national" to the "international." To discern the nation building phenomenon through cinematic presentations it is pertinent to look at the development of Chinese cinema over the past few decades.

Evolution of Chinese Cinema

The trajectory of Chinese cinema has meandered through a challenging conduit since the first Chinese movie *The battle of Dingjunshan* was released in 1905.[6] Endorsing the disposition of the political ambiance, the 1930s marked the beginning of a "leftist" cinema. Most prominent examples being Cheng Bugao's *Spring Silkworms* (1933), Sun Yu's *The Big Road* (1935), and Wu Yonggang's *The Goddess* (1934), all of which were noted for their emphasis on class struggle and external threats (Japanese aggression), as well as on their focus on common people, such as a family of silk farmers in *Spring Silkworms* and a prostitute in *The Goddess*.[7] Acclaimed as the first "golden era" of the Chinese cinema, this period was characterised by the emergence of three production companies: the newly formed *Lianhua* (United China), the older and larger *Mingxing* and *Tianyi*[8]. Yingjin Zhang has dealt quite extensively with the influence of the political atmosphere on the development of the Chinese national cinema during the twentieth century in his works on the Chinese national cinema.

This period also witnessed the transition of Chinese cinema from a leisurely activity based on appeal amongst masses to a narrative art. There was an evident tussle between the foreign businessmen who had to rely on traditional entertainment venues to attract Chinese audiences to the newly imported "western shadow plays" and the Chinese who insisted on claiming credit for the invention of cinema by tracing comparable shadow plays in their *national traditions*. The rift between the nationalists and communists was also transposed to their control over the production houses and it reflected in the quality of work produced during this tenure.[9] The legacy of the enlightenment spirit and the discourse of nationalism prevalent in the late Qing and during the May Fourth movement period became prominent in the way the film studios were named like "Xinmin" and "Minxin", both pointing to "new people" of China. The nationalist manoeuvring was also visible in the outright preference shown to the mandarin-dialect films over the Cantonese ones.[10]

The euphoria however, came to an abrupt end with the Japanese invasion of China and only those capable of circumventing the Japanese pressures survived in the market.[11] Consequentially, the late 1940s witnessed an inundation of anti-Japanese aggression movies which depicted the life of the survivors and their sufferings. *Myriads of Lights* (1948), *The Spring River Flows East* (1947), and *Crows and Sparrows* (1949) were especially notable for their depiction of social reality. Given the immediate acrimonious background these movies exhibited intense nationalistic sentiments. Most of them effectively demonstrated the application of two-pronged strategy utilised by the Japanese during the war.[12] They further portrayed the disillusionment with the nationalist party under Chiang Kai-Shek. This should not be read to mean that all movies produced during this time were nationalistic in content. Movies like *Spring in a small town* broke the monolith of the mainstream by their light-witted humour and artistic quality and later on came to be acclaimed as one of the greatest Chinese movie ever made (its popularity led to a remake in 2002 by Tian Zhuangzhuang).

The establishment of the communist government in PRC in 1949 gave rise to the proclivity of using motion pictures as a tool for mass propaganda. Movies like *Bridge* (1949) and *The White Haired Girl* (1950) based on lives of the peasants, soldiers and workers kindled nationalist responses.[13] In 1952 most of the KMT/GMD supported film studios were nationalised through confiscation by the CCP and most other private studios and converted them to three state-run studios at Northeast, Beijing and Shanghai. Throughout the period from 1949–1978, the film industry experienced the propagandist compulsions of the CCP. Censorship committees formed under the supervision of Yuan Muzhi, Cai Chusheng and Shi Dungshen took control of distribution and exhibition.[14]

Movies like *From Victory to Victory* depicted the civil war scenario between the KMT and CCP and class struggles between the peasants (*nongmin*) and the landlords. According to Shu Xiaoming, the socialist cinema of these times was characterized by—"a direct service to the politics, a lack of psychological depth, a distance from the artistic achievements of foreign films and the undeveloped research on the ontology of film."[15] With the establishment of the Beijing Film Academy in 1956, massive shades of folk arts, such as papercuts, shadow plays, puppetry and traditional paintings were used for popular entertainment. The *Red Detachment of Women* (1961) and *Stage Sisters* produced by the renowned filmmaker Xie Jin also exhibited explicit Soviet influence.

The subsequent period marred by the detriments of Cultural Revolution witnessed a slouching growth in the film industry. Films produced during earlier period were dubbed as detrimental to state interests and barred from reaching the common masses through a severe restriction on circulation of their prints. The *Lin family shop*, the *Life of Wu Xun* and *Sorrows of the Forbidden City* (a Hong Kong Court drama) were all dubbed as "poisonous weeds" and counter-revolutionary in spirit.[16] At the same time the period demonstrated a lack of distinct studio styles. There were also visible attempts by the CCP and more so by Jiang Qing, Mao's third wife, to warn the masses of what referred to counter-revolutionary by showcasing more than 20 films as targets of a massive campaign of film criticism. Several talents in the field of cinema were lost due to inveterate criticism of their works by their leaders.

Continuities were evident in portrayal of civil war situations in movies like *the liberation of the Shizhijuang*. The movie is a synoptic imagery of the guerilla tactics employed in capturing the industrious city of Shizhijuang. The Cultural Revolution period was characterised by the development of the new proletarian art and culture.[17] Mao's theory of "continuing revolution under the proletarian dictatorship" was implemented in the staged confrontations against class enemies and revisionists. The theatre works as well as the movies were galvanized to create the "Mao cult." It was only by 1974 that this propagandist tenor was abated with the internal friction rising between the Maoists and the ultra-leftists. *Breaking with old ideas* (*Juelie*, directed by Li Wenhua, 1975) is one such movie which captures the intricacies of the internal struggle in the Chinese political sphere. In their attempt to wrest space in public arena the evolving revisionist directors contended with several inconsistencies since the stereotypical heroes could not be framed given the two bifurcated stream of thoughts. These films tried to balance the pressures of political conformation with mass appeal by making the hero a man of the masses while having him always in agreement with the Party.[18]

Overall the period from 1977 to the mid-1980s was a period of recovery for Chinese cinema. Besides exposing the Gang of Four which was held attributable for the dilapidated condition of the film industry, the movies during this period portrayed a reconnection to the tradition of socialist realism and higher standards of achievement which could compete with international cinema and culture. The opening of the Beijing film academy to accommodate new students who would in future become the fifth-generation of Chinese filmmakers provided a new springboard for the Chinese film industry.[19] The legitimising efforts of the CCP by trying to formulate a historical discourse during the previous decades became secondary while developing an industry meant for entertainment purposes became their primary concern.

The emerging genre of Chinese cinema began to experiment with new interpretations of Chinese history and culture; thereby marking a paradigmatic shift in the organisation of the film industry. The bifurcation between the three streams[20] of Chinese cinema became more prominent during this phase. Critical issues like the return of the sovereignty of Hong Kong to China became the most-palpable theme in cinematic imagination. The movies also endorsed a more avant-garde style of weaving identity issues into the plain narrative of the movie. This shift was largely attributed to the political reforms of the 1978 under Deng Xiaoping who encompassed the modernisation of the film industry as a part of the larger apparatus of his four modernisations programme and the rising tide of commercialism.[21]

Independent Filmmakers and the National Cinema

Since cinema provides the most vivid perceptions of a country's popular social mores and its political overtures, the contemporary perceptions of Chinese nationalism can also be best determined by a preview of the post-1980s cinematic genres. As stated before, while deliberating on the intricacies of the Chinese national cinema, it is to be borne in mind that the articulation happens keeping both the domestic as well as the international audience in purview. The relations between censorship, post-release response and the construction of a national-cultural specificity that are engendered within the custody of a state–society relationship provide the message content which influence nationalism.

It is often suggested that a film narrative typically includes an argument for industrial self-legitimacy, a second argument qualifying the film's address (addressed to the censorship board), a third in possibly providing the pedagogic-instructional aspects guiding spectatorial action.[22] For delineating these purposes in the Chinese cinema, the contemporary genres can be divided into three categories: firstly, those movies dealing with Sino–Japanese relations, second, those dealing with the historical representations of the nation and its identity consolidation and third, the more general cornucopia of movies based on a commercialised market or situating the role of media in the state apparatus. The ability of these representations to bring together ethnic bondages through shared myths and ideologies with a contemporary mass perception exhibits the potential of the non-state apparatuses in whipping up nationalism. There are two core concerns which one has to keep in consideration while analysing the nationalist prime-movers behind such representations. First, how does the interaction between globalisation and nationalism effect the film industry's development? Second, does the state constantly intervene in the cinematic picturisation of nationalism and if yes, then to what extent? Third, how is the discourse on Chinese nationalism reinforced by such portrayals?

Historical Representations of the Nation

A prominent genre in the Chinese cinematic exposés is the reconstruction of Chinese nation through the use of its historical past. Most striking is its ability as an art to recreate the nation's history in a form with which one and all can identify. Since nationalism as a phenomenon constantly juggles between its past, present and future, these representations exhibit a "cultural baggage" which stimulate similar reactions and bring the people together. Most often such endeavours have gyrated around the themes of the warring states period, the imperial dynastic legends, the establishment of the republican era followed by the attempts at understanding the Cultural Revolution, and the corresponding ideologies of the historical times.

In the contemporary dynamics these efforts have yet again tried to renew the understanding of China's cultural past, and provide the new generations a glimpse into the legacy of the nation called China. The present section traces the career and works of the renowned film-maker Zhang Yimou, whose movies deal with such subjects at length. The fifth generation of film-makers to which Zhang Yimou belongs, to begin with demonstrated an anti-statist stance. Having been born and brought up during the Cultural Revolution period, this generation extremely abhorred the constraints placed on the creative potentials and individual freedom of expression, thus, the movie was an attempt to override the official lines of propaganda and search for the real identity with which these generations could redefine themselves.

To begin with, a highly innovative perspective was visible in Zhang Yimou's direction of the movie—*Red Sorghum/Hong Gaoliang* (1987). The movie based on the novel by Mo Yan, depicted a search for the narrator's identity and extendedly a search for the identity of an entire generation of Chinese who were victims of the Japanese aggression. Though the movie does not match up to the intensity and the canvas that Mo Yan is able to weave in his novel, it does portray the dilemmas of the generation which was a stalwart in overthrowing the yoke of the monarchical regime: precisely the reason why the identity of the narrator is not revealed in the movie at all. The movie situated in the Northeast Gaomi Township in an eastern province of China: Shandong, the birth place of Confucius, is woven around the experiences of the narrator's grandparents. The movie conjoins the depth of the novel through its effective use of folklore.

Throughout the narrative there is an obsession with the need for standing up against the Japanese who would otherwise ruin the Chinese civilization.

There is a consistent stress on the need for physical strength reflected in the song

> "If you drink our wine,
> You'll breathe well and you won't cough;
> If you drink our wine,
> You'll be well and your mouth won't smell bad...
> If you drink our wine,
> You won't kow-tow to the emperor..." (Annexure I (1))

A strong anti-Japanese element was also evident in the songs compiled by the author of the novel. "Northeast Gaomi Township, so many men, at Black Water River the battle began, Commander Yu raised his hand, cannon fire to heaven, Jap souls scattered across the plain, never to rise again; the beautiful champion of women, Dai Fenglian, ordered rakes for a barrier, the Jap attack broken..."[23] Simultaneously the traditional definitions of several norms also broke down "Who's a bandit? Who isn't a bandit? Anyone who fights the Japanese is a national hero. Last year I knocked off three Japanese sentries and inherited three automatic rifles. You are no bandit, but how many Japs have you killed? You haven't taken a hair off a single Jap!"[24]

These repertoires represent the deep-seated desire among the villagers to oppose ruthless suppression both by indigenous elements (monarchy) or the outsiders (Japanese). The *mise en scenes* are built with a magnitude which not only revels in the rural virility and simplicity of life but also provides for community based acceptance system which allows the narrator to accept Jiang wen as the "Grandpa" though he is not legally wedded to Jiu'er (Gong Li). An inherent questioning of China's roots and the heritage of how the Chinese ancestors came about is juxtaposed with the metaphor of sorghum and how it came to flourish in the eastern part of China.[25] In a way, the auteur exposes the inability of the larger Confucian ideology to effectively check norms in the hinterland. The external threat of the Japanese invasion also allows the breakdown of such customs without much ado since the attention is diverted significantly. Thus, the movie showcases the ability of challenging circumstances to create scope for social and gender mobility, which is otherwise denied in a stable societal order.

The movie draws upon folksongs from traditional times to knit the canvas of Chinese cultural richness, which is portrayed in the demeanour of the sedan-bearers who are responsible for delivering the bride to the master. They not only celebrate the occasion by entertaining the bride on the way while jostling her palanquin but also fight for her honour as a way of expressing their allegiance to their master. The expressions borrowed from the novel like "the Heavens have smiled on you" to denote the escape of a co-fighter from death by a Japanese bullet and drawing from the colour of Sorghum like—"the Sorghum is red; the Japanese are coming; compatriots, get ready; fire your rifles and cannons" also bring out the perceptions of Chinese village brigades towards their invaders. The movie highlights these ties of interdependence as providing a stable societal basis and enhancing the fabric of Chinese society during early times. Similarly, in the last scene the folklore is used to reinforce the mesmerising impact of cinematography and give an expression to the inner feelings of the narrator's father and grandfather.

Besides the community-bred life, the film also portrays the return to the "carnal" which governs the priorities of the village life instead of ideological influences propagated by the state or the nationalist parties. It repudiates the refined and sophisticated notions of Chinese culture awakening the viewer to more primal instincts. The significance attached to the wine brewing process and the centrality of the wine in their lives brings out the streaks of nature-worship that have been an intrinsic part of the traditional Chinese culture. Given the auteur's personal predilection of disparaging the state's attempt at propagandising several themes, the director has intentionally kept any ideological influence away from the script of the movie. However, the angst against the Japanese that the director has brought in is a reflection of a non-state generated, popular current in the Chinese intellectual sphere or simply the public sphere, while using the magnificent red colour to symbolise the angst against the "red sun"—the symbol of the Japanese flag and bloodshed (Annexure I (5)).

The reception of the movie within China was initially, severely restricted due to the state pressure and Zhang received almost ten thousand letters accusing him of treason.[26] The Chinese state also banned Zhang's later movies from being screened in China keeping in view his revisionist endeavours. Several Chinese film critics and scholars expressed their unacceptability, for instance, Dai Jinhua challenged Zhang's creation of the Chinese national myth and attacks in Red Sorghum as not only false but also "foreign to the Chinese reality and national culture in the East." In a similar vein, Zhang Yiwu even pronounces that Fifth Generation filmmaking is "an aberration from the Chinese tradition" and "a bizarre phenomenon outside the history of Chinese film."[27] Despite the log jams, the movie has been hailed as "presenting a perfect answer to what the country needed at that particular point in time." And while the movie does not embark upon showcasing a strong nationalist predilection, it contributes to the larger corpus of building a cultural discourse away from the gaze of the state.

Zhang continued with this quest of redefining the Chinese identity as it transited into the contemporary realm away from the accepted norms of a Confucian order in the movie *Ju Dou* (1990). He brought out the dilemma of a young woman (Gong Li) who is sold off as a wife to a vat-dyer named Yang Jinshan (Li Wei) and is maltreated on account of being unable to bear him a child. Besides positing the human need for love and care in an illicit relationship between Ju Dou and Yang Tianqing, Zhang employs the notion of a decadent and feudal system which has past its heyday and is on a brink of collapse comparing it with the old husband, while the younger nephew or the modern thought is exalted as the future of the country. The disillusionment of the protagonist at the end is the final culmination of the tussle between the contending streams of thoughts (Annexure I (2)). However, deeper entanglement with the political questions is witnessed in his later endeavours like *Raise the Red Lantern* (1991) and *To Live* (1994).

Raise the Red Lantern delves into deeper questions of privileging certain sections in the society over others under the tutelage of the power-bearer while denying the same to others. Yet again construed through the theme of man–women relationships, the movie runs along two parallel ethnoscapes: on the much obvious scale, a feudal setup wherein the patriarch chooses the liberty of his womenfolk depending on his predilections. On the other plane it engages with the issue of the CCP being the patriarch in the Chinese political order which chooses the privileges or denial of those privileges to those in obedience or opposition to its dictum. Historically situated in the warlord era of early 1920s, it is based on the novel *Wives and concubines* by Su Tong. The lives of the four mistresses revolve around the constant competition or struggle for their husband's affection and the benefits that come along with it. Wading through a web of internal intrigues and tales of jealousy and deceit, the auteur draws attention to the inability of an individual to live through the restrictions on his freedom of mobility and speech (Annexure I (3)). The loss of mental cognisance on part of the protagonist can be discerned to symbolise the agony of those political prisoners who are devoid of all kinds of freedom under the stronghold of the state.

To Live again deals with the difficulties faced by the common masses under the CCP's stewardship during the Cultural Revolution. The movie provides an accurate account of the social conditions during the decades prior and in continuation of the Cultural Revolution. The movie effectively utilises the allegories of folklore, the striking ability of the propaganda posters and the organisational capacity of the social fabric to wade through four generations of a single working class family in its struggle for survival (Annexure I (4)). Besides drawing attention to issues like the prioritisation of a son-child, the lack of proper medical care due to castigation of the doctors as the bourgeois elite, and endorsement of the Maoist aphorisms by the common populace, the movie presents the drab nature of the peasant and working class lives.

The anti-communist tenor of the movie earned it a ban in China for quite some time. Nevertheless, the auteur's attempt to expose the drawbacks of the Cultural Revolution provides an opportunity to gauge the revisionist attempt in constructing the state history. Despite the best attempts of the state to strictly define the contours of operation of the boundaries of film industry, continuous endeavours to escape those limits are palpable. The consecutive endeavours by Zhang Yimou focused more on revisiting the issues of national honour and international compliance. For this purpose he returned to historical accounts and tried to understand them through the prism of contemporary conceptualisation.

In *Hero* (2000), Zhang revisited the conventional understanding of national-heroes and redefined it under a predominant nationalist influence. True to its aphorism "in any war there are heroes on both sides", the movie is set in a dichotomy of "true peace for all" though "through the path of bloodshed"[28] and depicts the simultaneous journeys of two heroes. First, the journey of a nameless assassin (Jet Li) who becomes a great warrior-hero inspired by the spirit of reclaiming honour, the restoration of his self-identity and the clan-honour of his native Zhao state and finally the realization of a grand vision of his opponent and his submission to the same, while on the other hand, the journey of a tyrant whose visions of unifying the kingdom under a single rule manifests him into an epitome of a nationalist vision-bearer.

The historicism of the warring states and the prelude of the plot as the conflict between the king of Qin and King Wuling (325-299 B.C.) of Zhao have been corroborated by the Records of the Historian (*Shiji*) written by Sima Qian, the grand historian of the Emperor Wu (141-87 B.C.) of the former Han dynasty.[29] However, the authenticity of a group of assassins was difficult to verify and it would be appropriate to qualify them as additional fictional elements brought in to enhance the narrative. Incorporating an effective blend of dialogue and flashback, the movie is encrypted in the court of the Qin-emperor (Chen Daoming) who being wary of his three assassins keeps his visitors symbolically hundred paces away from his throne. The king impressed by the warrior who claims to have killed the three assassins and places their swords in front of the king, beckons him to sit within ten paces of his throne and narrate the manner of his duels with the legendary-three: Flying Snow (Maggie Cheung), Broken Sword (Tony Leung) and Long Sky (Donnie Yen). The warrior narrates his duel with Long Sky at the Weiqi parlour in terms of a mind game, while his encounter with the other two as a tale of distrust and jealousy sown through Flying Snow's illicit relationship with Long Sky and consequentially Broken Sword's with his apprentice Moon (Zhang Ziyi).

The king however, refuses to accept the explanation and affirms his belief in the character of the two assassins to be men/women of honour as a memory from his experience with them three years ago. Thus, discerning the loopholes in the warrior's story he gives him his own version. Consequently, the warrior discloses his true identity and narrates the actual truth of his existence and the resistance shown by Sword towards the assassination plan by construing the vision of "*Tian Xia*" (Annexure I (5)) "All under Heaven"/ "Our Land."

The king is astonished with Sword's ability to comprehend his visions and throws the sword to the warrior/assassin to execute him while he stares on Sword's scroll which is inscribed with the definition of an ultimate warrior — "the one who has no desire to fight." The warrior however realises the significance of Sword's words and leaves the king alive and treads the path of self-sacrifice. The emperor is however, traditionally bound to execute the assassin as preordained by the traditions of the country and to set it as an example before others. Notwithstanding, after the execution, the warrior receives a hero's burial given his ultimate realisation of the emperor's vision.

The consequential unification of China and the formation of the Chinese nation as an entity were followed *historically* by the unification of Chinese language, its weights and measures system and the completion of the Great Wall of China. The movie thus encapsulates in a mere two hour depiction the history of formation of the *zhong guo*/"middle kingdom." However, the director's efforts of portraying a revisionist version of a tyrant who is seen differently in the Chinese culture—as a father figure and a monarch with the capability to unite the nation had restricted appeal internationally.

The subtle presentation of art and culture from the ancient times through incorporating instances like "music and martial art sharing the same principles" as well as "the basic similarities in a person's way of writing calligraphy and his ability of wielding the sword as being similar" bring out the significance attached to certain beliefs of the ancient period. However, the most laudable tenet of the movie is the auteur's ability to accommodate modern cinematographic effects into a historical Chinese discourse.[30]

The culmination of the vision into the two words that have since time immemorial defined the Chinese international political vision, *tian xia*, further is an attempt by the auteur to posit the larger interest of the humanity against the limited nationalistic visions. Though it cannot be established that the author intended to juxtapose the same with the current CCP ideology of harmonious development and peaceful rise, it definitely is a statement of the civilisational foresee-ability of the Chinese ancestral leaders and a eulogy of their past achievements. The director showcases the age-old traditional techniques mentioned in the *Spring and Autumn Period* which had come to be established by then as well as martial arts known by the time King Wuling of the state of Zhao during the warring states period ruled inspiring cultural pride.

The national and international responses further place the movie in a context of the ideological divide between the East and the West, that is, the beliefs of communitarian visions vis-à-vis individualistic tenors. The film has been criticised by the Western media for its pro-totalitarian overtures and a preference of stability and security over liberty and human rights and was released after a deliberation of almost two years.[31] However, being one of the first films to endorse this dichotomy of Asian values, this movie can be hailed as a successful attempt by the filmmaker in providing a different perspective about China. Zhang further, ventured onto issues of state and society relationship during ancient times in his film *House of the Flying Daggers* (2004), which was situated in the later times of the ailing Tang dynasty. The movie brings out the nuances of state of affairs between the government and a rebel group called the *House of the flying daggers*. Outraged by corruption and inefficiency of the ruling government, such groups had taken up the role of the saviours of the general poor, and thereby, earned their trust and loyalty. However, the storyline is woven around a plot where the government forces are successful in assassinating the leader of this group and the new leadership vows to avenge their leader's death.

Set in 859 AD, corresponding with the decline of the Tang Dynasty, the story revolves around a blind-girl Mei (Zhang Ziyi) who feigns the identity of the daughter of the late-leader and has been assigned by the society the task of bringing the chief police/police captain of the general's troops to the headquarters of the secret society so as to enable the government to declare a war with the "house of flying daggers." It would be easy to dismiss the movie as yet another martial art romance capturing the sophisticated emotions of deceit, love and duty. However, the director's subtlety in portraying several shades embedded in the overall canvas which would otherwise be unnoticeable to the common eye is remarkable.

One such instance is the opening song of the movie in which the female protagonist recognizes the similarities between woman and a nation.[32] (Annexure I (6)). By way of this song the allegory of the "nation as a woman" and the "woman as a nation" is marvellously constructed. As a woman becomes the matter of contention between these two captains, in a similar way, a piece of land invariably beckons a master-ship which is earned by the victor by overwhelming the defeated. Moreover, the constructs of honour, duty and self-sacrifice that a nation demands from its citizens can be compared at the level which men are willing to go in pursuit of upholding the honour of their womenfolk. The song is an adaptation of a poem written by the Han dynasty poet Li Yannian and via this song the director has tried to incorporate the traditional notions of the nation juxtaposing it with a contemporary framework of international relations.

The cinematography of the movie has also relied on the paintings of the earlier period to give it an authentic flavour and showcase to the common masses the historical/traditional tenors of singing and dancing. The contextualisation of most of the plot in a bamboo forest has been engendered with a view to showcasing the immense traditional value associated with the bamboo in the Chinese culture. Also this has to be read in context of the spread of the Chinese soft power through positing their cities and renowned landmarks as places of tourist attraction, which is another way of promoting the country. In the auteur's conception, the pursuit of nations as a territorial unit and the border issues for which the two contenders are willing to go to war are rendered futile in the inherent message of the movie as the director eulogises the values of harmony and peace through mutual understanding in the concluding scenes. The movie tries to extol the larger internationalist attempts at seeking mutual understanding and the significance of deliberative consensus while highlighting the stalemate or lose-lose situation of both the opponents in case of a war.

The responses to the movie on the national and the international front depict the restricted reception of an internationalist perspective by the Chinese government which ostensibly criticised the movie for lacking any substantive storyline and as a mere attempt to appease the Western audience. On the other hand, while the movie was internationally acclaimed for the effective utilisation of strong visual effects and the computer-generated imagery, the endorsements have not come for the substantive message or character of the story-building but for the colourful picturisation and the standards that it sets in production and entertainment.

Similarly, in the *Curse of the Golden Flower* (2006) set against the historical backgrounds of the like of Forbidden City and the Summer Palace, the author embarks on an understanding of historical lineages. Along with the exhaustive ornamentation and use of antique armour to reduplicate the aura of the imperial armies, the movie meanders through a web of intrigues and illicit relationships to elucidate the collapse of Confucian ethics which earlier provided the basis for a stable societal arrangement. The ambiguity in the manner the auteur has brought the curtain down in the final scenes, provides for two parallel conjectures that can be drawn.

Primarily, the norms and values of filial piety and adherence to the order of relationship were no more the driving forces behind the emergent political relationships within the given time reference, thereby bringing instability and ruin of the Tang dynasty and thus, venerating the utility and moral uprightness of the Confucian order. However, on the other hand the movie questions the intentions of the monarch who is under the traditional order a *son of the heaven* and hence is responsible for delivering to the expectations of his near and dear ones. Zhang questions this premise by depicting the selfish motives of the Emperor Ping (Chow Yun-Fat) and the lack of wisdom in catering to the interests of his relatives. While the traditional mores beckoned upon the imperial family to set the norms and standards for its masses, the auteur engages with the question as to "what kind of an example could an embittered, internally divisive family put to its masses?"

Bringing out the nitty-gritty's of the fractionalisation of the imperial household into two opponent camps, he unveils the malignant intentions of the king in tending to the queen's medicines and similarly the queen's (Empress Liang, Gong Li) clandestine efforts of crowning her birth-son, Prince Jai (Jay Chou) to the throne through the "revolution of the chrysanthemums."

The ultimate doom which is inevitable is unravelled through an avalanche of events further buttressing the superfluous nature of the imperial household (Annexure I (7)). Thus, the afore-mentioned movies depict certain historical constructions of the theme of nation and how nationalism has meant different things to different people.

The Avant-garde in Chinese Cinema

Besides these historical conceptualisations, several avant-garde movies take a look into the unfolding dynamics of state-society relationships. Not being critical of the state in the strict sense of the term, "Not One Less" (*yi ge dou bu neng shao*) (1999) portrays the positive impact of the interaction of media with the rural hinterlands where the state control is relatively loose and autonomy in many senses becomes synonymous with indifference. The story is situated in a small village in the countryside where poverty and illiteracy hamper the day-to-day life of the people and the "dream of the city" lures small children out of the love and care of their parents into a struggle for earning a livelihood thus, rendering them exposed to the brutalities of a fast-paced life at a young age.

The movie revolves around a thirteen-year-old substitute school teacher who is assigned with the responsibility of teaching students of different grades in a school which somehow manages to survive despite its dilapidated condition and is the only source of information for people around the village. The abject poverty is picturised in stark contrast to the shining cities, affluent with the rich culture begotten from the capitalist boom. While the city-bred students receive best of the education and amenities, these students have to struggle for basic sustenance and many times even provide for other members of the family. In her determination to bring her student Zhang Huike back to school, she embarks on a sojourn to the city and finds herself lost in the quagmire of lofty buildings and a non-ending labyrinth of crossroads. She is finally reunited with her student with the help of the media, which further takes on the responsibility of exposing the dearth of facilities in the village and bringing to attention the state-of-affairs in the rural hinterland.

The movie is one of such a genre of depictions which is increasingly trying to bridge the gap between the state and the society. The watchdog role played by such cinema is less critical of the state and rather prompts the state to get entangled with the welfare mechanisms which ought to be the responsibility of the state authorities. The movie also sheds light on the intriguing relationship between the state and the educational system at large. The state recruitment policy of picking the best athletes from far of regions and training them under state supervision is highlighted through the instance of a student of Wei's school who is picked up by the state recruitment organizers. Moreover, the nationalist tenors are evident in the manner of how the students are taught to handle the flag and the national song, which provide testimony to the didactic overtones of rural existence (Annexure I (8)).

The modernist approaches in the new movies have led to several scholars in dubbing these as non-nationalist. Paul Clark, a scholar on Chinese film, writes that the images of China in Fifth Generation films "reflect a profoundly ambivalent nationalism." However, it is not sufficient to dub the new tenors as ambivalent nationalism, as the redefinition of the nation is a process that is constantly evolving through this medium. And the cinematic representations remain the only medium through which the state is able to bring the rural hinterland within the canopy of its nationalist goals. Cinema thus, provides a scope for redefining of national culture and influencing a stratum of society which is otherwise marginalised in the purview of state. Various attempts by directors, actors and the involvement of the audience allow the nation to be rejuvenated and a sense of identity established by questioning and reaffirming their legacies. Nationalism is consistently generated in the responses that these movies are able to elicit nationally and internationally.

Anti-Japanese Nationalism in Chinese Cinema

Another theme which is preponderantly depicted in Chinese movies is the intricacies of the Sino-Japanese history and diplomatic undercurrents which have been attempted in earlier movies like the *Liberation of Nanjing* (four parts). For instance, *Devils on the doorstep* directed by Jiang Wen which was released in 2000 attempted to understand the Sino-Japanese relations and the war memories in a highly unconventional way. Being one of the fifth-generation directors, Jiang Wen tried to articulate a non-state perspective of the Japanese soldiers during the Second World War. The movie utilized a comical depiction of the interface between the Chinese and Japanese during the Second World War to exhibit the ground realities about the local people and the prisoners of war. Distinctly, it remains one of the rare black and white productions of the contemporary era which endeavoured to authenticate its *mise en scenes* through an impressive non-use of colour.

The movie was partly an adaptation of the novel *Survival* by You Fengwei and narrated the experience of a peasant Ma Dasan (Jiang Wen) a mysterious figure, in a village named "rack-armor terrace" in Hebei province, who is forced by circumstances to take two prisoners as captive in his home. The movie absolves Ma Dasan's efforts to save a man who in the end becomes his own persecutor (Annexure I (9)). One of the significant aims of projecting such a plot by the maker seems to be an attempt at debunking the passivity of the Chinese peasants or citizens as receptors of Japanese aggression.

The depiction illustrates how peasants experienced a multiplicity of choices while undergoing the struggle against the Japanese. Not only was there a chance for survival through executing the two prisoners right at the beginning of the movie, but also a choice of whether to accept the trade-off between the two prisoners and the army for just some sacks of grains. The peasant's acceptability of entering this agreement demonstrated how issues of nationalism and national honour took a back seat when contextualised against the chances of survival in a war-torn rural China. The auteur sets the issues of loyalty and honour in the backdrop of daily necessities which governed the basic life of the people in such far away regions.

In the movie, the auteur tried to delve into the psychological need of blaming the "other" as the perpetrator of crime against a "passive self" which identifies with being a victim especially as a theme in Chinese literature. The movie also highlighted the gamut of misrepresentations that occur when two people of unknown languages are brought face-to-face. In this particular case, the attempt by the interpreter in the movie to deliberately misconstrue the sergeant's words for the sake of his own survival also provides testimony to the individual's need of survival which operates beyond the larger super-structures of economy and polity and influences the outcome of any event.

The movie interestingly portrays the major atrocities committed by Japan into a comical sequence presenting a light-weighted argument which moves away from the traditional staunch anti-Japanese propaganda. The juxtaposition of a fatal strike by an executioner with an art of pleasure further demonstrates the non-traditional approach of the director in dealing with such issues. Given its radical revisionist tinge, the movie was declared banned in China by the Chinese Film Bureau, while it premiered at the Cannes film festival in 2000 and clinched several awards abroad.[33] The director was also threatened with dire consequences—a seven year ban on his direction, in case of proliferating such thinking as depicted in his movie. Several reservations were raised regarding Jiang's visit to the Yasukuni Shrine, which the director clarified later to be motivated by the need to gather historical facts from old records.[34]

These responses to the movie highlight the discomfort of the Chinese government with popular perceptions that try to re-examine or re-evaluate the historic Sino-Japanese relations, especially if they project a stance different from that of the government. Thus, the government's non-acceptability and the resultant ban of this movie depict the intention of the state on controlling the nature of discourse that circulates in the public sphere. While Jiang provides interesting insights of the similarities in culture of the two countries such an attempt is considered blasphemous in the eyes of the state. Though the movie also juxtaposes the relatively humble nature of the Chinese peasants against the aggressive nature of the Japanese soldiers, these instances are easily overlooked by the state administration due to the overall revisionist image of the movie. The state authorities even declared that given his desire to adhere to the commercial atmosphere of the globalised scenario, the director has unnecessarily hurt the national feelings.

In contrast the movie *City of Life and Death/Nanjing Nanjing* by Lu Chuan released in 2009, which was lauded as a tribute to the 60 years of Chinese state-existence, portrays the Japanese atrocities during the siege of the city of Nanjing in 1937. This was yet another movie utilising shades of white and black to give a realistic touch to its depiction and avoid anachronism and is swathed of nationalist depictions. The movie was both economically and culturally a massive experiment with the local aspirations and understandings.[35] The Nanjing massacre in which more than 3,00,000 Chinese were killed, remains one of the most poignant episodes in Chinese history and rekindles several atavistic memories amongst the Chinese people. In contrast to the previous movie, the director's attempts have been lauded as a tribute to the unwavering spirit of the Chinese people of resisting against evil.

It shares the theme of deconstructing the passivity of Chinese as silent sufferers with the above-mentioned movie but is significantly different in the image projection of the scale of brutality on part of the Japanese. Unlike the comical or much repressed tenor of the previous movie, it brings in unfathomable derision for the Japanese actions into its cinematography. With a considerable number of scenes showcasing rape and murder, the picturisation of brutality has earned it the "honour" of being one of the most nationalistic representations in contemporary portrayals so far.

The movie showcases several shades of Chinese experiences beginning with the Japanese army entering the gates and taking charge of the internal divisions. While most of the male citizens lose their lives fighting for control and trying to save what is left of the city, the females are concealed under the tutelage of a foreign missionary and a German businessman, John Rabe, managing director of Siemens China, (John Paisley) who organised the International Committee for the Nanjing Safety Zone. Despite the efforts of these missionaries and the businessmen, the Japanese soldiers are able to negotiate the provision of several Chinese women as sex-workers in lieu of leaving the rest of the women in peace (Annexure I (10)). These instances of defiling the sanctity of the Chinese women are often adduced by the Chinese state to elicit nationalistic responses from its citizens.

Besides showing the ineffective war-methods of the Chinese soldiers, the movie also depicts how Mr Tang's (Fan Wei), a teacher at the Nanjing University, tries to bargain for his survival by appeasing the Japanese soldiers through buying a permit and a flag cover from the Japanese establishment but in the end remains unsuccessful in his feat. The resistance shown by the Chinese on their part results in one of the soldier throwing away a young girl (the daughter of Mr. & Mrs. Tang) out of the window. Thus, driven by personal loss and anger the parents decide to leave for Shanghai. The war situation turns increasingly unendurable forcing many missionaries and officials to leave. Any effort of empathy is met by punishment for the Japanese soldiers, as in the case of Mr. Tang cited in the movie, who was shot the instance it was known that he let someone else leave for offshore in his lieu. These instances elucidate how bilateral relations driven by war become overbearing on the representatives of each side even though they might believe differently on a personal scale.

The nationalist responses to the movie were tremendous and varied from segment to segment among the citizens. The movie also got mixed response for its sympathetic portrayal of a Japanese soldier, Kadokawa (Hideo Nakaizumi), who was equally affected by the depredations of war. Some amongst the several instances where he is shown as being considerate are when he helps a sex-worker, a father-son duo whom he releases to atone for his stance during the war, as well as a female Chinese non-conformist, who is captured during her efforts to help those people who need assistance. The tremendous pangs of guilt that he experiences while the rest of the army is busy rejoicing the absolute establishment of their authority through a ceremonial commemoration of its martyred soldiers finally lead him to commit suicide. Thus, the movie revived national sentiments by reminiscing personal traumatic experiences, while the ultra-nationalist sections in the Chinese community showed their resentment to the views of the director, who has consequentially received death threats.[36]

Some popular perceptions can be gauged by the following reactions aired by the Chinese netizens on popular forums: "The crimes of the Japanese were much worse (than those showed in the movie). I especially cannot accept the image of Kadokawa", an 87-year-old Nanjing citizen Zhang Zhenqing opined after watching the movie. "Perhaps Lu Chuan is too young to understand our feelings," said Zhao, who survived the massacre.[37] "I remember coming out from the screening with tears in my eyes. It was powerful", said Bey Logan, vice president of Asian Acquisitions and Co-production, the Weinstein Company, an independent American film studio. He further confessed that "the film presents history in very human terms, which is why it's so moving. I think a one-note film about heroic Chinese soldiers and evil Japanese soldiers might be epic, but it wouldn't be nearly as engaging emotionally, as this one is."

The movie ends with the father and son duo sharing the joy of liberation and rejoicing in the fresh air of countryside which seems to have escaped the destruction spread by the war. The final message which is transmitted to the viewers is a veneration of the ability of the Chinese to start afresh despite the atrocities suffered over previous centuries and celebrates their perseverance and will for freedom and survival (Annexure I (10)). The movie bears several precedents like *Nanjing* which had earlier (2007), in a similar fashion, capitalised on several historical documents and interviews and brought to fore the condition of the prisoners of war under the Japanese supervision. However, the ability of the auteur to audaciously portray the evils of the significant "other" (Japanese) earned the movie a significant response and marked it as different from the rest of the movies in the same genre.

As mentioned earlier, the reason why most cinematic representations keep reinvigorating the anti-Japanese sentiments is given the belief of the Chinese people that Japan has not fully recognised the war crimes and sincerely apologised for them. However, some Japanese historians and government officials often claim that the demonisation of the Japanese soldiers takes place as the "massacre has been exaggerated or even fabricated for the purposes of political propaganda" by the Chinese state.[38] What is most significant about the propagation of such movies is the inability of the Sino-Japanese bilateral relationship to move over these historical issues while dealing with each other bilaterally.

Though the movie tries to develop a new perspective on understanding a Japanese soldier, nationalist considerations have rendered the case to be shown as one in a million and not as a majority phenomenon. For the Japanese actors the movie has been a rare exposure as they have been made witness to the horrible crimes that their nation is held responsible for and the crimes of their ancestors which derelicts their identity for more than half a century now. The Japanese actors believe that the possibility of revising critical episodes in history could also provide for revision of relations between the two countries later on. In sum, the director put his intentions well when he opined that "to continue to wail and whine to the world about the sufferings we had experienced will not work. We need to probe deeply into how and why the war happened."[39]

The movie is being increasingly compared with the Florian Gallanberger directed *John Rabe/La bei ri ji* released around the same period which looked at the Nanjing massacre solely through the prism of the German businessman and is set to reinstate for him, his deserved historical fame.[40] Due to alternative claims, several controversies have arisen which have further flamed nationalist responses from the Chinese people. Some have however, reacted differently, for instance, Tang Daoluan opined that "denying and downplaying Rabe's contribution is unfair to Rabe, to history, and to the cause of international humanitarianism, and it makes us look like ungrateful people."[41]

This contestation of fact and fiction in cinematic presentations is largely given the aspiration of an auteur in trying to recreate historical characters in a manner which substantiates the national goals. While both the movies have garnered substantial gains at the Chinese box office, the former has definitely become associated with the larger goals of presenting historical images of the Chinese nation. And despite the auteur's reiteration that the movie does not seek to build on a legacy of nationalistic cinema it has irrevocably generated jingoistic responses.[42]

Besides these, several anti-Japanese films like *Ye ask* and *forever enthralled/*

Mei Lanfang (2008), directed by Chen Kaige, reflect strong traces of nationalism. While the former portrays the life and times of a real historical figure who was born in Foshan, Guangdong Province, and used the Chinese martial arts to resist Japanese aggression, the latter is a biopic of an opera artist who refused to sing for the Japanese imperial army despite the high official position bestowed on him. The two films have effectively utilised drama and folklore as processes depicting nationalism.

Interestingly, besides these overtly explicit anti-Japanese aggression movies, there exist several movies which try to provide unconventional views of how internal divisions within Japan often result in bifurcated conceptualisations of the Yasukuni shrine as a symbol of the nation. Li Ying in his documentary *Yasukuni* (2008) probes this dilemma by deconstructing the nature of controversy surrounding the official visits by the Japanese to this shrine commemorating war victims. These visits have often been construed by the Chinese government and citizens as insensitive to the Chinese sentiments, as the place was earlier used to manufacture swords that were employed against the Chinese.[43]

The documentary is woven around a dialogue with the oldest sword-smith Kariya Naoji of Japan who oblivious to the consequences or purposes of his profession keeps working with utmost precision. On the other hand, several interest groups within the Japanese political paraphernalia continue to struggle with their conceptualisation of the Yasukuni shrine. Through a dialogue with the sword-maker, the auteur tries to gauge the historical dimensions of the war and whether the Japanese accept the scale of loot and plunder that was manifested on the Chinese soil.

The sword-maker while demonstrating the art of sword-making and engraving the central icon—saber called "the body of Shinto," acquiesces to most of the allegations while staying mute over critical issues that might reflect on Japan as a nation. The documentation is done through questioning several original sources of war and verifying their authenticity with the help of the sword-maker. The parallel sketch of a ceremonial salute taking place in the premises of the shrine on the occasion of the 60th anniversary of Japan's surrender that is, on August 15, 2005, is depicted by the director to provide a glimpse into the routinisation of this cult. While the Japanese official troops carry out their duty-call, several other passers-by are amused with their alacrity and solemnity. An American supporter of this ritual however, arouses concern when he parades around with an American flag and is consequentially asked by the authorities to leave the ground or else put the flag aside. During these sequences, yet another incident unfolds where two young protestors who try to disrupt this ceremony are reprimanded for their stance and shooed away rather acrimoniously (Annexure I (11)).

The documentary has been shot with more an intention to provoke further research on the issue rather than leaving a message with the viewers. Being funded by the Japanese government the director has refrained from colouring the documentary with anti-Japanese tenor while it shrewdly indicates towards the authoritarianism of the ultra-right wing. The movie concludes rather abruptly and refrains from propagating any statist perspective. Rather the movie has been viewed as an appeasing effort by the Chinese towards the otherwise much disliked Japanese patriots. While aesthetically the documentary fails to conform to the expected levels, it does provoke strong reactions from both Chinese and Japanese communities. While the Japanese banned the screening of this documentary dubbing it as a propagandist attempt against the building of a strong venerable feeling amongst the Japanese community, the Chinese have shown mixed reactions.[44]

Similarly, in the movie *Little Soldier Zhang,* directed by Sun Lijun, nationalist dispositions are brought to the fore even if it means a reiteration of historical resentment against a neighbouring country (Japan). The movie depicts the life story of a cute 12-year-old boy during the 1930s, who seeks revenge from the Japanese for having killed his grandmother, by joining an underground Red Army detachment.[45] Chinese nationalism, thus, has come to be increasingly "other" directed on the international scenario and acquired a tenor of a zealous unifying force within the domestic context. While China has been involved in various controversies, textbook controversy with Japan who eulogize criminals as war heroes, the Yasukuni Shrine issue and a relatively insecure border in terms of dissenting ethnicities, it has simultaneously advanced a foreign policy that avers an "inclusive peaceful growth" for the region.

The high reception of such movies amongst Chinese audience shows that the anti-Japanese streak in the Chinese cinema quite obsessively conjures up nationalistic feelings. Pictographic angst-inspiring sequences are often buttressed with the state's responses which either help or deter the promotion of the movie depending on its capacity to endorse the foreign policy goals of the central government. These cinematic representations which easily get engraved in the memory of the common masses help in keeping alive the rhetoric of nationalist agenda, thereby, legitimizing the authority of the state as the stalwart of national interests and dreams and ambitions of the Chinese people. These movies authenticate the function delineated by Nairn who declares that "Nationalism is always Janus-faced. Not only does it look both backward and forward, it simultaneously embodies claim to distinctive cultural identities and social solidarities and to legitimate global standing and at least partial sovereignty."[46] With many scholars asserting that the film is a medium born to become a depot of history'[47] such depictions have become more and more palpable in cinema. Besides the thematic representations, the nationalist tinge is evident in also the television and media series, which are aired from time to time.

Nation in Popular Constructions—'Da Guo Jue Qi'

In a documentary television series aired in 2006 by the CCTV, a set of Chinese historians discussed the rise of great powers and the character of their rule. The "Rise of the Great Powers/Da Guo Jue Qi" traverses through the experience of nine countries viz. Portugal, Spain, the Netherlands, the United Kingdom, France, Germany, Japan, Russia (Soviet Union), and the United States to determine the elements of nationalist assertion and hegemonic intentions in the region. This was one of the first attempts whereby China posited internationally that it was willing to discuss its own position at length with other powers in the world. Trying to justify its intent of "peaceful rise" there was a deliberate attempt by Chinese policy-makers to learn from the mistakes of other nations whose rise had created a shift in power balance at the international level. The series identifies certain historical landmark years, that is, 1688, 1789, 1871 which changed the face of world history and through an ostensibly more open attitude towards history it aims to assuage the US' qualms about China's aggressive rise (Annexure I). It is now also available with the History Channel. Several other popular soaps and series have also been adduced to strengthen the discourse of nationalism and elicit patriotic reactions.

The CCTV itself has been implicitly drawn upon for nationalist propagandas. It has been constantly harrowed by the Publicity Department of the CPCCC and the SARFT to abide by the censorship rules of the government and is headed by a Vice-Minister of the State Council, being considered one of the "big three" in Chinese media. Most controversies surrounding broadcast on this network gyrate around the maintenance and preservation of China's international image. *Focus*, a programme aired by the CCTV has been long watched by the Chinese government with skepticism. It is one of the rare projections which have managed to criticize the government lackadaisical approach as well as gain its support by showcasing the government's response to cases of corruption.[48] The extensive rights given by the Chinese government to broadcast the Beijing Olympics also substantiate the notion of government support for this channel. This practice of strengthening a local enterprise to project itself internationally is not typical of China alone. Most nations including the US have been observed to extend protection to their enterprises abroad to attain national goals. In India a parallel could be drawn with the Doordarshan which is aimed at concretizing the process of nation-building though driven by comparatively lesser propaganda.

Such attempts have however been subject to domestic criticisms in China. In January 2009, Chinese intellectuals signed an open letter calling for the boycott of state television news programme on the ground that it had turned its news and historical drama series into propaganda to brainwash its audience.[49] The author of the letter also contextualized his claims against the argument that China often accuses the West of biased coverage about its history and politics but instances like these show that China itself was no exception to twisting facts and figures. These reactions have forced China to reconsider its stance on visual media and the themes and manner in which these are projected.

In sum, through effective use of visual aids the Chinese authorities have further reinforced the Janus of nationalism. The discourse has not only employed revival of historical notions of empire, republic or ethnicity but also impinges on the nature of transactions between national and international media houses. While the state completely controls certain production companies and tries to limit their area of operation and experimentation, the ones outside the direct supervision of state tend to tread with caution lest they earn the governments wrath. And though various scholars have argued the need for transiting from a perspective based on "national cinema" to that of "cinema and the national"[50] both are interlocked in inseparable ways. The more internationally competitive the Chinese cinema surfaces, the more a discourse on the "national" will become palpable in its functioning.

NOTES

1. The Chinese cinema has had three distinctive historical trends: Hong Kong Cinema, Taiwan cinema (For a detailed history of Taiwanese cinema see—Yingjin Zhang-Chinese national cinema) and Mainland cinema. However, for the purpose of this work the focus has been restricted to the representations of the mainland China.
2. Hillary Brenhouse, "As its Box Office Booms, Chinese Cinema Makes a 3-D Push, *Time*, 31 January 2011, Online URL: *http://www.time.com/time/world/article/0,8599,2044888,00.html*
3. Beginning from 1896 till the 1980s five generations have been identified. First one reigning between 1896–1940s, second from late 1940s to 1950, third between 1950s and 1960s, fourth one being witnessed during 1960s–1980s and contemporarily fifth and sixth from the 1980s to the present.
4. Yingjin Zhang, *Chinese national Cinema*, Routledge, New York and London, 2004, p. 6.
5. Yingchi Chu, *Hong Kong Cinema: Colonizer, motherland and self*, Routledge Curzon, London & New York, 2003, p.xiv. The author argues that the national film industry produces films that mainly target its national community.
6. Though the first documentary was presented on 28 December 1895 by the Lumière brothers at the Grand Café in Paris, the first indigenous Chinese movie was released in 1905. Along with cinema, theatre continued to be an important medium of influence on the general masses.
7. Zhang, Ch. 4, no. 4, p. 6.
8. The period also produced the first big Chinese movie stars, namely Hu Die, Ruan Lingyu, Zhou Xuan, Zhao Dan and Jin Yan.
9. Zhang, Ch. 4, no. 4, pp. 54–57.
10. Ibid., p. 71.
11. The Shanghai film industry survived the Japanese control by making films like the Greater East Asia Co-Prosperity Sphere, which promoted *Eternity* (1943).
12. Mao in his work 'On Diplomacy' delineated these two strategies as being firstly, "using Chinese to subdue Chinese," a sinister device of the Japanese imperialists in

their aggression against China. By creating divisions within the country they cultivated various Chinese elements to serve as their stooges. After the outbreak of the war they not only employed the openly pro-Japanese clique headed by Wang Jingwei within the Kuomintang, but also made use of Chiang *kai-shek's* clique as it could put a check on the communist party, which was most resolute in resisting Japan. Secondly, "Sustaining war by means of war" referring to Japanese imperialist policy of ruthless plunder of the Chinese areas under Japanese occupation to meet the expenses of their aggressive war. "Mopping up campaigns" was a euphemism for their barbarous policy of triple atrocity—'burning all, killing all and looting all'—Mao Zedong, *On Diplomacy*, Foreign Language Press, Beijing.

13. Li Xiao, 'Film industry in China,' *China.org.cn*, 17 January 2004, Online URL: *http://www.china.org.cn/english/features/film/84966.htm*
14. Zhang, Ch. 4, no. 4, p. 191.
15. Ibid., p. 212.
16. Ibid., p. 217.
17. Ibid., p. 219. The author explains that the principle of three prominences was duly translated into a set of formulae in film production. In frame composition, the hero must be located at the centre and the villain at the fringes. In camera positioning, the hero must be shot from a low angle and the villain from a high angle. In proportions, the hero must appear large and the villain small. In colour scheme, the hero must be bathed in warm colours and the villain in cold tones. In lighting, the hero must be bright and the villain dark. Although formulaic, these principles governed film production for almost a decade and left indelible marks on a wide range of artistic works.
18. Chris Berry, *Post-socialist cinema in post-Mao China*, Routledge, Francis & Taylor, London & New York, 2004.
19. Ibid., p. 222. The word filmmaker in the text has been used in the larger connotations of directors, producers as well as actors and actresses who form the cornucopia of the film industry.
20. The three streams refer to Chinese language Cinema along with Cinema of Hong Kong and Cinema of Taiwan.
21. Berry, Ch. 4, no. 18, pp. 7–12. He dubs this genre as the post-socialist Chinese cinema.
22. Ashish Rajadhyaksha, 'A Theory of Cinema that can account for Indian Cinema', Chitra Keralam Bilingual monthly cited in *The Book Review*, Vol. XXXIII, February 2009, p. 4.
23. Mo Yan, *Red Sorghum, A Novel of China*, Translated from the Chinese by Howard Goldblatt, Viking Penguin, USA, 1993, p. 13.
24. Ibid., p. 27.
25. David Neo, Red Sorghum, A search for Roots, *Senses of Cinema*, 28, 2009, Online URL: *http://www.sensesofcinema.com/2003/cteq/red_sorghum/*
26. Tina Gianoulis, *Review of Red Sorghum*, Online URL: *http://www.filmreference.com/Films-Ra-Ro/Red-Sorghum.html*
27. Pi-Chun Chang, Globalized Chinese Cinema and Localized Western Theory, *China Media Research*, 5(1), p.14.
28. "People give up their lives for many reasons, for love, enemy an ideal and kill for the same reasons. Before china was one great country, it was divided into seven warring states. In the kingdom of Qin was a ruthless ruler. He had a vision to unite the land, to put an end once and for all to war, it was his idea soaked in the blood of his enemies"—the opening lines from the movie.
29. Haraprasad Ray, Ch. 2, no. 2, p.14.
30. The methods of combat being visualised in the mind or the battle of minds, which

bear precedence in Western movies like the *Matrix*, reflect the increasing rapprochement between Chinese and Western methods of film-making.

31. 'Hero to premier in US,' *Xinhua*, 17 August 2004, Online URL: *http://news.xinhuanet.com/english/2004-08/17/content_1804195.htm*
32. *Béifāng you jiārén, juéshì ér dúlì., Yí gù qīng rén chéng, zài gù qīng rén guó, Nìng bù zhī qīng chéng yu qīng guó, Jiārén nán zài dé.* Annexure I (10) 'A rare beauty in the north, she's the finest lady on earth, A glance from her, the whole city falls; a second glance leaves the whole nation in ruins, There exists no city or nation, that has been more cherished, Than a beauty like this'
33. 'Responses to Jiang's Devils screened illegally in Japan', *Meiri Xinbao*, Online URL: *http://ent.sina.com.cn/m/c/2002-06-27/89146.html*
34. Numerous voices—Reactions to screening of devils in Japan', *Nanfang Dushibao*, Tianjin, 26 June 2005, Online URL: *http://ent.163.com/edit/020701/020701_124728(1).html*
35. It took the director nearly four years to bring this venture out and cost US$ 11 million after the final making.
36. Nanjing massacre film 'Nanking Nanking' attacks by ultra-nationalist on film director Lu Chuan, FRI, 11 May 2009, Online URL: www.rfi.fr/actucn/articles/113/article_13669.asp
37. Lu Chuan's Interview, 'Nanjing is not Nationalism', 14 April 2009, Online URL: www.china.com.cn/info/movies/2009-04/14/content_17600311_2.htm
38. Tadao & Ohara, *The alleged Nanking Massacre, Japan's rebuttal to China's forged claims*, Meisei-sha, Tokyo, p. 1–30, The authors examine the historical records to testify that the number of casualties the scales of atrocities have been highly exaggerated in response to Iris Chang's book (1999) the Rape of Nanjing.
39. "City of Life and Death," A director's odyssey, *Xinhua*, 21 April 2009, Online URL: *http://news.xinhuanet.com/english/2009-04/21/content_11228660_2.htm*
40. Most of the instances are based on Rabe's diary uncovered in the custody of his granddaughter Ursula Reinhardt, during historian Iris Chang's research for the book 'Rape of Nanking'.
41. City of sorrow: Competing film portrayals of the Nanjing Massacre, China.Org.cn, 30 April 2009, Online URL: *http://www.china.org.cn/culture/2009-04/30/content_17702091_2.htm*
42. 'Drama Nationalism', *China Youth Daily*, 8 February 2009, Online URL: www.insun.com.cn/Html/dyfxb/special/media/0992410.html
43. Founded in 1869, Tokyo's Yasukuni ("peaceful country") is a Shinto monument in which 2.5 million Japanese war-dead are enshrined, including some designated Class A war criminals. This makes it a target of protest by Taiwanese, Koreans and Chinese who see Yasukuni as an enabler—a reassuring testament to Japanese hegemony and the occasional atrocity committed in the name of the emperor.
44. Sword smith Wants Out: 'Yasukuni director suspects political Meddling, *Japan Beyond Stereotypes*, 11 April 2008, Online URL: *http://weblog.naruhodo.com/index.html?blog=36*
45. Why China loves to hate Japan, *The Peking Duck*, 11 December 2005, Online URL: *http://www.pekingduck.org/archives/003251.php*
46. Nairn Tom, *Janus Revisited*, Verso, London, 1998.
47. Ashish Rajadhyaksha, Ch. 4, no. 22.
48. Susan L Shirk, *China: Fragile Superpower*, Oxford University Press, USA, 2007.
49. Shirong Chen, China TV faces Propaganda Charge, 12 January 2009, BBC News, Online URL: *http://news.bbc.co.uk/2/hi/asia-pacific/7824255.stm*
50. Berry and Farquhar, *China on Screen: Cinema and Nation*, Columbia University Press, New York, USA, 2006.

5

Nationalism in China's Sports

> *"Whether on the soccer field or the battlefield, it has almost always proved easier to mobilize popular passions in the national rather than the international cause."*[1]

Sports present the most prominent dais for expression of vicarious sentiments at both individual as well as national levels in the realm of public culture. The value-neutrality associated with sports has long lost its credibility and cross-cultural comparisons have led to sensitive perceptions. Today, sports exemplify the complex relations between several sets of social relations operating in different nations. While many scholars have often cautioned against the juxtaposition of nationalism with sports and professed "to associate nationalism would be the end of sports", the two have become intertwined in an inseparable way in contemporary times.

Sports not only function as an important means of bringing cohesiveness to the national social order but also reflect significant changes in the state's policy and behaviour. Every sports event whether it is hosted within the geographical precincts of a particular country or on a foreign territory provides an opportunity for it to express either solidarity with international expectations or show reservations with international norms. These public events also provide a country an opportunity to manoeuvre on the international stage to pursue its own interests. In this sense, since sports provide a dais for symbolic competition between nations, sports competitions often reflect national conflict.

Yet the nexus between sports and politics is not entirely new. Precedents exist in several countries where since a long time organized sports have been used to fulfil state objectives. E.P. Thompson, in his book *The Making of the English Working Class,* referred to the propensity of the sports being used for systematic repression of working class, leisure in the nineteenth century.

Similarly, Louis Althusser viewed sports as a cultural apparatus of the state—a structure in which ideology is given a free rein and becomes an actual expression, which functions to reproduce undeterred, the social relations of a modern capitalist production. He identified sports as being inextricably linked with individual competitiveness, chauvinism, nationalism and sexism.[2]

Meanwhile, Bordieu construed the role of sports under the concept of "Habitus", which signifies a set of beliefs, dispositions and behaviour patterns which produce a unified structure that invariably reproduces the dominant social and cultural relations. He also postulated that the field of sporting practices is the site of struggle over the definitions of legitimate bodies and the use of a particular legitimate body in the sport. George Orwell, for his part, described international sports as a "mimic warfare," while Foucault believed that the impact of sports as a spectacle adduced in building ideologies.

Since sports is a socially mediated phenomenon which takes different ideological forms, it has to be looked at through the prism of the media coverage whose "naturalizing tendencies" with a focus on televised sports reveal the character of the dominant ideology of a nation. National sports have long been a powerful rallying point for many nations, and China is no exception. It is being argued here, that in the Chinese domain the interaction of sports (*tiyu*) with political ideology has been from the beginning steered under a nationalistic banner.

Juxtaposing Sports and Nation: Historical Lineages and Construction of the Discourse

Sports or physical exercises have occupied a significant place in the Chinese history and have left a remarkable legacy which is today recognised among numerous categories of modern sports. The lifting of bronze tripods and archery, which is endowed with an honourable status in the modern Olympic Games, are believed to have been practiced in China as far back as the Western Zhou Dynasty[3] that is c.11th century–771 B.C. Most of these sports were characterised according to their utility and purposes: performing and entertaining sports, "keep-fit activities," activities with a military purpose and others which could amalgamate two or more of these functions. These sports were not only aimed at promoting physical fitness but primarily at building a coordination of the mind and body which is seen as an essential part of the Chinese culture.

The significance attached with sports historically in the Chinese culture is known to the contemporary generations through allegories and beautiful legends such as *Hou Yi Shoot Suns* and *Kua Fu Runs after the Sun*.[4] The earliest instances of competitive sports have been discovered in the murals of the Potala Palace in Lhasa which depict a congregation of more than a hundred sportsperson of Tibetan, Mongolian and Han nationalities "representing the best of musclepower" of those times.[5] The legend of *Nen-Jiecen,* a famous Tibetan archer who was renowned for his ability to split the sides of a flying eagle with an arrow, and *Peigodtungjam* are oft-quoted to inspire the Chinese youth in present times, keeping in sync with their belief of learning from history.[6]

The Chinese are also known to have built gigantic sports architectures like the *Hanguang Hall* and Sports ground at Xi'an, the ancient capital of Shaanxi Province during the Tang dynasty, which is corroborated by the stone tablet excavated in Xi'an.[7] Instances have also substantiated the role of sports during diplomatic exchanges and parleys where it served both the purposes of competition and entertainment. For instance, in 710 A.D., Emperor Zhong Zong organised a polo (*jiju/pulu* (in Tibet)) game in the Hanguang sports arena to entertain an envoy from the Turpan people living in the south western part of China. The envoy requested to take part in the match and won several games following which the emperor ordered four people including his son-in-law, to play against the envoy's team of ten. The host team was finally able to defeat the guest team.[8] Thus, these incidents elucidate the significant role that sports played in diplomatic confabulations during ancient times.

The cultural supremacy of the athletes was evident in the fact that sports became the major determinant of not only selecting soldiers for war but also son-in-laws. Strategists like Wu Qi (warring states period) and the Ming patriotic general Qi Jiguang (1528–1587) surmised that "surprise speed is the key to success in a war."[9] Also, under the stewardship of Kublai Khan, emperor of Yuan in 1287, a separate contingent of Royal guards called the "*Gui Chi Guards*" was brought together to include all the fastest running athletes.[10]

Several other sports like bullfighting (*jiaodixi*) and *baixi* (a variety show including dancing, singing, instrumental music, acrobatics, magic, wrestling and boxing), have been vividly portrayed in Chinese paintings and scrolls which have been co-opted as themes by modern Chinese acrobatic troupes. The popularity of *xiangpu* (wrestling) during the Qing dynasty demonstrates the use of the game to enhance national unity as it requested the presence of important personages from minority communities of the remote regions of Inner Mongolia, Tibet and Xinjiang and the ceremonies allowed the Qing emperor to instate the honours of '*Imperial Bukus*', thus, vesting the supreme sovereignty over these regions in the Chinese emperor.[11]

The popularity of ice sports is known as early as the first emperor of Qing dynasty, when ice-sports meets were organized in the Taiyi Pool (the present Beihai Park and Zhongnanhai Lake in Beijing) during the winter solstice. The dexterity of the ancient Chinese people at swimming is also known from *The Book of Songs,* the earliest collection of Chinese poems compiled during the *Spring and Autumn period.* Even football was practiced in different forms as illustrated in the "*playing football*" painting by Qian Xuan which is currently placed at the Shanghai Museum.[12] This image of sports of a diplomatic tool was transformed to that of a nuisance which needed to be best kept at bay during the late nineteenth century and early twentieth century. Reminiscing about their glorious past, the common Chinese masses questioned the degradation that had set into their sports culture during this century of humiliation. Following which the educated elite framed several arguments and discourses which began circulating and led to the revival of the sports and its association with building a national character.

Chinese Sports in the Twentieth Century

One of the most venerated figures in the history of Chinese sports is Zhang Bolin, the man who is widely believed to have brought the Olympics to China. He terminated his military career to pursue his dream of educating China by establishing the *Nankai Schools* in Tianjin. He laid heavy stress on physical education for the development of China. In his article "Modernising China through education" he wrote:

> "the purpose of education is to modernize China, our country so that China will find its proper place in the world and will not be eliminated. We must take appropriate measures namely: building up people's bodies through physical education…to strengthen our nation, we should first make our people strong, which can only be achieved by exercise and physical education aimed at "cultivating all-rounded character characterised by unity, cooperation and integrity."[13]

He believed that the three aspects of education: morality, intellect and physique should develop in a balanced way and since China was a late-comer on the international stage given the semi-colonial experience; he proclaimed that "physical education is (should be) the top priority for a strong Chinese nation ... people used to associate the strength of a nation with military forces and weaponry that was not right. It is closely related to physical fitness of individuals."[14]

In 1903 the Qing government implemented a new policy—*Regulations of Teaching Institutes* that included physical education in school curriculum as a compulsory subject. On October 24, 1907, Zhang Bolin made a speech *The Olympics in Athens* in the closing ceremony of the Fifth Associated Sports Meet of Tianjin Schools held in the YMCA auditorium. In 1908, the English language magazine *"Tianjin Youth magazine"* published an article *"On Sports competition"*, quoting Zhang Bolin—"how long must the Chinese wait to win a medal in the Olympic Games?" The author appealed to the government to take responsibility for developing sports and to host the Olympics.[15]

In January 1909, Zhang Bolin yet again asked the government to promote the Olympic movement in China in his speech "China and the International Olympic committee." The same year, Xu Yibing, a famous sports advocate tried to mobilise the Chinese sports personnel under the motto "Strengthen the Chinese national physique, wipe out the shame of the "sick man of Asia"![16] Further, the nationalist tendencies became palpable in the 1920s when faced with difficulties and the struggle for influence among types of physical exercises, sports promoters alleged that sports had been actually invented in China.[17]

The sports promoters even tried to ride on the nationalist wave of the 1920s (attributed to the May 4th Movement) in order to gain support for sports to the status of a legitimate form of physical exercise.[18] This led to a distinction between "ancient sports" (*gudai tiyu*) and traditional sports (*guocao tiyu*). A further re-evaluation and return to values from Chinese antiquity invoked favourable responses to the role of sports by many scholars like Wang Geng and Hao Gengsheng who maintained that indulging in sports no longer constituted a submission to barbarism but rather a celebration of national history.[19] In fact they were ready to learn from the West, popularly called as "learning the superior techniques of the foreign barbarians to control the foreign barbarians" as put forward by the reformists Gong Zizhen and Wei Yuan.[20]

Within the structure of this discourse lay an inherent fear of national decline and the intellectuals of the early twentieth century visualised a solution in developing physical strength along with moral strength as they associated physical education with national strength. Several constitutional reformers used the body as a metaphor for a nation or national system. Similar trend was observed in the Swedish nationalist movement of the early twentieth century where the early organized sports movement wanted to make a connection between enterprise and national tradition.[21] These observations deeply influenced Mao, who in his first article, *A Study of Physical Culture*, published in *New Youth* in April 1917 as part of the "28 paintings of health", argued,

> "Our country is being drained of its strength. Public interest in martial arts is flagging. The people's health is declining with each passing day. These phenomenon deserve serious concern… this is because external forces have little appeal to a public that is unaware of the real significance of physical education."[22]

Sports were seen as a significant part of China's new culture and were thus, imbibed with strong nationalist rhetoric. In the same line of argument as Mao, Feng Wenbin, the inaugural president of the All-China Sports Federation, spelled out the task of physical culture at the 1949 meeting of the federation, where he stated that the motto of the New Democratic Physical Culture was "to develop sports for people's health, New Democratic Construction, and the people's national defence."[23] There was also a strong emphasis on Sports ethics and the restraint from bringing shame to their motherland.

He visualised sports as contributing to Communist political action, which formed a systematic united front against imperialism and feudalism (the overriding discourse of the 1930s-1960s). It was viewed as serving and belonging to the masses. The older forms of sports associated with US imperialism were denounced and a lot was adopted from the Soviet sports system. In a speech at a preparatory meeting of the National Physical Culture Committee in 1950, Vice Chairman Zhu De insisted, "We shall learn from the Soviet Union."[24]

The Soviet Union adhered to the Voluntary Sports Societies (VSS) system during this time which instated the trade unions as sponsors of developing mass physical culture and sports and to provide facilities and conditions for sports training and improvement in athletes' skills. Together with the Dinamo Sports Societies and Armed Forces Sports Societies, they provided facilities to the athletes from factory and vocational schools.[25]

Taking cue from the "Labour-Defence System" of the Soviet Union, China adopted a national fitness programme. It imbibed many influences in its "physical culture institutes", government financing and control of sports, trade union sports societies, clubs and sponsorships, Sports boarding schools and sports programmes for women. Physical education was reiterated as a compulsory part of education after the establishment of the PRC and Ma Xulun, the Minister of Education, laid out the policy and task of education in 1951 as:

> "The physical culture committee should be established to guide all schools in faithfully carrying out the policy of "health above all", in reducing the student's amount of class work and after class activities, to promote sports activities and recreation activities."[26]

The Common Programme of the Chinese People's Political Consultative Conference (CPPCC) of 1949, adopted by the First Plenary Session of the CPPCC on 29 September 1949 in Beijing stated in its Article 48, "national sports shall be promoted. Public health and medical work shall be expected and attention shall be paid to safeguarding the health of the mothers, infants and children."[27] The transformation effected through these changes was seen to be credible enough by Mao to have remarked,

> "China used to be stigmatized as a decrepit empire, "the sick man of Asia", a country with a backward economy and a backward culture, with no hygiene, poor at ball games and swimming, where the women had bound feet, the men wore pigtails and eunuchs could still be found, and where the moon did not shine as bright as in the foreign lands. In short, there was much bad in China. But after six years' work of transformation we have changed the face of China. No one can deny our achievements."[28]

In 1952 at the inaugural meeting of the All-China Sports Federation

(ACSF), Mao urged people to "develop physical culture and sports, and strengthen the physique of the people." He argued that Chinese sport was national and "it opposed imperialist oppression." His understanding of sports constituted a specific ideology that combined Chinese nationalism and the ideology of communist revolution. Mao presided over the meeting of the Central Politburo, where the National Sports Commission submitted to the Central Party Group—"on strengthening the work of the people's sport." He remarked "improving people's health status and enhancing the people's physique is an important task of the party." Further in his "on correct handling of the contradictions among the people", Mao pointed out "our education policy should stress on the moral, intellectual, physical aspects of education to build a generation of young people who are physically fit and help to improve the national physique and pride."[29]

The National Education Committee of the CCP Central Committee Party endorsed the significance of raising the level of movement technology in September 1958 in its report "on the sports report of the Ten-Year Plan" and acclaimed the new records created in 1956 through these policies (Chen Jingkai won the first honour for the nation, followed by Rong Guotan). This led to the establishment of a nation-wide sports system which however, received a temporary setback during the Great Leap Forward.

The "Ten year guidelines for Sports development" that called for "40 million people to achieve the standard of the labour defence system, 8 million people to achieve the basic sports standards, and 5000 people to become top athletes" also witnessed a setback.[30] The Cultural Revolution also hindered the development of competitive sports as the training system was dismantled; the sports schools were closed, the participation of Chinese teams was discontinued in overseas competition and the outstanding athletes were persecuted as the offspring of the bourgeoisie.[31] *New Physical Culture* and *Physical Culture News* were forced to cease publication. Several prominent athletes were dubbed as spies and tortured by the Maoist regime and sports was replaced by activities expressing loyalty to Chairman Mao. At the same time, martial arts competitions were replaced by the development and promotion of "loyalty boxing."

Premier Zhou Enlai in 1971, made an attempt to restore the sports training programmes, competitions, schools, organisations and administration that had been discontinued between 1966 and 1970. He permitted the *Physical Culture Daily* to resume publication despite efforts by Mao to undermine his authority. Hereafter, most of the efforts by Mao and the Cultural Revolution began to be criticised amongst the historians and writers writing about sports who believed that the Cultural Revolution had destroyed sports development. For instance, Gu Shiquan and Wu Shaozu, the former director of the State General Sports Administration agreed with the official resolution of Party History of 1981 in condemning the losses of the former period.

The CCP Central Committee in its report "on the further development of sports" announced the building of a new China and a resurrecting of the "golden age" of China. The adoption of the "Nagoya Resolution" in 1979 in consonance with the International Olympic Committee's suggestions ushered an era of success for the PRC.[32] The Nagoya Resolution recognised the National Olympic Committees of the PRC as distinct from the ROC based on its name, flag, anthem, emblem and constitution. As a result of this stipulation, neither the phrase "Republic of China," nor its associated flag, anthem nor emblem could be used in venues conducting International Olympics Committee (IOC)—approved activities.

These were followed by Deng's "open door" policies which encouraged the development of sports and international participation and encouraged aspirations to achieve the highest level of sports performance. Deng Xiaoping encouraged "promoting sports for the nation's pride", in *Tiyu Bao* on 15 September 1983.[33] China noted that sports could be profitable and could prove an effective tool of bolstering nationalism. He believed that sports reflected a country's economy and civilisation and hence it became state policy to undertake sports under the direct control of the State Council. He further called on them to—"follow the rhythm of reform and opening up, China's rapid development of sports, the pace of the world cannot be stopped."[34]

Chinese Sports Beyond 80's

The focus of sports development under Deng adopted an increasingly nationalistic tenor as it became a cultural arena for establishing the state's sovereignty. Keeping in view the delineations or compulsions of its ideology, the government approved two key documents in 1984 and 1986. A CCP Central Committee dispatch, "*a notification about moving further ahead in sports development*," sent to all sports official stated, "Chinese sports had developed well in the 1980s proving Chinese sports were approaching world levels of performance and had the potential to further promote Chinese national pride and self-confidence, as well as patriotism and support outside China. There was still a gap at the very top level of international sport which could be reduced by a truly popular sports policy."[35]

With this aim the government decided to increase the sports budget and political functions of sports were highlighted towards the aim of building a socialist thinking and a cultured civilization. The commission published another document in 1986 espousing a reform of the sports system. Thus, besides the notion of a physically fit nation, the discourse of nationalism was intermingled with the ideologies of socialist thinking, civilisation's resurrection and cultural revival. These traits marked the beginning of the development of sports as a national symbol.

Susan Brownell,[36] who earned both a gold medal in the heptathlon during the 1986 National College Games of the PRC and fame throughout China as "the American girl who won glory for Beijing University", recapitulates in

Pic. 5.1

Source: IISH Collection.*

her book *Training the body for China* she notes that as an athlete representing the Chinese, she was consistently encouraged by the slogans like

> "train the body! (*duanlian shenti*)
> study diligently,
> train the body!
> bravely scale the peaks,
> train the body!,
> carry out the four modernizations,
> train the body!,
> defend the nation!"[37]

She recounts the experience of training the body under an authoritarian regime and states that the development of a physical culture was disseminated in the 1980s in a massive way to form the national consciousness through informal as well as formal structures.[38] This period also witnessed the metamorphosis of sports culture from that of a centrally controlled endeavour to a one based on consumerist trends.[39] This consumer-driven attitude towards sports was followed by a more starkly visible phenomenon viz. the growing popularity of sports spectacles and the growing political actions around sports events. There were mass instances of hooliganism and fan-violence.

In 1985, soccer fans in Beijing rioted after China lost the world cup qualifying round to Hong Kong.[40] The 1994 Asian Games and 1998 world championships summoned reactive nationalism as they shed a negative light

*The two posters, part of the propaganda posters of the CCP, express the shift from Mao's emphasis on hygiene to Deng's emphasis on sport as contributing to the nation's strength. Stefan R. Landsberger. http://www.iisg.nl/~landsberger/

on the Chinese sports authorities and the national leadership, due to the embarrassing doping scandals which were criticised worldwide.[41] The government disparaged the attempts by the other countries to propagate an image of China whereby it was seen as a power seeking to win by whatever means and at the expense of honest and hard working athletes. The government tried to salvage its tattered reputation by escalating efforts to organise sports under state direction.

The sports-related law of 1995 passed during the tenure of Jiang Zemin, stated that the "athletes should be instructed on patriotism, collectivism and socialism." Besides the reiteration of requirement amongst the citizens to enhance their health and physique through sports, the *Physical Culture Law* also visualised a "National Health Plan." With an emphasis on younger people and children, this programme proposed that everyone should engage in at least one sports activity daily, master at least two body-building methods and have a health examination every year. It laid down that sports development was an integral part of economic construction, defence mobilisation and social development. It further required that physical culture departments at all levels would help individuals to create health-building activities that fitted in with their work and school commitments (Article 4). The Law stipulated the development of sports in ethnic minority areas for the purpose of dissemination of state-of-the-art technologies to the ethnic minorities in Article 6 of the document (See Annexure V).[42]

The law vowed to protect traditional sports and the government at all levels was to take measures for the elderly, the disabled to participate in sports activities with ease (Article 15). Schools were directed to implement national standards for physical training of students in school sports during the day time without exception. In Article 33, the provision for an arbitration council was laid which would be responsible for conciliation, arbitration and settlement of disputes in competitive sports. The Sports Arbitration Body set up methods and the scope of the arbitration provided for by the State Council separately. Thus, the vision was institutionalised and furthered to build "national athletes."

Jiang Zemin also related the sports spirit of the young athletes with the Chinese nation's precious spiritual wealth. In July 2002, the CCP Central Committee issued the document—"Circular on Further Strengthening and Improving the Work of the Views of the New Era of Sports." It emphasised the need to speed up China's sports undertakings in the comprehensive development of the broad masses of people to meet the growing demand for sports and culture, and to promote China's social and material and spiritual civilisation building and fulfilling the common task of development of people of all nationalities.

The sports development during this period enunciated the efforts of the Chinese leadership to move into the global system, though remarkably on its own terms. A predominant influence of the government on sports continued which was noticeable during the Asian games when China tried to boost the morale of its people through control over television and print news coverage. Over the past few years, the schools have become an important dais for "embodiment" of morality and state ideology through physical education (though contrary views exist)[43] and international sports events have increasingly evinced nationalist moorings. The 2004 Asian Cup Soccer tournament at the worker's stadium at Beijing in China, where China lost to Japan (3-1) in the finals, instigated massive protests.

The anti-Japanese nationalist reaction derided the games as being unfair. Television replays of Japan's key second goal seemed to show that a Japanese player illegally touched the ball with his hands. Even during the match proceedings, the Chinese fans threw garbage and plastic bottles on the Japanese supporters and shouted "May a big sword chop off the Japanese heads." During the Japanese national anthem Chinese fans showed disrespect despite messages like "be civilised spectators! Show a civilised manner!" being screened on the scoreboard.[44] They even burnt the Japanese flag and damaged the Japanese ambassador's car. These incidents occurred despite the 1998 Friendship Treaty signed between China and Japan which was signed to ward off similar instances. In the East Asian Championships in Chongqing (2008), China and Japan again came to loggerheads. The rhetoric of the historical differences was again and again refurbished by the Chinese fans. This depicted the undying patriotic fervour and the inability of the Chinese youth to take a different perspective to the Japanese image as opposed to that of popular perceptions.

The above-cited incidences further called for massive efforts by the government to protect the athletes of the international community and resulted in a series of measures by the government on the ground as well as the internet where most of the popular nationalism was being fanned. The increasing significance attached by the CCP to the task of nation-building through sports was also persistent in the Eleventh Five-year Plan (2006-10) where the government declared that—"sports and social sciences were to inform development planning." According to the CCP Central Committee, the State Sports General Administration of Sports (SSGA) was to be responsible for promoting the spirit of social science research and decision-making. The report lauded the SSGA's accomplishments of establishing 25 sports and social sciences key research base and its ability to cultivate a group of academic leaders and theoretical talents.

The law promulgated that there was a severe need for instantaneous research given the state's requirement of hosting the Olympics in 2008, which demanded an in-depth analysis of competitive and mass-sports as well as of the economic impacts of a burgeoning sports sector. Aspiring for sustainable development the document prescribed:

> "In the development of sports and social sciences, the guiding ideology is: adhere to Marxism-Leninism, Mao Zedong Thought, Deng Xiaoping Theory and "Three Represents." Comprehensively implement the scientific concept of development, adhere to the practice of sports services, integrating theory with practice and research-orientation. Emancipate our minds, seek truth from facts, advance with the times and actively promote theoretical innovation."[45]

The document was not only a statement of the policy layout but also evinced the keen interest of the government to use sports as an arena of national contestation. Thus, the prescriptive tones exhibited a compulsive manifestation which was staked on national image creation. The establishment of the *Institute of Sports and Nutrition* at the East China Normal University depicted the rising significance being given by the government to the sports organisation. These tendencies substantiate the goals of the CCP in trying to create a populist base for its ideological legitimacy. In addition to the role of sports as contributing to national prestige, the government has realised the scope of economic gains from sports as a mature market. While the government continues to propose and implement reforms in the sports sector, recognising both economic and national advantages, jingoistic euphoria and national ambitions operate under high government influence. The orientation of Chinese sports remains by far nationalistic in essence. Winning athletes become enhancers of a nation's self-esteem or the new breed of national soldiers and also provide diversions from the internal dissentions of the society.

China—The Olympic Sojourn

The emphasis on physical activities and sports in Chinese culture was not only a driver for institutionalisation of such activities in the school curriculum but also in its quest for international recognition through participation in larger sports events like the Olympics and the Asian games. The history of Olympics reflects a history of political manoeuvring since its very inception, prominently after the end of the nineteenth century.[46] The 1936 Summer Olympics held in Berlin best illustrate the use of sports to strengthen an ideology and spread it through propaganda. The boycott by the US and similarly politically aligned nations of the 1980 Summer Olympics and by the Soviet Union of the 1984 Summer Olympics was a direct consequence of the Cold War politics.[47] Similarly, competitive sports in South Africa faced a conscientious opposition due to the policy of apartheid being followed there.

Many African nations boycotted the 1976 Summer Olympics in Montreal, as a result of then New Zealand Prime Minister Robert Muldoon allowing "All Blacks to Tour South Africa." The nationalistic Italian fascists even created volata as their own home-grown alternative to soccer and Rugby, which was intended to be a replacement for the popular British games that would be of a more local character, tracing its heritage back to the earlier Italian games of Harpastum and Calcio Fiorentino. However, the history of Volata as a sport was short-lived and is no longer played. Similarly, the policy of Spanish football team Athletic Bilbao of picking only Basque players is strongly linked to Basque nationalism. Thus, sports have become a dais for presenting national proclivities as well as international dispositions depending on the participant's geo-political situation.

In the Chinese case such predispositions have been perceptible in Chinese sports since the very beginning of its inclusion into the system of nation-states and the Olympic community. The Chinese Olympic tradition in particular demonstrates the association between Chinese sports and nationalism. The China National Amateur Athletic Federation was established in 1921 and was subsequently recognized by the International Olympics Committee (IOC) as the Chinese Olympic Committee. In 1922, when Wang Zhengting became the first Chinese member of the IOC, his election symbolised the beginning of China's official link with the Olympic movement.

Interestingly, China's participation in the Olympic Games came about largely for diplomatic reasons and buttressing of its national identity. That is in the backdrop of Japan trying to legitimise its control of Manchukuo with a plan of sending a team to the 1932 Los Angeles Olympics to represent China and aimed at hindering the other's membership from the Olympic family. China responded to the Japanese intentions by sending sprinter Liu Changchun, who was recognized in the official 1932 Olympic Games report as the "sole representative of 400 million Chinese."[48]

Pic 5.2

Source: IISH Collection.*

*Stefan R. Landsberger http://www.iisg.nl/~landsberger/

Chinese athletes took part in both the 1936 and the 1948 Olympics despite a long war with Japan, under the Nationalist regime. The period between 1950s and 1970s became major struggle tenure as it saw both Beijing and Taipei claiming to represent China and each doing everything possible to block the other. Heated disputes regarding their exclusive membership claims plagued the international Olympic movement for many years. However, in 1958, to protest Taiwan's membership in the Olympic family, Beijing withdrew from the Olympic movement, and did not return until 1979.

China further boycotted the 1980 Moscow Olympics following suit with US and finally returned to the Olympic community in 1984 once again at the Los Angeles games where it had made its beginning. The 1990s brought for the Chinese nationalists a mixed bag of responses. Since it had returned after a long gap, China envisioned marking a credible performance, however, many Chinese athletes were found tangled in doping cases and hence, the Olympic hopes were dashed for the time being and projected into the future.

Embarrassing doping scandals at the 1994 Asian Games and 1998 world championships shed a negative light on the Chinese sports authorities and the national leadership which were criticised worldwide.[49] China's achievements are commendable considering the span of 24 years, when it had returned to the Olympics, and today is espousing to become the next sports superpower. It is within this ambit of adhering to international norms and image projection that one can construe the significance of Olympics for the Chinese state and its people.

Image politics has become central to the conduct of international relations. Concepts such as strategic public communication, national image building, and media diplomacy have often been used to refer to the purposeful enhancement of a nation's image as a tool of foreign policy. Beijing also realised that the Olympiad is a powerful instrument for state legitimization and national cohesion and hence the Olympics in the 21st century witnessed a growing aggressive stance by China to rejuvenate its national image and power.[50] Though it has been generally suggested that the Olympic games are short-term mega sporting events that generate enthusiasm and national pride, which have long-term consequences for the host cities and the citizens of the country.[51] China has provided a new dimension by using the idea of sports to save the nation and join the world as an equal and respected member. China's hosting of Olympics has become juxtaposed against its search for a new national identity.[52]

The outstanding extravaganza displayed by the Chinese government has put an end to the spirit of "games for games sake"[53] which was inherently the primary reason behind the revival of these games by Pierre de Coubertin 113 Years ago (1896). Reviving the ancient Greek tradition of sports espousing it to improve the education of young people through organised sports and cultivation of moral and social strength, Pierre de Coubertin envisioned the

Olympics to serve the purpose of building peace, solidarity and integration amongst various nations. Nevertheless, through the course of the previous century the fair and just notions associated with competitive sports have all been lost and the games have metamorphosed into a plank of showcasing a country's comprehensive national strength, which explains the behaviour of spending an estimated US$ 45 billion (Xinhua, 2008)[54] by the Chinese government and eliciting the efforts of 1.7 million volunteers for presenting an unprecedented spectacle.

It is spectacular how far the itinerary of sports has travelled in the Chinese temporality. More than a century earlier, Wu Tingfang, an ambassador and minister during the Qing dynasty, had codified the reticence of the Chinese people in endorsing sports as a medium of amusement let alone a diplomatic tool, in his book "America through the spectacles of an Oriental diplomat"—

> "Perhaps in nothing do the Chinese differ from their Western friends in the matters of amusements more than in sports. The Chinese would never think of assembling in thousands just to see a game played. We are not modernized enough to care to spend half-a-day watching others play... I much doubt if sports will ever be really popular among my people. They are too violent, and from the oriental standpoint lacking in dignity."[55] It is by far sardonic that such a nation today has presented the world with the most unforgettable of all Olympics."

To begin with, China's chase of the Olympic dream commenced as a continuum of its successfully hosting the 11th Asian games in 1990 that were considered by the international community as a dress rehearsal for the 2000 Olympic Games. The "2000 Olympics Games Bidding Committee" formed in April 1991 presented the application of Beijing as the candidate city for the Summer Olympics to the IOC in 1992. However, competing against its international competitors, Beijing lost the selection to Sydney by two votes. Amongst the various reasons adduced by the Western countries for this rejection, primary explication was given in reference to the situation of human rights and the violent suppression of the student protest in 1989. Nonetheless, China still enthusiastically participated and won the 3rd position behind USA and Russia with 28 gold, 16 silver and 15 bronze medals.[56]

Indicating its capability as a well-deserved participant, China reaffirmed its resolve to demonstrate not only its ability as a player but also its competence as a host at the onset of the Olympics. The "Beijing 2008 Olympic Games Bid Committee" (BOBICO) under the presidency of Beijing's Mayor Liu Qi meticulously presented Beijing's application to the IOC in 2000-01. The aims and aspirations of the Chinese people were reflected in the Commission's exhortation—"we believe that the Beijing Games would leave a unique legacy to China and to sport and we are confident that Beijing could organize excellent Games."[57]

Fortunately for it, China realised its objective on 13 July 2001 under the maxim of presenting a "Green Olympics" and declared to the world its intent to stage a high level Olympics with distinctive "Chinese characteristics."[58] Li Lanqing, vice-premier of China stated at the winning of the bid: "the winning of the 2008 Olympic bid is an example of the international recognition of China's social stability, economic progress and the healthy life of the Chinese people."[59] Additionally, China assured the international community of its efforts in the direction of improvements in human rights, press freedoms and environmental concerns in various ways to allay the fears, which had earlier hindered the acceptability of its vision by the others on the global front.

The Beijing Olympics

The Beijing Olympics marked a critical signpost in China's sojourn from the "sick man of Asia" to an "impending superpower." The symbolism endemic in its rhetoric of presenting the world with the best games ever continued to be inspired by its quest for an achievement of a "great-power" status. In this endeavour, besides capitalising on its economic and military strength, China increasingly forayed into non-traditional arenas of image enhancement and building soft-power resources. The Beijing Olympics meant a lot to China in terms of sustaining its nationalism. The national character was presented to the world through a plethora of architectural and human infrastructure, accompanied by the symbolism of the ceremonies.

With the principal objective of "presenting a modern and dynamic China through its sporting prowess," the Beijing Olympics were inaugurated by the Chinese government on 8 August 2008. Beginning with the torch relay which was schematised to be "a journey of harmony, bringing friendship and respect to the people of different nationalities, races and creeds", the leadership visualised the games to posit China on the world plinth. By citing the goal of Olympics from the Olympic Charter, China made believe its intentions were completely in sync with the global aspirations.

The significance of hosting Olympics held gigantic proportions for China as it recognised the potential of advertising its global power through the non threatening medium of sports. This rare opportunity that could aid the further integration of the Chinese in to the world coincided with the 30th anniversary of China's reform and opening up and was thus intrinsically dabbed of an emotional tenor. The leadership further expected to raise China's global profile and depict a "democratic, open, civilized, friendly and harmonious" China through the medium of Olympics. Moreover, it recognised the potential of the games in welding the nation through promoting national pride.

At the same time, China also saw these games as a unique opportunity for projecting its universalistic goals and employing the tools of cultural diplomacy. Building on the precedent of the 1970s whereby Sino-US relations witnessed a thaw via the Ping Pong diplomacy under President Nixon and

Premier Zhou Enlai, the games were meant to showcase China's policy of peaceful development and scientific outlook. According to the Foreign Affairs Minister Yang Jiechi, the games were also meant to help people in other countries "better appreciate and support China's domestic and foreign policies."

In the economic realm China wanted to utilise this opportunity to emerge as the world's top tourism destination (replacing France by 2014) and accruing maximum benefits for its manufacturing industry amid a rising fascination with Chinese objects, besides escalating its GDP growth. Olympics were seen as a springboard for the ushering of "Chinese brands" and bringing Chinese enterprises on the world stage along with changes in consumption patterns. The Chinese government envisaged a tremendous boost to regional industrial development as well as inter-regional exchanges and cooperation. Moreover, it wanted to bolster domestic and foreign investor confidence through "system and mechanism innovation." With these aspirations in mind China embarked on the trajectory of achieving a most extraordinary feat, voiced under the catchphrase "one world, one dream" to showcase international aspirations and "nothing is impossible" encouraging national participation.

The National Architecture

Most often certain architectural monuments become a symbol for a countries identity or historical legacy. While the Statue of Liberty is symbolic of American ideals, the Eiffel Tower instantly denotes France. Similarly, while Taj Mahal becomes synonymous to India, the Great Wall symbolizes China. Given the symbolic significance attached to monuments of a country, the architectural representation within the spectacle of a global event takes immense proportions. The manifestation of China's vision began with the establishment of the BOCOG under the stewardship of Wang Wei, which conceptualized the "Olympic Activity Plan" in June 2003 for the infrastructural development of Beijing, improvement of its modern communication facilities; build up of modern sporting venues, modernization of its tourist accommodation facilities and investment in alternative sources of energy.

The Ministry of science and technology of China undertook several initiatives as early as 2001 when the BECAPEX project (Beijing City Air Pollution Observation Field Experiment) provided a detailed three-dimensional description of the dynamic and thermal structure of Beijing's urban atmospheric environment and helped in curbing the effects of dust storms that formed a canopy over the city.[60] This was followed by application of solar energy to light lawns, courtyards and streets at several venues including the Olympics village. The national stadium itself was lit by a 130 KW photovoltaic system and a 27KW photovoltaic system was used to supply energy to the Feng Tai baseball stadium. Solar heating, geothermal and heat pump technologies were extensively used in the other venues. Several automobiles were taken off the road to reduce pollution levels of the city.

A massive expanse of projects were undertaken by the Chinese government, for instance the construction of the Bird's Nest Stadium, which was designed by architects from Herzog and de Meuron, with Li Xinggang from China Architecture Design & Research group taking care of inner details, the National Aquatics Centre more famous as the Water Cube, the Laoshan Velodrome, Olympic Green Tennis Centre and the Beijing University Technology Gymnasium and several other among the 37 stadiums chosen to host the events. China also constructed high-altitude training bases in Duoba in the northwest, canoeing, rowing facility at Thousand Island Lake, southwest of Shanghai, Zinjiang Sports training base and the most successful of them, Shichahai sports school for training many promising athletes. 200,000 employees in the tourism industries were trained in etiquette and foreign languages, while 50 lithium battery-powered (eco-friendly) buses were deployed to take media persons and fans to the various game venues.[61]

The enhancement of transportation amenities took centrestage during the allocation of funds. Several foreign companies bidding to develop telecommunications network were allowed to enter the Chinese market and assistance sought from several renowned architects like Lord Norman Foster, who designed the exemplary new terminal 3 at the Beijing airport.[62] The state had set a target of repairing more than 40 main roads and constructing 27 artery roads and nine expressways by the year 2007 in its preparation for the 2008 Olympic Games, with a total investment of 870m Yuan (US$ 111.5 million) and repairing and renovating the east-west artery Changan Avenue which was accomplished before the designated time.[63]

Pic. 5.3: The Bird's Nest Stadium at Beijing

Source: China Today.com

The Beijing south railway station and inter-city rail were also opened for public transport. Mobilisation of resources in form of human capital was done through the spread of the "Green Olympics" concept through a variety of measures in cooperation with the government ministries, the city council, schools, the private sector and local communities. Over 550 schools including 200 in Beijing were nominated as the Olympic Model schools where Olympic values including the environment were being promoted. Primary schools were asked to take part in "Reserve a Barrel of water this summer" to promote water saving.[64]

The Chinese government opened fascinating avenues for tourists at large that enhanced the national revenue collection. The industry was observed to be growing at a constant pace of 7 per cent of which tourism alone accounted for 8 per cent of the city's GDP. The government also took some measures at the school level, for instance, it launched a campaign of an art contest at Fuxue Primary School, featuring Olympic Games posters to be extended to 500 primary schools with an aim to spread Olympic culture. The Beijing administration further set aside thousands of hospital facilities for emergency use during the 2008 Olympics games in case of outbreak of infectious diseases.

The government relocated several events to be held outside Beijing namely football in Qinhuangdao, Shanghai, Shenyang and Tianjin; sailing in Qingdao primarily due to "uncertainties of equine diseases and major difficulties in establishing a disease free zone." This reflected the need for the government to project only the best of their country. The Central government also heavily clamped down on the provincial governments, which according to the National Bureau of Statistics had failed to provide reliable statistics concerning energy and environment.[65] The massive input that the government propelled into building these architectural facilities demonstrated its desire to establish national architectures, which is yet again a part of the soft-power resource base that China intended to develop as a part of its comprehensive national power.

The Chinese Central government, Beijing Municipal Government and the BOCOG attached great significance to media services providing a floor space of 62,000 square meters for the MPC which became the largest media center in Olympic history.[66] As early as 31 December 2006, China had begun relaxing norms for the media services. In a text report by Josephine Ma in Beijing, "New games rules for HK media", published by Hong Kong newspaper *Sunday Morning Post* on 31 December, China stated that "beginning 1 January 2007 till 17 October 2008, Hong Kong and Macau reporters would be allowed to interview individuals and organisations. They would be able to get multiple-entry visas to the mainland because of their Olympics accreditation and other valid travel documents." The new regulations would also allow Hong Kong reporters to hire mainlanders to help them. But an official from the Hong Kong and Macau Affairs Office maintained that mainland citizens could only work as assistants to the journalists and were unlikely to be granted press accreditation. Cai Wu, minister of the State Council Information Office, also remarked on the possibility that the regulations might be extended even after the Olympic Games were over.[67]

However, of the 971 workstations constructed for media facilitation 680 were equipped with electrical and network interface features to provide optimal communication capabilities and the remaining were made available to photographers. Sun Weide, deputy director of the BOCOG Media and Communications Department and Sha Wanquan, director of MPC stated "providing cutting edge technology capabilities and top service setting new Olympic precedents with offerings had been the committee's goal."[68] Demonstrating additional enthusiasm, the MPC announced that all journalists who were going to have their birthdays in China would receive best wishes and would be made to feel at home in China.

The humongous scale of planned efforts was also palpable in the formulation of a systematic plan to identify sports yielding better results and allocating funds for their activities. Among various other sources, according to the General Administration of Sport, funds were raised through budget allocation, a national lottery to the National Olympic Committee and donations from overseas Chinese. Besides formulating the Project 119 Strategy,[69] the Chinese government hired the best coaches from around the world for increasing the leverage of its participants against the well-trained professionals of the Western countries. These systematic plans were accompanied by severe protocols on behalf of the athletes who were expected to spend long hours in training rooms and were allowed little freedom of personal choice. The Chinese government even increased the salaries of migrant workers by 30 to 100 percent to meet the demand for labour on the construction of Olympic Games venue.[70]

Most of all the Chinese government effectively employed cultural diplomacy in selection of the Olympics mascot- *fuwa,* the five dolls, which were done in a way to represent the hospitality of the Chinese people. The Fuwas: Beibei, Jingjing, Huanhuan, Yingying and Nini which are the duplication of the words *"Beijing huanying ni"* meaning "Beijing welcomes you" also represented the five colours of the Olympic rings. The idea of a harmonious world fervidly pursued by the Chinese leadership was innately built into the opening and closing ceremonies of the event. Zhang Yimou, the renowned Chinese filmmaker, who was chosen to direct the ceremonies along with co-director Zhang Jigang, who together splendidly brought out the essence of the harmony and peace (*he*) an ideal critical to Chinese culture and gave voice to the spirit of 1.3 billion Chinese citizens. The theme underlying his venture—"conflict of man foretells the desire for inner peace" encapsulated in a single mould not only the civilisational history of a nation but also the vision of the Chinese leadership for China's prospective moral fibre.

Constraints[71]

China faced several constraints in delivering to the expectations of international bodies and media who had voiced concerns regarding Beijing's credibility on hosting such a prestigious event and its lack of conformity to international behaviour. Prominently, concerns of terrorism and dissent loomed large dampening the Olympic fervour. Despite massive efforts initiated on the environmental front for instance, the creation of an enormous Olympic forest spread across 580 hectares with a lake that resembled a dragon's tail symbolising the balance between *yin* and *yang*, which are intrinsic to the Chinese culture, the pollution levels remained very high as compared to the international standards. While Beijing as the host city amassed certain benefits from the green technology deployment, the neighbouring provinces of Hebei and Shandong which were the main contaminants for Beijing city to begin with, still additionally contribute to pollution as the provincial leaders continue to ignore most of the environmental laws and edicts. Beijing's refusal to use the kind of tax policies and market-oriented incentives for conservation, which were adopted in Japan and many European countries, evinces the partial approach to adopting foreign technologies thereby, hindering the complete implementation of policies. At the end China was unable to allocate more than US$ 7 billion for environmental clean up against the initially pledged investment of US$ 12 billion.

Another major hurdle that the Chinese authorities had to face was provision of space for accommodation. *Hutongs*, the traditional Chinese tenement housing system which are deemed to be the repositories of Chinese cultural past were fastidiously demolished or relocated to create avenues for commercial tourist accommodations which were a severe loss in terms of cultural legacy. It was ironic that the city clad to receive the world's citizens became quite inaccessible to its own. Most commoners were cordoned off given the expensive pricing of tickets (50-100 Yuan) that went beyond the reach of common Beijing citizens.

Rising GDP figures due to investment in venues did not lead to generation of wealth for the lowest margins and rising income inequalities which were palpable on a large scale. A serious issue was raised by the residents of Beijing who were forced to relocate when several of them put up allegations against the government for not compensating them for their properties. While the government alleged that families who could prove ownership were compensated on an average with about US$ 87,500, the local residents disputed the fact. The lack of transparency during this massive relocation called for international criticism on the human rights front.[72] The dislocation was also followed by an increase in the value of real estate which made housing unaffordable for the common masses shifting from those areas.[73]

The banning of ethnic Tibetans from working in Beijing for the duration of the games barred the state from appropriating the opportunity to normalize its relation with the Tibetan Autonomous Region (TAR). The constraints of the Chinese government became more palpable in comparison to the developed countries, which had a vibrant and burgeoning sports culture as compared to China. The Chinese sports industry believed to be still in a transitional phase and not yet adapted to the needs of economic development had to massively gear up for the production required on mass scale. Most of the Chinese products were refused accreditation by the international bodies, which resulted from the constraint of capital and inexperience of market manoeuvrability. Despite the above-cited constraints the nationalistic responses elicited by the Beijing Olympics were commendable.

Opening and Closing Ceremonies: The Art of Myth Creation and Beckoning History to Serve the Present

> *"For the 1.3 billion Chinese, today's opening of the 29th Summer Olympics in Beijing is nothing short of history itself... Asian and now global giant has been waiting 100 years to host the biggest athletic festival on the planet."*
>
> —***Chinese President Hu Jintao*** during the opening ceremony of Beijing Olympics

The capacity of the Olympics to create a spectacle was very much recognised by the leadership and hence the perfect representation through the opening and closing ceremonies held prime significance in marking the historical moment for the nation. And since the formulation of a nationalist discourse builds upon the impressionistic values of public display, the opening and closing ceremonies of the Beijing Olympics provided a platform for China to effectively use allegory to surmise the achievements of its people and culture. Beginning with the display of the mariners' compass which inaugurated the official countdown to the events, the ceremony adduced the electrifying energy of the youth to demonstrate the traditional glory of the Chinese civilization.

Manifesting the efforts of a three year unbridled effort of coordination and hard slog, it became an unparalleled saga of demonstrating splendour through the silver clad stalwarts of nationalism. Bringing out the significance of the four great inventions that China has contributed to the world, the director Zhang Yimou, successfully portrayed the architectural canvas of the China's history. Through an audacious use of gold and red, he not only demonstrated the intricacies of the ancient art of paper-making and religious mores but also traced the trajectory to its industrial development and the accomplishment of the lunar probe-Chang'e. The rumbling of the drums and the unravelling of the scroll which became the centre stage of all performances

Pic. 5.4: The unravelling of cultural elements through the formations on the scroll

Source: Google images.

Pic. 5.5: Portrayal of the cultural legacy of the Chinese civilisation

Source: Google images.

brought out the ethnic mores and the specificities associated with the various minorities of the Chinese state.

The image projection through this medium not only reminded the global community of its inheritance from the Chinese civilization but also provided a glimpse of the future potential of the nation. The participation of the Chinese youth on such humongous scales demonstrated the inimitable cohesion in the aspirations of the Chinese people and their faith in their nation's providence. Zhang Yimou in his interview to the *Nanfang Daily* on 14 August 2008 highlighted the difficulties that he faced in bringing science and tradition together to reproduce the images of the past, yet his determination was strong as he could not afford to let down his country.[74]

The state of the art technology bought by the Chinese government to assist in the ceremonial burlesque provided as many challenges as much assistance. The successful outcome was not only a result of their hard work and continuous practice but also a consequence of a fear psychosis where failure to deliver to the national expectations mounted heavily on everybody's minds. Zhang Yimou further elaborated on the perceptions of the West as China being a very serious and repressed country. Contrary to this he endeavoured to present a more fantasised and romanticised nation which believed in fun and amusement as much in struggle and revolution.

The director's efforts were nevertheless regulated to a large extent by the Chinese media since he had been notorious in the previous years for his non conformist views. He covertly expressed concerns over the level of regulation of creativity to maintain the ideological apparatus of the state. He acquiesced to the overwhelming capacity of the state to manoeuvre the artistic forms of representations for its own purposes and commented on the nature of trade-offs in the organizational sphere of such events. The state's sense of presenting a flawless image worked itself to the hilt in the lip-reading of the song "ode to the motherland" by a child artist who is believed to have not actually sung it. "The main consideration was the national interest", said Chen Qigang, the show's musical designer. "The child on the screen should be flawless in image, in her internal feelings, and in her expression." While the patriotism of the child singer was palpable in her statement- "I am proud to have been chosen to sing at all."[75]

The success of Zhang's efforts in creating a national spectacle is however, palpable from the lasting impact which his composition was able to create on people's psyche. In an interview by Xinhua News Agency, several local citizens in Beijing evinced the pride they felt as a consequence of being able to share the pleasure of hosting these games. "Usually I don't watch sports too much on TV, but I couldn't miss it this time. Our country is getting stronger every day. I think all of us should be proud," said 22-year-old Zhou Xiaobing.[76] "All those audio and video technologies in the performance made me feel like in the space age" said Su, another local resident. What impressed her most was "footprints" made by fireworks. "It looks like deities walking by or UFO landing ... the firework performance was so wonderful. It reminded people that it is the Chinese who invented gunpowder." Thus, Zhang Yimou attained for the Chinese state its foremost objective of the etching the memory of Chinese Olympics and a reason for national pride which is so crucial to the formation of a nationalist discourse.

The most significant outcome of the Opening ceremony was the cohesiveness brought amongst the far off regions which is otherwise impossible to generate given their backwardness. Most citizens in the far off western regions could associate intensively with the "coming out party" of the Chinese nation. A huge screen was erected in front of the landmark Potala

Palace in central Lhasa, the capital of the Tibet Autonomous Region, attracting hundreds of viewers who cheered and applauded the performances. At Lhasa's Jokhang Temple, one of the most sacred temples of Tibetan Buddhism, monks held a special prayer ceremony for the newly opened Games, according to monk Ngawang Qoizha.[77] The ceremonies also reminded one of the ancient customs of hospitality and warmth, which the Chinese believed were intrinsic to their culture. Also in the diplomatic realms, the ceremony evinced a most appropriate revival of the history to serve its present. Culturally, the centuries old "loose-rein" (*jimi*) and "kind treatment" (*huairou*) policy was deemed to serve similar purposes in the ancient times that the Beijing Olympics have been adduced to do today.[78]

The closing ceremony though in a continuum, demonstrated a completely different tenor of the Chinese worldview. It presented a more modern and scientifically led China which was moving into the global state-system with promising state of affairs. It symbolised the rebirth of a nation through the transcendence into a realm of contemporary realities which was evident in the lighter shade of presentations. The assertive nationalism witnessed during the pre-ceremonial episode was transformed into a benign and inclusive stance which recognised the current multi-polarity and stated its intent to not disturb the global order by any assertive stances.

Pic. 5.6

Source: Google images.

The closing ceremony however, did bring to centre-stage the sense of accomplishment which bound the various nationalities into a single whole. The spectacle and memory entrenched into the minds of the common man has laid a strong base for future patriotic revivals. The exclamatory renewal of folklore traditions which toured around during the Olympic renaissance and the use of allegory by the citizens to buttress the nationalist fervour on the internet sites provide corroboration to the increasing penetration of nationalist rhetoric in mass portals. Most of all along with the ceremonies, the mascots and maxims utilized during the Olympics served well to provide legitimacy to the government. The idea of a harmonious world fervidly pursued by the Chinese leadership was innately built into the opening and closing ceremonies.

This kind of ceremonial depiction was instrumental in achieving the transformation of China's national image. The strategic concern of the government to allay the fear of China threat was achieved by the effective application of cultural diplomacy. On the other hand it also led to harmonization of interests at the global level by bringing China as an equal member amongst the determinative entities on world stage and earning international respect and prestige for the country. However, the international response varied due to different interpretations of the Chinese overtures by various countries. Despite the above-cited convivial efforts of the auteur's of the Olympic ceremony, a desire to capitalise on ethnic minority symbols for drawing them into the larger corpus was visibly absent. The intentional restriction of the usage of symbols adhering to mainland Chinese conceptions is significant keeping in view the fact that use of singing and dancing minorities to symbolise national unity is often resorted to by China.[79]

Nationalist Dimensions in Beijing Olympics

The Beijing Olympics are largely believed to have engendered a highly nationalistic response from the Chinese citizens. In particular the feelings of the residents of Beijing were so strong so as to lead to the coining of the phrase —"Beijingoism."[80] The assertive stance of Chinese nationalism was seen most vividly in the ferocity of the Chinese state towards foreign media coverage of the incidents within the Chinese domain. For instance, China was very apprehensive about the coverage of the Tibetan protests and at the protests that greeted the Olympic torch relay in some Western countries. Several sinologists postulate that this high occurrence of nationalism is a consequence of the CCP having dumped its previous ideology of Marxism–Leninism, and now looking towards economic prosperity and national image projection as its saviour.[81]

From the citizen's perspective, the nationalism exhibited during the Olympics also had a strong populist base. This nationalism was manifested as an outcome of how national interests were prioritized by the state and whereby the citizens were made to consider the threat of secession and separatism as being detrimental to the overall image of China. This discourse came to be increasingly tested during the Olympics. The oft-claimed national homogeneity was facing a bitter struggle from the internal dissensions which espousing to make use of the opportunity to the hilt. These demonstrations were strongest with regards to the Tibetan and Taiwanese questions.

Throughout the preparation time of the Olympics, the rhetoric of opposing Taiwan's independence held prime significance. Spokesman Yang Yi of the Taiwan Affairs Office of the State Council said at a press conference on 18 January 2007, that cross-strait relations would face severe challenges in the year as Taiwan authorities tried to seek "de jure independence" through the so-called "constitutional reform" which might enter into a "substantive" stage. He further expressed "We will make the utmost efforts to seek peaceful reunification with maximum sincerity. We cannot tolerate "Taiwan independence" and will not allow Taiwan to secede from China by any means."[82]

To avoid any secessionist activities the Chinese government had approved 3,752 Taiwan-funded projects in 2006 and the contracted investment of these projects was more than worth of US$ 11.34 billion. A post-facto analysis reveals that this decision taken by the Chinese government has immensely benefitted the cross-straits relations by strengthening the "third link" of the entrepreneurial interests amongst the two. The Taiwanese concerns however were visible in a statement made by the former Taiwanese President, Lee Teng Hui, "2008 will be the most flamboyant year in the history of China and "Chinese Nationalism" will be grotesquely powerful."[83] Moreover, the Taiwanese government showed apprehension about the "Olympics diplomacy" that China would try to forge as a way of distracting international attention from domestic concerns.[84]

Keeping in view China's vision of a unified nation, several Taiwanese asserted that the Olympics meant a game of personal-upmanship whereby Hu Jintao was trying to consolidate his position as a president.[85] These remarks called for a vehement criticism by the Chinese government which alleged that Taiwan was trying to sabotage the glory associated with Olympics. China however, failed to encash the opportunity provided by the "international spotlight effect" to reflect on the solutions to the Taiwanese question. Interestingly, Taiwan as a constituent of Chinese sovereignty marks both a national as well as international constraint. The refusal by the head of the Taiwan's Olympic Committee, Tsai Chen Wei, to participate in the relay as it compromised the island's sovereignty was supported by several international elements that rallied for Taiwan to be allowed to participate in the games under a flag of its own preference. The final outlet by which the torch was allowed to pass from Vietnam's Ho Chi Minh City to Taipei and then to Hong Kong provided some leverage to Taiwan which stated that the route allowed it to be a part of the international leg, while the Chinese government for its part intentionally tried to blur the distinction between the domestic and international legs.

Taiwan's experience with Olympics had also been quite out of the ordinary. While Taiwan had participated by and large in the earlier Olympics under the name of "ROC" and avoided any confrontation with the Chinese name, the 1981 Olympics marked a critical watershed in this regard. Rising Chinese nationalism endorsed by the Chinese leadership and asserted at the IOC level, beckoned that some kind of Chineseness be assimilated within

Taiwan's identity, for it to be able to compete in the games. Thus, in 1981 an ambiguous term "Chinese Taipei" came to be formulated to allow Taiwan to become a part of the Olympic family.[86] Unfortunately, at this time the Taiwanese citizens are believed to have had very little say in their government's foreign policy decision-making.

A significant opportunity for asserting its own identity by Taiwan was already lost in the 1976 Montreal Olympic Games, when the then IOC chairman Lord Killanin had tried to negotiate with the Canadian government several times from May to July 1976. By the eve of the 1976 Games opening ceremony, the IOC had already downgraded Taiwan's position by asking the ROC to use its national flag and anthem but under the name "Taiwan" or under the Olympic or no-name plaque. However, then-president Chiang Ching-kuo declared that each element of the "trinity"—national name, flag and anthem—was de rigueur. IOC and Canadian authorities' suggestions on using "Taiwan" for the Olympics or the no-name plaque were all unacceptable to ROC at that time. As a result, the ROC withdrew completely from the 1976 Olympic Games.

While the Taiwanese community believed that by denying the use of any nomenclature suggested by the international community it had re-established its historical Chinese legacy and claimed itself as the more legitimate government, on the international front this move was seen as a diplomatic failure. During further negotiations at the international level, the international community supported the PRC, largely guided by its geographical size and proportion and blocked all ways of returning to the original-ROC formula, making it a diplomatic success for the Chinese mainland. Recently, when the Chinese government hosted the Olympics on its own land, the naming and participation again became a critical issue for nationalist stalwarts as it provided an opportunity to voice their concerns regarding the mainland.

Taiwan for its part attempted to curb all kinds of misleading (as per the official perception) Olympic propaganda by China and thwart all attempts being made to subvert Taiwanese sovereignty.[87] In a more competitive gesture the Taiwanese government came up with an introductory video clip of the 2009 World Games that were to be hosted in Taiwan in 2009. These efforts were contextualised in Taiwan's intentions of seceding from the mainland and its search for an identity away from the PRC's international image and backing. Thus, these actions became an immense source of concern for the Chinese government.

Another dilemma surrounding the implications of Beijing Olympics on China's nationalism was whether such an event instigated exaggerated pride and exaggerated rhetoric, thus rendering a real China threat to the international community. The successful holding of the Beijing Olympics has engendered a process of introspection among the Western countries who with their dwindling architecture and much needed reform have begun to rephrase their own capabilities to beckon such massive responses from their own people. While, they are cognisant that the Olympics showcased China at its best, they are equally aware of the future potential that this giant nation inherits.

However, several common arguments by international scholars and strategists also look at these efforts by China as mere half-truths and call for a need for looking at the larger picture of China. In an interview with a former political prisoner and now a political economist-Minqi Li conducted by Paul Jay, Minqi Li commented on the doubtable character of the nationalism generated by the Olympics. He suggested that given the different political tendencies and intellectual tendencies and the different degree of association with the state, the nationalism is quite elitist and north centric. He differentiated between the left aligned who were critical of globalisation and the neo-liberal tendencies of the state and the right wingers who favoured neo-liberal policies and directed their nationalism towards an anti-Japanese stance. He believed that there is a huge bank of people who do not associate with any nationalist feelings at all.

Further, he elaborated on the exclusivity of this new nationalism as it did not affect the peasants and workers in any substantial manner which was the case during Mao's era when the peasants and the workers held centrestage in the political arena. He postulated that this new nationalism was centred on the urban middle class, intellectuals, manager-technicians, college students and the overseas Chinese who tended to associate with the identity more strongly due to their accessibility and stakes in the system. The circulation of such opinions in the media led the government to revise its stance and try and derive more broad-based nationalistic responses during the Olympics.

The Olympics demonstrated a two-pronged development for the Chinese realm: it instilled not only nationalist tendencies and national pride buttressed by the developmental mode of Chinese nationalism, but also established beyond comparison the hold of the state on private spheres in the Chinese public sphere. Though no massive student protests tried to destabilize the political leadership as feared by Susan L Shirk,[88] the dissidence was seen more from secessionist agendas. The organizational capacity demonstrated by the Chinese state remains a feat which was unconceivable in any other state which relies on the voluntary will of the people or to put it differently, which would have been difficult to sustain among democratic structures. Thus, the manoeuvrability of the Chinese state remains high in construing and managing public sentiments for the benefit of their country.

Despite this the hyper-nationalism evinced by the netizens during the course of Olympics beckoned a serious effort by the government to control the overly jingoistic behaviour from its netizens.

The government has been hard put to constrain the so called separatist elements in the state.[89] In the first official statistics on China's security crackdown in advance of the Beijing Olympics, a report published in an official newspaper said 1,154 people had been indicted in the western region of Xinjiang on suspicion of "endangering state security" in the first 11 months of the year 2008. The report said that prosecutors' departments in Xinjiang, home to the Turkic-speaking Muslim Uyghurs, approved 1,295 arrests of individuals and indicted 1,154. In 2007 the number of people arrested across all of China on suspicion of endangering state security was 742 according to government statistics. Also, several ethnic-Tibetan supporters of regional autonomy in TAR were also detained.

The most intriguing aspect of this new nationalism was that given the nature of image projection on the wider scale, the citizens preferred patriotic state sycophancy over democratic predilections. The indispensability of the state was further established through the legitimacy it derived from its capability to provide guidance and leadership with utmost precision and the successful execution of the games. While on the international stage, the state gained legitimacy by portraying its capability of curbing the prejudiced tendencies within the populist nationalism. Given the significance of the Tibetan question the PRC carried out a systematic and vigorous effort to create linkages between the Tibetans and the Han Chinese people. This was done through a huge propaganda to fan nationalism amongst Tibetans with leanings towards the Chinese state and fanning hatred towards the "Dalai clique" (as asserted by China) amongst the Chinese people. Thus, nationalism was used by the state as a double-edged sword to substantiate both its internal and external authority in the aftermath of the Beijing Olympics.

The management of patriotism is generally done through a process of inculcation via the curriculum of the schools where values like friendship, fair competition and excellence are taught alongside patriotism and loyalty to China's one-party political system. In an article on the sina.com, it was demonstrated how students proudly walked through the school's version of a Greek arbour with plastic grapes overhead at the Yangfangdian and other schools around the Olympic. At the same time several exchange programmes were conducted by "moral education" teachers who focused on discipline and instilling pride about China and the games amongst its citizens. The program was thick with nationalism, making a case for the fact that China was a force for "civilized progress."[90] The penetration of the nationalist discourse in the education system from the very basic levels accounts for the uncontrolled expression of the patriotic fervour. Susan Brownell, observed that this Olympic education was not about China's image in the world or propping up the CCP but was directed at shaping the "next generation of Chinese in a way the government believed it would best serve China's economic development and political stability."[91] The futuristic undertones remained at the heart of the developmental genre of nationalism endorsed by the state. The state wove a discourse around the three facets of globalization, nationalism and development rendering it impossible for the popular spaces to stay away from its propagandist tenor. Political will was certainly a major factor, and unlike many Western democracies where "individual choice" is promoted as the holy grail of society, the centralised system of government in China made it much easier for its political will to be translated into reality.

Nationalism as Evident in International Response

The international responses to Beijing Olympics were a significant indicator of how Chinese nationalism was being perceived. A dual analysis through the medium of pre-Olympic and post-Olympic developments and the difference between China's perceptions vis-à-vis the international community's perception will help clarify this in detail. Perceptibly, there was a critical disjuncture between what China expected from these Olympics for its status enhancement and what the international community expected from these Olympics to patent in the Chinese polity. While the pre-Olympic international concerns were voiced largely under environmental concerns, the post- Olympic circumstances evinced a more complex approach.

Pre-Olympic Developments

The torch relay itself became a matter of contest as enthusiastic Chinese citizens tried to up the ante against the protesters trying to pull it away from the prescribed runners from Paris to Seoul. Within the Chinese mainland the reactions became manifest in a rising tide of Chinese nationalism as angry crowds of Chinese showed outrage at the treatment of the runners.[92] In fact, two local protesters shocked hundreds of cheering bystanders by unexpectedly extinguishing the Olympic Torch near the "Window of the World," a theme park in the Shenzhen industrial zone near Hong Kong gaining the state's ire. The immense nationalistic sentiments generated by the incident came to be regarded by several countries as a manifestation of Chinese triumphalism rather than a symbol of international brotherhood of sport. The pre-Olympic euphoria in the Chinese realm was marred by the Tibetan riots that perplexed the Chinese government by their scale and timing of demonstrations. Given the unrest and the inhibition to participate in the Olympic torch relay by several countries, China became beset by internal protests and international condemnation contrary to the expectations of an emergent "responsible stakeholder."

On the other hand, the international community had expected that the global nature of the games would help in toning down the loyalist elements of Chinese nationalism. The global community had also expected that the Beijing Olympics would catalyze a move towards democratization and had hoped an emulation of the Seoul Games model of 1988 which unfortunately did not materialize.[93] While the Chinese government viewed the developments prior to the Olympics as being constrained by the dynamics of its geo-polity, the Western community dabbed these as unacceptable and hindering liberal progress. Several Nobel laureates, journalists, non-governmental organizations criticised the Chinese suppression and such brutal application of force.

Hollywood director, Steven Spielberg, who was earlier approached by the Chinese government to direct the Olympic ceremonies, had denied contributing to this Chinese enterprise unless political change was effected in China. French President Nicholas Sarkozy expressed concern over the human rights conditions in Tibet. He along with the European Commission chief Jose Manuel Barroso opposed the boycott of French supermarket chain Carrefour and other French goods inspired by a wave of anti-French sentiment and Chinese nationalism that swept the nation.[94] This was deemed by China as interference by France in the internal affairs of the Chinese government.

The Amnesty International in its review of the run-up to Olympics chided that the Chinese authorities had failed to deliver their promises. The Chinese authorities locked up, put under house arrest and forcibly removed individuals who they believed would threaten the image of "stability" and "harmony" that they wanted to present to the world. Despite guarantees of unfettered internet access, the Beijing Organizing Committee announced in late July that China would allow "convenient" access, still blocking sites the PRC deemed inappropriate, particularly those critical of China's stance in Tibet, Darfur, Myanmar and 1989 protests at Tiananmen Square. Several foreign journalists were denied visas despite Prime Minister Wen Jiabao's signing of the decree dealing with the regulations for foreign journalists regarding reporting of the vents around the Olympiad in December 2006.[95]

The Olympics witnessed the CCP reassert an authoritarian grip over Beijing. It used the pretext of an alleged terrorist threat to impose a restrictive security cordon on the city and curtail visas even for harmless businessmen. Anxious to prevent protests, the authorities have suppressed dissidents with more than usual vigour. Several foreign participants, who had arrived in China with hopes of sharing good experiences and reinforcing the Olympic spirit, felt dismayed by the claim of the Chinese to the sports event as their moment of glory and theirs alone and the boisterous rhetoric and excessive discourse of the "China Rise" syndrome. The Human Rights Watch also condemned the systematic surveillance system, obstruction and intimidation of sources and pressure on the local assistants by the Chinese government that in turn instigated the foreign correspondents to pursue investigative stories.[96]

However, the Chinese citizens lamented the fact their national vision and endeavours were misconstrued. Most sections of the educated Chinese people endorsed the government's responses to the prevailing situations and disliked the western media for making unwarranted criticisms of China and its people.

Meanwhile, the international media continued to believe that such explicit support for their country was not based on rational conclusions but a virulent nationalism that had extracted tremendous appeal from the people based on projecting a Chinese image to the world.[97]

Post-Olympic Developments

All international criticism evident before the Olympics was maimed in the aftermath of the event. The temporary mismatch in perspectives between the Chinese establishment and foreign countries was dissolved considering the larger economic and strategic ties which gained priority. The Beijing Olympic opening ceremony was attended by over 100 heads of states who hoped that their presence would enable them to cultivate better ties with this Asian economic giant. The French president had to give due consideration to the historic ties between China and France which were posited to mark the 45th anniversary of Sino–French relationship. Chairman of French supermarket chain Jose Luis Duran denied any efforts to support the Tibetan secessionist movement. Even Steven Spielberg acclaimed the efforts made by Zhang Yimou in his brilliant portrayal of Chinese aspirations. He exclaimed, "in one evening of visual and emotional splendour, he educated, enlightened and entertained us all."[98]

The post-Olympic report released by the United Nations Environment Programme (UNEP) at Nairobi also lauded China's efforts in the direction of environmental sustainability. The report underlined that though more could have been done on engaging the NGOs and cutting the Olympic and Paralympic games' carbon footprint. But overall "Beijing raised the environmental bar and the games left a lasting legacy for the city." It further stated that "these achievements are all the more impressive given that the Games were held in a rapidly developing city in a country facing multiple development challenges in the first decade of the 21st century."[99] Moreover, it mentioned several areas where the Chinese Olympics actually exceeded the expectations of various international organising bodies. The CCP also reacted swiftly to these international comments. Thus, the post-Olympics exigencies elicited a pro-Chinese response internationally.

Contextualising Beijing Olympics in the Nationalist Discourse

Despite the initial misgivings and apprehensions, the 2008 Beijing Olympics marked a watershed event in China's nation-building process. Its significance emerged prominently from the economic benefits which accrued to Chinese economy from the consistent double-digit growth of GDP over the seven years of planning and preparation for the event and the boost given to its tourist industry and merchandise industry during the follow-up period to the games. The games also metaphorically presented China's cultural advancement and exuberance to the world. Radiating the confidence of a modernised civilization which was set to reclaim its long due position, casting away the blues of humiliation and disparagement, China demonstrated its resolve towards its much-desired "peaceful rise."

Since the interest in Olympics is commonly believed to have coincided with China's search for a new national identity and a move towards internationalisation, the games marked a great leap in its diplomatic undertakings. In the final culmination the Beijing Olympics primarily substantiated—the PRC taking its rightful place in the world (official Chinese rhetoric), a process that began with its inclusion into the UN in 1972. The Beijing Olympics successfully staged the emergence of an impending superpower and welded the nation together on an unprecedented scale.

The three concepts of "Green Olympics", "High-tech Olympics" and "People"s Olympics"[100] that the Chinese government framed to assert its capability were concomitant to its ideological vision of the country. The manoeuvrability of Taiwanese military high-end technologies for the mainland concerns represented the amalgamating potential of the Olympics games. While international acclaim for instance—the IOC president Jacques Rogge acquiescing to the "truly exceptional" character of Beijing Olympics and announcing during the closing ceremony that the IOC had "absolutely no regrets" in choosing Beijing to host the 2008 games, buttressed the distinctive nature of the Beijing Olympics.

Despite initial reservations, all but one (Brunei) of the NOCs (205 countries) participated in the games. Hailed as a "logistic success" in the international media, the Beijing games demonstrated the fulfilment of expectations of the Chinese people from their government as surmised by Liu Qi "the Chinese people, filled with enthusiasm, have honoured the commitments they solemnly made."[101] While there was a mixed response from the international community in construing the impact of the games, most of the states believed that the Olympics provided an atmosphere for engendering relatively open and mature attitudes in a more confident nation. The success had rekindled the patriotic leanings of its citizens.

On the flipside, given the enormous responses of the Chinese masses to this spectacle, Chinese nationalism was feared to have spiralled out of control.[102] Increasing mass dimension on chat rooms like *Tianya* and "shut-up CNN" t-shirts that did a round on Internet-sales blogs demonstrated the intensity of the mass resentment. The emergence of "blind nationalism" provoked a circumspect response from the international community which warned China of catastrophic ramifications in case the state was unable to manage it properly. Given this dangerous trend, the government initiated several efforts to focus on the discourse of harmony and world peace and "peaceful Olympics", thereby engendering some mechanisms to establish the peaceful nature of these sports events.

Also, the Olympics episode regenerated an apprehension amongst the Western nations that "a country on its way to becoming a superpower may turn out to be more dangerous" than the optimists had hoped it would not. Since sports is said to provide opportunities for release of long-standing tensions within communities, potential for channelising aggression under socially-controlled conditions and harmonising potentially disruptive divisions in society, the international community banked on it to provide enduring resolution of the "China threat" prospect.

Another question that bothered the international players was whether all the changes that had become manifest during the Olympics were merely temporary in nature or would produce long-lasting systemic changes. They are perplexed with the question of reversibility of the Chinese government to pre-Olympic restrictions once the global community left the Chinese territory. They believed that with sports emerging as a ritualistic struggle of a national community against the others, the Olympic athletes would become some kind of soldiers who after strong indoctrination will work under severe pressures of upholding the national prestige.

Moreover, though the Olympics are capable of generating nationalism at an unprecedented scale, the question is also whether this nationalism can be effectively sustained. Being a spectacle-natured event it whipped up sentiments to fuel legitimising tendencies, nonetheless, this kind of sports legitimacy could only be reinvented once in four years. The time gap allowed for what one could call the relative "erosion of memory" which is more likely given the role of globalisation and hence, such kind of nationalist fervour would exist in that particular moment if not sustained thereafter. The significance of Olympics as an event would thus depend on how effectively the leadership or the public discourse would utilise or continuously build on the legacy of Olympics in future its discourse.

In future, the Communist Party stakes its survival and legitimacy on tight political control, economic advance and management of nationalist pride. The Beijing Olympics not only signify the ultimate rise of China as a sports power but also regurgitate the relentless embracement of Chinese nationalism. As far as the future of sports in China is concerned, the combination of "demographics, desire and application" will almost certainly mean that China will come to dominate many of the sporting events the West once considered its own as observed by Andrew Hamilton. And though the athletes are generally sought from myriad sections of the society, a larger nationalist goal has an overbearing presence in their minds given the discourse that is built through instutionalisation from primary stages. In the final analysis, though the Chinese government claims its strict adherence to the Olympic charter which states "the goal of Olympism is to place sports at the service of the harmonious development of man"; it has redefined the meaning of cultural extravaganza and thereby, redefined nationalism and the meaning of sports.

With the 2012 Olympics in Britain approaching, the Chinese "nationalist" athletes will yet again experience the weight of the national aspiration and work towards fulfilment of their national goals.

NOTES

1. Simon Schama, "Mr. Europe," *The New Yorker*, 28 April 1997.
2. Jeniffer Hargreaves, *Sport, Culture and Ideology*, Routledge and Kegan Paul, London, 1985, pp. 15–25.
3. *Sports and Games in Ancient China* China Spotlight Series, Beijing: New World Press, China, 1986, p. 5.
4. Ibid., pp. 7–27. This is somewhat similar to the mythical heroism in the resplendent portrayals of Indian mythologies which eulogize the courage and zeal of their idealised warriors, like in the Mahabharata, Ramayana and various historical accounts of ancient warriors. The cited text—Huai Nan Zi, a history textbook written by Liu An in the western Han dynasty (206 BC–24 AD), tells the story of a mythological archer named Hou Yi who shot down the nine suns with his bows and arrows to help his countrymen overcome the wrath of the heavens.
5. Ibid., p. 9.
6. The ancient jade thimble discovered from Fuhao's tomb among the Yin Dynasty (c. 1324–1066 B.C.) ruins near a village in Anyang County, Henan Province, provides substantiation for the earliest woman archer and general yet known.
7. According to historical records, the emperor after feasting with his courtiers would invite them to watch a game of polo at the playground behind the Hanguang Hall.
8. Ibid., p. 15.
9. Ibid., p. 42.
10. According to the Historical records of the Yuan Dynasty, quoted from Sports and Games in Ancient China.
11. Most of the paintings depicting these historical paintings are instated in the gallery of Palace Museum in Beijing.
12. Ibid., p. 87.
13. *The Man who Brought the Olympics to China: the Story of Zhang Boling*, Compiled by Sun Hailin, New World Press, Beijing, China, 2008, pp. 13–14.
14. Ibid., p. 14.
15. Shiming Luo, *Zhongguo jindai tiyu bianqian de wenhua jiedu* (Interpretation of the transformation of physical culture in modern China), Beijing University Press, Beijing, 2007, p. 122.
16. Gao Cui, '*Cong dongya bingfu dao tiyu qiangguo*' (From sick man of Asia to Sports Superpower), chengdu, Sichuan renmin chubanshe, 2003, p.9, quoted in 'Sport, Maoism and the Beijing Olympics' Dong-Jhy Hwang and Li Ke Chang, *China Perspectives*, No. 2008/1. p. 4.
17. During the nineteenth and early twentieth century the perspectives of the Chinese differed from the Western idea of sports; sports was regarded as a Western import and looked down upon. Except for a few isolated attempts by Chinese students returning from the United States and Great Britain, it was primarily under the vanguard of YMCA that sports were revived.
18. Aurelien Boucher, 'The Introduction of Sports in China', *China Perspectives*, No. 2008/1, p. 50.
19. Ibid., p. 52.
20. *The Man who Brought The Olympics to China, the Story of Zhang Boling* (2008), no. 401, p. 16.

21. Nils-Olof Zethrin, *'Sports and Nationalism, The Ideological Development of Swedish sport,'* International Olympic Academy, 1997, Online URL: *ioa.org.gr/en/proceedings/special-sessions/doc*_download/15-1997. Also see Sport, Nationalism and Globalization: European and North American Perspectives by Alan Bariner, Suny Press.
22. Cheng and Jiangtao 'Central collective leadership and concern for the Beijing Olympic Games Chronicle', *People's Daily*, 29 July 2008, Online URL: *http://cpc.people.com.cn/GB/64093/64094/7575649.html* Also see Chen Duxiu, "Jin ri zhi jiao yu fang zhen (Present educational policy)," *New Youth*, 1(2), 1915, pp. 1–4.
23. Maurice Meisner, *Mao's China and After: A History of the People's Republic*, Free Press, a Division of The Macmillan Company, New York, USA, 1999, pp. 380–82.
24. Hwang and Chang, Ch. 5, no. 16, p. 8.
25. Voluntary Sports Societies of the Soviet Union, Online URL: *http://en.wikipedia.org/wiki/Voluntary_Sports_Societies_of_the_Soviet_Union*
26. "Minister of education Ma Hsu-lun Reports on education Accomplishments During the past year," in survey of Mainland Press (142) 25 July, 1951, pp. 5–12, quoted from Hwang and Chang, no. 404.
27. The Important Documents of the First Plenary Session of the Chinese People's Political Consultative Conference Foreign Languages press, Peking, 1949, pp. 1–20. Internet accessed—Modern History source book, Online URL: *http://www.fordham.edu//halsall/mod/modsbook.html*
28. Ibid.
29. Xu Jialin The Fundamental Guiding Principle of China's Vocational Education, "On correctly handling contradictions among the people", *Mao Zedong Thought*, 2006, Online URL: www.mzdthought.com/html/sxyj/jysx/2006/0830/8516.html
30. Roderick Mac Farquhar, *China under Mao: Politics takes command*, The Massachusetts Institute of technology, Massachusetts, 1972, p. 467.
31. Hwang and Chang, Ch. 5, no. 16, p. 11.
32. Chronicle of PRC, 1 January 1979, *China Culture*, 1979, Online URL: *http://chineseculture.about.com/library/china/history/blsyear1979.htm.*
33. Ibid., p. 15.
34. Cheng and Jiangtao, Ch. 5, no. 22.
35. For further details about the policy see *'Sport and Political Ideology'*, Hoberman, London, 1984.
36. An anthropologist who is presently an adviser to the IOC's Olympic Studies Centre in Lausanne, Switzerland.
37. Susan Brownell, *Training the body for China, Sports in the moral order of the People's Republic*, University of Chicago Press, Chicago, 1995, p. 4.
38. Ibid., pp. 67–71.
39. She provides a detailed account of the propaganda slogans used in the official doctrines from the First National Games (1959) to the present and delves closely into the traditional and modern aspects of Sports as they developed in China.
40. Soccer in China, Facts and Details, Online URL: *http://factsanddetails.com/china.php?itemid=278&catid=12&subcatid=78*
41. Yang, Dali L and Alan Leung, 'The politics of Sports Anti-Doping in China: Crisis, Governance and International Compliance', *China: An International Journal*, 6(1), 2008, pp. 121–48.
42. Zhonghua Renmin Gongheguo Tiyu Fa (The Sports Law of the PRC), Released on 29 August 1995, Quzhou City Sports Council, Information Centre, Online URL: *http://qzty.qz.gov.cn/Article/ShowArticle.asp?ArticleID=97*
43. In case study of Hebei province Gladys Chicharro-Saito examines the disciplinary, military and collectivist aspects of Chinese sports and concludes that the obsession

of the state with taming the bodies of children has dwindled given the lack of initiative by the only-child generation and it rather focuses on stressing collectivity to counter individualism: 'Physical education and embodiment of morality in primary schools of the PRC', *China Perspectives*, pp. 29–39, 2008.

44. Soccer and Nationalism, China versus Japan, Online URL: *http://www.pantown.com/board.php?id=4805&area=1&name=board2&topic=175&action=view*
45. General administration of sport of China, Online URL: *http://www.sport.gov.cn/n16/n1152/n2523/n377568/n377598/n377673/397019.html*
46. The Olympics were accompanied by truces, as all hostilities were suspended during the Olympic Games as demanded by the tradition of "ekecheiria." Only athletes who proved excellent from both the athletic and the "whole-person" perspective were able to enter Olympia cited from "Olympism and Japan's Future" by Seiko Hashimoto, AJISS-Commentary No.132, *http://www.jiia.or.jp/en_commentary/201110/05-1.html*
47. An American movie-'miracle' brings out the entire discourse of the cold war alignments and usage of sports slogans by America to force USSR to stay out of its operations in Afghanistan.
48. Xu Guoji, 'Sports, Nationalism and Global politics: Why China Wanted the Olympics', Online URL: *http://www.britannica.com/blogs/2008/08/sports/nationalism-and-global-politics*
49. Yang and Leung, 'The politics of sports anti-doping in China: crisis, governance and international compliance,' 2009 Online URL: *http://www.thefreelibrary.com/The+politics+of+ sports+antidoping+in+China%3A+crisis,+governance+and...-a0176775932*
50. Ni Jianping, 'The Beijing Olympics and China's National Image Building', Shanghai Institute of American Studies, Hong Kong, 28 May 2008, Online URL: *http://www.cctr.ust.hk/materials/conference/workshop/14/nizp_olympics.pdf*
51. Waitt and Roche, cited from 'The mega-event as a strategy in spatial planning: starting from the olympic city of Barcelona,' by Lei Qu and Marjolein Spaans, paper presented at The 4th International Conference of the International Forum on Urbanism (IFoU) 2009 Amsterdam/Delft, available at Online URL: *http://newurbanquestion.ifou.org/proceedings/9%20Changing%20Planning%20Cultures/full%20papers/F030_Qu_Lei_Spaans_%20Marjolein_The%20mega%20event%20as%20a%20strategy%20in%20spatial%20planning_261009.pdf*
52. Suisheng Zhao, "The Olympics and Nationalism," *China Security*, 4(3) Summer 2008, World Security Institute, pp. 48–57.
53. Much in consonance with the ideas of its helmsman Mao who at the Yenan Forum articulated the non-detachment of arts or sports from politics.
54. Of which US$ 40 billion or 280 billion Yuan was spent exclusively on infrastructure projects and the cost could probably be more considering the effort of past seven years. Domestic and overseas firms spent 65 billion U.S. dollars advertising in China in 2008.
55. Andrew D Morris, *Marrow of the Nation, A history of Sport and Physical culture in Republican China*, University of California Press, Los Angeles, 2004, p. 1.
56. BOCOG Official releases, Press Conference on Beijing Olympics games and China's economic Development, Online URL: *http://china.org.cn/webcast/2008-08/17/content_16251146.htm*
57. Ibid.
58. Ibid.
59. Ibid.
60. Xiangde Xu, 'Beijing tackles its Environmental problems with a new field

experiment', *Environmental Health Perspectives*, 110(9), September 2002, p. 501.

61. Beijing to clean sky for 2008 Olympic games, China Daily, 07-07-2003, Online URL: *http://www.chinadaily.com.cn/en/doc/2003-07/07/content_243610.htm*
62. Modern architecture in China, Online URL: *http://factsanddetails.com/china.php?itemid=1912&catid=7&subcatid=40*
63. 'Olympics get big green ticket', UNEP Report spotlights achievements and highlights some shortcomings of 2008 games- 25th session of UNEP's governing council/global ministerial environment forum 16–20 February, Online URL: *http://www.unep.org/Documents.Multilingual/Default.asp?DocumentID=562&ArticleID=6086&l=en*
64. Ibid.
65. China to improve evaluation of energy consumption, pollutant emission, Text of report in English by Xinhua (New China News Agency), 18 January 2007, BBC Monitoring Services Reports.
66. 'One month to go, MPC opens in Beijing,' Online URL: *http://www.aipsmedia.com/index.php/www.fiba.com/immagini/immagini01/index.php?page=news&cod=2349&tp=n&allcomm=1*
67. *Sunday Morning Post*, Hong Kong in English, 31 December 2006, BBC Monitoring Global services Reports.
68. 'Providing cutting edge technology: Aim of BOCOG,' Online URL: *http://en.beijing2008.cn/news/official/preparation/n214441189.shtml*
69. A project aimed at winning 119 gold medals in track and field, swimming, canoeing/kayaking, rowing and sailing. Controversially, the Chinese sports establishment has denied the existence of such a project at any time.
70. 'Beijing increases migrant workers' salary for construction of Olympic venues,' Xinhua, 18 January 2007, Online URL: *http://news.xinhuanet.com/english/2007-01/18/content_5623169.htm*
71. Some excerpts from this chapter were earlier published as 'Staging China: An Analysis of the Beijing Olympics,' *World Focus*, China Special Issue, March 2009, Vol. No. 351, pp. 95-101.
72. China defends Relocation Policy- Pre-Olympics Construction Pushes thousands from homes, Online URL: *http://www.washintonpost.com*
73. Chinese people seek 'affordable housing' in wake of land tax enforcement, Xinhua, 18 January 2007, BBC Monitoring Services.
74. Zhang Yimou's Interview, Accessed on 30 April 2009, Online URL: *http://www.nanfangdaily.com.cn/nfzm/200808140101.asp*
75. Beijing Olympics: Faking scandal over a girl who sang in opening ceremony at Beijing, The Telegraph, 12 August 2008, Online URL: *http://www.telegraph.co.uk/sport/olympics/*
76. 'China's night of joy, pride as Olympics ceremony captures world,' 8 August 2008, Online URL: *http://news.xinhuanet.com/english/2008-08/08/content_9061290.htm*
77. 'Chinese president encourages country's Paralympians,' 26 August 2008, Online URL: *http://handsoffchina.org/2008/08/chinese-president-encourages-countrys-paralympians/*
78. Haraprasad Ray, Ch. 2, no. 2, p. 4.
79. Susan Brownell, *Training the Body for China: Sports in the Moral Order of the People's Republic*, University of Chicago Press, Chicago, 1995.
80. The Challenge to Beijingoism, 26 December 2007, Online URL: *http://chinhdangvu.blogspot.in/2007/12/challenge-to-beijingoism.html*
81. Brownell, Ch. 5, no. 79.
82. 'Year 2000 crucial for opposing Taiwanese Independence,' *Xinhua*, 17 January 2007, Online URL: *http://www.china.org.cn/english/GS-e/196403.htm*

83. Yu Junwei, "China's Foreign Policy in Sport: The Primacy of National Security and Territorial Integrity Concerning the Taiwan Question," *The China Quarterly*, 191, 2008, pp. 294–308.
84. Liu Kuan-the, 'Fighting Beijing's Olympic Propaganda', *Taipei Times*, FBIS, OSC Transcribed text, 01 May 2007, Accession Number 243450049.
85. Evans Phidelis Aryabah, The role of the Beijing Olympics in china's public diplomacy and its impact on politics, economics and environment, June 2010, Online URL: *http://uscpublicdiplomacy.org/pdfs/Aryabaha.pdf*, Also see, Ogasawara Yoshiyuki (2001), Taiwanese Identity and the "One China Principle": Policies of the Lee Teng-hui Administration towards China, at *http://www.tufs.ac.jp/ts/personal/ogasawara/paper/epaper3.html*
86. K. Catherine Lin, 'How Chinese Taipei Came About', *Taipei Times*, August 5, 2008, OSC Transcribed Text, Document Number: 200808051477.1_a768019e07ca18f5.
87. Ibid.
88. Shirk, Ch. 4, no. 48, p. 39
89. Bob Dietz—a netizen posted a list of restrictions placed by the government for the behaviour of the journalists.
90. Teaching about Olympics reaches deep into China's schools (2007), Online URL: *http://english.sina.com/sports/1/2007/1218/137616.html*
91. Brownell, Ch. 5, no. 79.
92. 'Chinese Protesters in Shenzhen Attack Olympic Runners, Put out Flame,' Asia Sentinel correspondent, May 9, 2008, OSC Transcribed Text, Accession number 262101171.
93. Black and Bezanson, 'The Olympic Games, Human Rights and Democratization: Lessons from Seoul and implications for Beijing', *Third World Quarterly*, 25(7), 2004, pp. 1245–61.
94. 'Olympic Spirit: Countries Should Seek Cooperation amid Competition,' August 7, 2008, ROK editorial, OSC Transcribed Text, Accession Number 266600924.
95. Of the 5,600-press quota accredited by IOC to the NOCs, the foreign journalist filled a miniscule portion whereas the total figure was put at 20,000 journalists reporting the Beijing Olympics.
96. (2008) Human Rights Report: China (includes Tibet, Hong Kong and Macau) Bureau of democracy, Human rights, and Labor, 2008, Country Reports on Human Rights Practices Report 25 February 2009, Online URL: *http://www.state.gov/j/drl/rls/hrrpt/2008/eap/119037.htm*
97. Suisheng Zhao, *Chinese Foreign Policy: Pragmatism and Strategic Behavior*, Armonk, New York and London, Me Sharpe, 2004, pp. 48–57.
98. Stephen Speilberg , Zhang Yimou, *Time*, 17 December 2008, Online URL: *http://www.time.com/time/specials/packages/article/0,28804,1861543_1865103_1865107,00.html*
99. UNEP Report, Ch. 5, no. 63.
100. C.R. Pramod, 'The spectacle of the Beijing Olympics and the dynamics of the state-society relationship in PRC', *China Report* 44(2), 2008, 111–137.
101. Liu Qi's speech at the Closing Ceremony of the Beijing Olympics, 24 August 2008, Online URL: *http://en.beijing2008.cn/ceremonies/headlines/n214584104.shtml*
102. ROK Daily 'Chinese Nationalism Feared to Spiral Out of Control', 29 April 2008, OSC Transcribed Text, Accession number 261600129.

6

Cementing the Discourse: The Future of China's Nationalism

From the beginning of the twentieth century nationalism has been construed as a "search for national identity" which assumed even more urgency since the repudiation of the Marxist-Leninist symbol system that served to legitimate and unite China. Working under this assumption, several scholars like Joseph Levenson and Prasenjit Duara traced the intellectual evolution of nationalism through evaluating the traditional discourse of Chinese literati like Li Dazhao who imagined the "nation in the language of a class"—that the Chinese people were a national proletariat oppressed by the capitalists. This conception got engendered in the domestic scenario during the Cultural Revolution and instigated attempts to reshape the nation within an image of the idealized proletariat. Similarly, the elevation of Mao Zedong to a "role of the supreme theorist" and the creation of a Chinese model of revolutionary transformation in the late 1930s led to embodiment of "nationalist distinctiveness" in a model of class struggle.

With the ascendance of the post-Mao leadership economic nationalism gained prominence and the current leadership continues to build on the economic base to reproduce a populist form of nationalism that has attained substantive momentum. For nationalism to aid the economic and political development of the country, the leaders recognized the prerequisite of legitimizing agencies. While some in the international arena interpreted nationalism to be a part of a foreign policy of party-state elite[1] others saw it as an emergence of an assertive Chinese threat. Thus, with the help of media, leaders tried to promote favourable characterizations (*guoji xingxiang*) and ameliorate unfavourable stereotypes of themselves and the polities they represented.[2]

In sync with this attempt since the 1990s the CCP has issued several White

Papers to address sensitive issues like human rights, the situation in Tibet, China's national Defence and the environment and made a sustained effort to improve its relations with countries world over. Most notably, Peter Hays Gries studied the impact of student demonstrations, Chinese wall posters, editorials and movies being allowed in the Chinese media to understand whether it was a mainstream phenomenon or benign, dormant force. The construction of the discourse has been aided by a remarkable deployment of symbols and memories; the impact of which on image-creation in the public memory can hardly be overestimated. The reactions to popular media like cinema and sports buttress this discursive character of contemporary Chinese nationalism.

Maintaining international and domestic legitimacy remains at the forefront of this huge "enterprise" that China has publicized as nationalism over a century. This is starkly evident in the statements made by the leaders both domestically and internationally. For instance, Liu Qi, the president of BOCOG claimed that "owing to the Games, people have been united as one Olympic family, regardless of their nationalities, ethnic origins and cultural backgrounds. Their understanding has been deepened and their friendship renewed. The Chinese people, teeming with enthusiasm, have honoured the commitments they solemnly made" in 2008.[3] While the successful culmination of Beijing Olympics helped to "keep the face" of the nation, the ensuing international responses have further boosted its morale.

On the other hand, Lee Teng-Hui, the former Taiwanese President had verbalised his apprehensions claiming—"2008 will be the most flamboyant year in the history of China and "Chinese Nationalism" will be grotesquely powerful"[4] which was not only verified in retrospect but has also diminished Taiwan's likelihood of getting international recognition as a country let alone as the official and original China. It was the aim of this work to assess and analyse the nature of Chinese nationalism through delineating the institutions and processes which helped its resurgence. On the basis of the previous chapters, certain observations are being made here on the futuristic dimensions of Chinese nationalism and how it is likely to be shaped through geopolitical exigencies.

The manifestation of Chinese nationalism has been different for different sections of its society. For the educated, it might suffice to say a techno-nationalism is emerging as argued by Christopher Hughes, while for the peasants and workers it is largely the cinematic representations which form a link between the state and ideology, and for the youth, it draws upon myriad forms of apparatuses to gain legitimacy. Hence, a syncretism in its approach towards its people is visible. Conceptualising nationalism through cultural processes and delineating its trends through institutional analysis not only establishes the existence of a nation in a psychological commitment as proposed by Anthony Smith or an imaginary bonding as construed by

Benedict Anderson, but also within the constantly evolving discourse in the realms of manifestation. With the Chinese leadership steering an active discourse of nationalism, the future trajectory of China as a nation will continue to amalgamate institutions and processes to strengthen its bulwark.

Perceptibly, new symbols and cultural repertoires have come to occupy the centrestage and will be instrumental in weaving the national image in future. Most often in the Chinese case, the proliferation of its nationalist image and discourse occurs within a controlled and managed demeanour guided by the Chinese government which is likely to be questioned and become the primary arena of contestation in the future. The folklore celebrations which create an arena, "a social context and a tangible product into which these ideas are concretized"[5] are pruned by the state agencies which institutionalise and activate these attitudes in the public sphere. This also will emerge as a playground for sparring entities. A glance into how cinematic representations or sports are utilized guided by the state's concern for building a national image provides testimony for the hypotheses that management of nationalism through redefining identities as well as redefining several traditional concepts is constantly underway in the contemporary Chinese domains.

The rhetoric of accommodation internally as well as internationally has been put into place through jargons like "peaceful rise", "harmonious development", and "friendly neighbourhood policy", but is largely blinkered by nationalist visions and the Internet, media and literature play critical role in this process. The management, realignment and curbing of spaces created by global forces have been pursued systematically by the government. There is a constant tussle between the citizens and the government over the issues of how to and how much freedom is to be relegated to the public sphere. Several government units, scholarly associations and different arrays of organisations (dubbed as GONGOs) aid the state in disseminating its national discourse by producing books, movies and material artefacts to promote symbols of Chinese culture. These activities occur within a context that is "intensely national" but avowedly international. The growth of organisations like the Falun Gong, and various internal developments like increasing access to Internet and hi-tech facilities, which make the state management of opinion a cumbersome process provide both an opportunity as well as act as an impediment for the rise of the discourse on nationalism.

The process of "eliciting future hopes for the destiny of a nation" along with constantly seeking its legitimacy in the nation's history is a practice gaining pre-eminence in the rhetoric of the nationalist discourse, something akin to the manifest destiny syndrome in the US history. It is no more the "wounded or reactive nationalism" that had been hitherto identified as the overarching trend in Chinese nationalism but the developmental face of nationalism that now symbolizes its identity. A prominent role is being played by the entrepreneur class, which is progressively getting involved in the issues of the state, while the nationalism that had a substantial peasant base during the early 1930s and 1950s is being relegated to the backdrop. The ascendance of the "party state developmental syndicate"[6] has marginalised the communist ideal of peasant nationalism and the populist base is being generated through vicarious experiences of sports and cinema.

This is largely a consequence of the institutional culture characterised by paternalistic ties within policy networks. While the elite sections have easy access to most organs utilised by the state, the common masses are left out to fend for themselves and grope for spaces to effect a critical contribution to the ideological leanings of their government. Rather, nationalism as an ideology acts a stratagem to divert their attention from everyday issues like corruption and indiscretion of government officials through increased focus on the larger international goals. For the Chinese government, nationalism has provided an effective device for management of change with least opposition and has become a *self-sustaining ideology* during a period of political and economic transition.

Several sections of the Chinese society can be seen as becoming active participants of the process and stalwarts of this new nationalism, primarily, the fourth-fifth generation of the Chinese leadership, the fifth and sixth generations of Chinese film-makers and intellectuals, the technologically driven educated elite and the economically well-off financial elite. Thus, cultural corroboration of the state perspective has assumed a privileged position given the state's recognition of the desirability of the soft power component. To reiterate, the two strands of statist nationalism and cultural nationalism do not necessarily exhibit a contradictory existence in the Chinese case as understood conventionally rather they complement each other. China being historically a "civilisation state" has inherently combined culturalism in its repertoire and the current realities exhibit a relocation of the state according to the previously espoused *sino-centric* order. "Learning from history to serve the present" continues to guide the Chinese in their drive towards identity consolidation.

Chinese Nationalism: Future Implications

The rising tide of Chinese nationalism forebodes several eminent transformations. It can be discerned that while the nature of contradictions between communism and capitalism might have become blurred in the Chinese political realm for the sake of upholding national interests, a new-fangled wave of protectionism is developing in terms of value-systems, creating space for populist endorsement of its nationalist ideology and goals. Some introspection has been nevertheless carried out by Chinese leaders who realise the potential of an overly jingoistic nationalism to create troublesome situations and hence, a toning down of the nationalist rhetoric has been effected. The endorsement of an internationalist stance is another move in this direction.

Yet the Chinese state is trying to cope with populist as well as international pressures generated as an aftermath of the image-projection exercise, especially the Beijing Olympics. Moreover, there is growing realisation of the presence of a large section of people who are dissatisfied with the policies of the state. Hence, the Chinese state is trying to bring in those people into its fold through capitalising on the nationalist discourse. Also in view of several international voices which claim that Chinese nationalism might be inimical to a stable international system the Chinese government has been hard pressed for populist reforms. In an attempt to attain the goal of a consensual polity the Chinese government is increasingly trying to get support from its hinterlands through monetary provisions and assimilation as well as acculturation.

Globalisation as a process has proved redundant as far as substituting homophilic tendencies is concerned and for the Chinese state it has rather proved to be an effective tool for reasserting its nationalism. China is constantly endeavouring to assert itself as a strong and powerful nation. Whether it becomes a "responsible stake-holder" or an upholder of multi-polarity remains to be seen in the future but for now China does seem to have emerged as the most probable challenger to the existing contemporary international status-quo. It is conspicuously managing and manufacturing consent for its vision indigenously and continues to be governed by the nationalist visions as was the nineteenth and twentieth century Europe. As astutely observed by Sahni- "the post-modernity of Europe is long way away from Asia... Asia is today living in the historical moment of political modernity: the principal driver of politics in Asia is the sovereign territorial state perfecting its sovereign territoriality."[7]

Noticeably, the official campaigning runs unchecked, uninhibited by foreign policy considerations or worries on jeopardizing bilateral relations due to popular nationalism as in the case of Japan. The recent upsurge of nationalism in China thus, has to be located within its changing geopolitical vicissitudes of international dynamics. The global dynamics of identity formation have dictated the assertion of a Chinese national identity based on a more populist notion of "rising China" vis-à-vis the others. Its unwillingness to give up claims in Taiwan, Tibet and Xinjiang, after the successful assimilation of Hong Kong and Macao under the "one country two systems" arrangement, despite international pressure reiterates its belief in a "unified China" and which is justified under the appendages of nationalism. Contrary to the often claim of an adherer of *"omni-directional diplomacy,"*[8] China has established a mission of unifying its territories internally and maintaining integrity through state policies which bolster nationalism. Despite the divisive forces fostered by globalization, the state policies have been claimed to be directed towards making nationalism more humane and accommodative.[9]

The minority issues provide one such tool of further analysis in understanding nationalism with regards to state policies. The discourse of pluralism and positive discrimination adopted by the state to assimilate the national minorities evinces the persistent persevering of the "unification" goal by the Chinese leadership. Hitherto ridden by pan-Han nationalist tendency the state has followed an authoritarian stance towards these communities. Thus, the management of these communities has become the greatest impediment to its nationalist vision. Much of this hindrance surfaces in the form of assertion of a regional, ethnic, racial and lingual disparity.

However, of late the state has begun to show accommodative gestures towards these minorities trying to bring them under the fold of Chinese national identity. The successful manifestation of economic reforms in Southeast China and the consequent influence of Hong Kong and Taiwanese culture are also leading to the development of a southern regional culture. Regional dialects have come to be more openly used and accommodated in official contexts. An increasing questioning of the superiority of the Han Chinese culture has led to ethnic tensions. The minorities also perceive distinctiveness based on what they believe as incomplete economic reforms. The proliferation of benefits accrued from the economic liberalization has not been affected in a rigorous manner in these marginalized societies which gives them a scope for preservation of local culture and traditions. However, the study of the process of their integration into the larger nationalist ambition remains to be studied further and is beyond the scope of this work.

It should be acknowledged here that given accessibility issues, the language barrier and the clustering of a literate intelligentsia the sources at the hands of a researcher are limited. Despite an effort of deconstruction through looking at the cinematic and sports dimensions, it was observed over the course of the research how both these public spaces are intertwined with the state apparatus. While cinema is largely meant for the public audience which constitutes the rural as well as urban populace, most of the responses from the common masses are not available in the media sources as they are repetitively censored. The study relies in many cases on circumstantial evidence and sources accrued through conduct of surveys and interviews with only certain sections of the common masses.

The study also establishes that most of these trends are elitist in character and the peasant nationalism is not visible in the discursive realm. While this trend is clear in the rising cases of dissent, it is largely not given credit in the literary or techno-representations in the public sphere. The Chinese state has strategically curbed the secessionist voices and the identity of new Chineseness is being formulated in terms of building a national image in sync with international sports, music and competitive engagement. A pride in the national heritage is being promoted to surpass the divisive tendencies leading to a more cohesive identity-formation; largely attributed to the propagation in the media. In fact a very significant manifestation of this engagement between the state and nationalism, which some scholars envisioned as an "ideology filling the vacuum" in absence of any other, is witnessed largely in its impact and deployment in the media.

Presently, state intervention in media activities can be corroborated by various illustrations, for instance, in an article published in *China rises- trusted voices*, named "dissent with a dose of nationalism", the overarching character of the state has been substantively portrayed. The article demonstrates how nationalist feelings get prioritized over personal, rational choices. To corroborate further, Tim Jhonson observed "a Chinese activist Guo Feixiong had been convicted and sentenced to five years in jail on account of illegal factory involvements." But the author claims he wasn't at all the kind of person which he was being portrayed. He was in fact an ardent nationalist who had deliberately, refused to help him (the author) expose the kind of prison labour practices adopted by the Chinese industries, by saying that "it would be highly detrimental for the image of his country and do more harm than good to the legal industries."[10] Such instances are widespread and exhibit the strong influence of indoctrination of nationalist agenda.

The reiteration of a more cogent belief-system has also been furthered by the adoption of a foreign policy favouring China's assertive engagement with the outside world which in turn reinforces domestic stability. The endeavour to expand as a world power has brought the reluctant forces under the scope of rapprochement. China's growing economic and military power, expanding political influence, "distinctive diplomatic voice"[11] and increasing involvement in multilateral regional institutions has fundamentally altered the power structures and the way China is perceived from within and outside.

Its increased pro-active stance with regards to neighbours is being conceived under the rhetoric of "peaceful China rise." This has enhanced its credibility amongst neighbours as a constructive partner, a careful listener, and a non-threatening regional power. Today, China claims and wants to be perceived as an exporter of "goodwill and consumer durables instead of revolution and weapons" and wants to allay all fears and skepticism on part of other East Asian Regional powers about the assertive nature of Chinese nationalism. It aims at abdicating the "China threat" theory propounded by various Western scholars and has bolstered a renewed feeling of pride among the Chinese citizens. China has proclaimed itself to be the leader of a quest towards a multi-polar world, which has further boosted its perception internationally. Its four-pronged strategy can be attributed to this shift in its image-perception: participation in regional organizations, establishment of strategic partnerships and deepening of bilateral relations, expansion of regional economic ties and reduction of distrust and anxiety in the security sphere.

Through participation in various organizations like the ASEAN, BRICS and SCO it has infiltrated its economic interests in different regions and invested massively through FDI mechanisms. A growing interdependence by regional entities also reiterates China's endorsement of inclusive growth pattern. A complex and dynamic environment has provided the spring board for redefining of the national interests to form a canopy engulfing various ethnic minorities and economically backward classes to propagate the ideology of the state which is exhibiting itself in an increasingly nationalist tenor. The propaganda in the media in terms of the "rising China" dictum has become one of the major apparatuses for the promulgation of its nationalism.

The policy-making procedures evince a continuous effort on part of the state to manage both domestic and international issues. It is possible, then, to agree with Townsend's proposition that the "Chinese attitudes towards the nation seem to have been flexible and pragmatic, enabling it to endure ruptures, discontinuities, contradictions and competing loyalties without disintegration." The Chinese identity, today, seeks to be progress driven that is encompassed by the success of the nation as an economy. However, this is also extremely dangerous as any bubble-burst in the economy could spiral the Chinese state into a legitimacy crisis. Nationalism as a phenomenon now addresses the concerns of the international dynamics by a way of depicting coherence within the state. The central apparatus has thus, adopted it as an intrinsic part of policy-making criterion which can help in the formulation of a more coherent entity. The people, it seems have accepted "their nation as 'theirs' be it good or bad" in its totality. While most commonly it is believed that "the official nation is one of aspiration, not social reality" but China definitely seems to have embarked upon a trajectory of making it one of both aspirations as well as a social reality accommodating the interests of its majority citizens.

NOTES

1. Barry Sautman, 'Peking man and the politics of Paleoanthropological Nationalism in China' in *The Journal of Asian studies*, 60(1), February 2001, pp. 95–124.
2. Hongying Wang, 'National Image building and Chinese foreign policy,' *China: An International Journal*, 2003, pp. 46–72.
3. Liu Qi, Beijing Games, 'grand celebration of sport, peace and friendship,' *Xinhua*, 24 August 2008, Online URL: *http://en.showchina.org/olympics/News/200808/t212309.htm*
4. Junwei Yu, 'China's Foreign Policy in Sport: The Primacy of National Security and Territorial Integrity Concerning the Taiwan Question,' *The China Quarterly*, 194, 2008, pp. 294–308.
5. Sue Tuohy, Cultural Metaphors and Reasoning: Folklore Scholarship and Ideology in Contemporary China,' *Asian Folklore Studies*, 50 (1), 1991, pp. 189–220.
6. Hsu Szu-Chien, 'The domestic origin of China's rise and its international impact: the party state developmental syndicate' in Hsin- Huang Michael Hsiao and Cheng-yi Lin (ed.) *Rise of China: Beijing's strategies and implications for the Asia-Pacific*, Politics

in Asia series, Routledge, Taylor and Francis Group, London & New York, 2009, pp. 55–83.

7. Varun Sahni, 'China-India partnership: Defining an agenda", *China Report*, 44(1), Jan–March 2008, New Delhi.
8. T Kojima, China's Omni-directional Diplomacy, cooperation with all, Emphasis on major powers, *Asia-Pacific Review*, 8(2), 1 November 2001, pp. 81–95, Online URL: *http://www.ingentaconnect.com/content/routledge/capr/2001/00000008/00000002/art00007*
9. Duara, no. 49.
10. Tim Johnson, (2007): 'Dissent with a dose of nationalism' in "China rises," Online URL: November 2007, Online URL: *http://washingtonbureau.typepad.com/China/2007/11/dissent-with-a.html*
11. David Shambaugh, "China engages Asia, Reshaping the regional order," *International Security* 29(3), pp. 64–99; also see David Shambaugh (ed.), *The Modern Chinese State*, Cambridge University Press, Cambridge, 2000.

Annexure I

Filmography

1.	Red Sorghum/ Hong Gaoliang	1987	婷高粱
2.	Ju Dou	1990	菊豆
3.	Raise the Red Lantern/Da Hong Denglong Gaogao Gua	1991	大ᴗ 灯ŏ 嫘嫘挂
4.	To Live/ Huo Zhe	1994	活着
5.	Hero/ Yingxiong	2000	英雄
6.	House of the Flying Daggers/ Shi mian mai fu	2004	十面埋伏
7.	The Curse of the Golden Flower/ the city of the Golden Armour/ Mancheng Jindai Huangjinjia	2006	啕城尽首黄金甲
8.	Not One Less/ Yi ge dou bu neng shao	1999	一个都不能少
9.	City of Life and Death/ Nanjing Nanjing	2009	南京南京
10.	Devils at the Doorstep	2000	鬼子来了
11.	Yasukuni	2008	靖国神社

ANNEXURE II

Media and Cultural Groups Founded by Falun Gong Actively Engaged in Contesting the Nationalist Perspectives of the State

Company	Earlier stages	Currently
Sound of Hope Network	Local Chinese language operations in San-Francisco, 2001	Broadcasts in five languages in 11 countries in North America, Europe and Asia and available online; also shortwave and satellite radio into China
New Tang Dynasty Television	Satellite broadcast in North America, 2002	Extended to Asia, Europe and Australia, with 24 hour broadcast in Chinese and English; also has interactive websites in a number of languages
The Epoch Times	Chinese Newspaper and online editions in New York 2003	Printed in 10 languages and distributed in 29 countries in North and South America, Europe and Asia with 17 languages on the web
Devine Performing Arts and Orchestra	Merger of performance groups from a Chinese New Year Cultural show, 2006	Puts on Chinese traditional culture shows, performed in about 30 cities in 2007
Shen Zhou Film Studio	Film Studio, 2006	Held first Shen Zhou International Film Festival in Washington, DC, in July 2007

Courtesy: Dong Xiang's article on Falun Gong and multiple internet sources.

ANNEXURE III

China's Policy on Tibet
(Selected Verbatim Excerpts)

'Social harmony is of the essence of socialism with Chinese characteristics. Tibet is an important border ethnic region of China; due to its particular geographical environment and history, it remains an undeveloped region, and is facing a sharp and complex anti-separatist struggle for a long time. Development and stability have always been two major affairs for Tibet, and in them lays the key to building a harmonious Tibet. In building a harmonious Tibet, we must comprehensively implement the scientific development concept, have a correct understanding of Tibet's special features, master the line of thought that understanding is the precursor, development the basis, stability the premise, solidarity the core, and work style the key, do a good job in this combination, and get a good grasp of implementation'...

... 'Tibet's strategic position is extremely important; it is an important security screen in China's southwest and also an important ecological screen. Tibet's special features in history, current state, environment, and geography determine that its development and stability are always closely linked to national sovereignty and security. Tibet is a focal point in our struggle with international anti-China forces; hostile forces' desire to finish us is not dead, their desire to throw us into chaos has not changed, and they have all along tried to make use of the so-called 'Tibet question' to contain and split China; supported by international anti-China forces, the Dalai clique has continually changed its methods, frequently caused incidents, damaged social stability, and plotted "Tibet independence"; it has all along been the greatest obstacle to Tibet's development and stability, and also the evil force sabotaging the unity of the motherland and ethnic solidarity. Our struggle against the Dalai clique and the western hostile forces supporting it is long term, sharp, and complex, and is even quite intense at times. The level of Tibet's productive forces is low, the infrastructure is weak, people's livelihood is difficult, and there is a shortage of talent of all types; in 2005 average per-capita GDP was 65.3 per cent of the national level, while net income of the peasants and herdsmen was 63.8 per cent of the national average; the overall level of economic and social development lags far behind that of China's interior'..

... 'We must tightly grasp the central authorities' strategy of continuing to carry out major development of west China, the intensified support for

Tibet, and the valuable opportunity provided by the opening of the Qinghai-Tibet railroad, comprehensively practice the economic development strategy of "improving standards in primary industry, grasping the focal points in secondary industry, and vigorously developing tertiary industry," persist in proceeding from reality, highlight the focal points, express the characteristics, increase the effect of the characteristics, promote industrial structure optimization and upgrading, spur the coordinated development of regional economy, and make efforts to press the region's economic development into the fast lane'...

... 'In building a harmonious Tibet, we must hold aloft the banner of patriotism, and guide the people of all ethnic groups to unite and strive together to promote prosperous development and create a happy and beautiful life'...

... 'Whatever the ethnic group, stratum, or religious belief, there is always identity on this fundamental issue of patriotism, and there cannot be the slightest wavering or ambiguity at any time and in any circumstances. We must step up education in history with patriotism as the core, to enable the people of all ethnic groups to know about the motherland's history and Tibet's history, and understand that the unity of the motherland is the fundamental guarantee for achieving the fundamental interests of the people of all ethnic groups. Preserving the motherland's unity and building and developing Tibet well is where the fundamental interests and also the fundamental responsibility of Tibet's 2.77 million people of all ethnic groups reside. Tibet's development and progress accord with the tide of history, and are also the common aspiration of the people of Tibet, and can only be realized under the socialist system in the great family of the Chinese nation. We must resolutely wage struggle against separatism, earnestly implement the work guidelines of "take a clear-cut stand, give tit for tat, take the initiative to put things in order, and strengthen and consolidate the base" and "cure both the symptoms and the cause, with the focus on the cause," unfold without the slightest relaxation education in "solidarity and stability are happiness, separatism and chaos are calamity" among the cadres and masses of all ethnic groups, firmly grasp the initiative in the struggle against separatism, and ensure the building of a harmonious Tibet amid a stable and orderly social environment'...

... 'Vigorously carry forward the spirit of the Chinese nation with patriotism as the core, build a system of socialist core values, launch in depth propaganda and education in ethnic solidarity, persist in the idea of "three cannot do withouts" (san libukai) and the "five lakes and four seas" principle, handle well relations between Tibetans and fraternal ethnic groups, speed up the development of minority ethnic groups, and continually strengthen solidarity between cadres and between masses of different ethnic groups, so that their feelings touch each other, their thoughts are exchanged, and they interact in work, and the socialist ethnic relations of equality, solidarity, mutual aid, and harmony are continually consolidated and developed'...

— 'Grasp the two major affairs of development and stability, promote the building of a harmonious Tibet' from '*Quishi* Website' posted by Zhang Qingli, secretary of Tibet Autonomous Region CCP Committee on 16 January 2007. Translated in BBC Monitoring Services Reports.

ANNEXURE IV

Education Law of the People's Republic of China

(Selected Verbatim Excerpts)

(Adopted at the third session of the eighth National People's Congress on March 18, 1995, promulgated by Order No.45 of the President of the People's Republic of China on March 18, 1995 and effective as of September 1, 1995)

Article 1 With a view to developing educational undertakings, improving the quality of the whole nationality, accelerating the construction of the socialist material and spiritual civilization and in accordance with the Constitution of the People's Republic of China, the present Law is hereby formulated.

... Article 3 In developing the socialist educational undertakings, the state shall uphold Marxism-Leninism, Mao Zedong Thought and the theories of Constructing socialism with Chinese characteristics as directives and comply with the basic principles of the Constitution.

Article 4 With education being the foundation for construction of socialist modernization, the state shall give priority to the development of educational undertakings...

..Article 6 The state shall conduct education among education receivers in patriotism, collectivism and socialism as well as in ideals, ethics, discipline, legality, national defence and ethnic unity.

Article 7 Education shall be carried out in the spirit of inheriting and expanding the fine historical and cultural traditions of the Chinese nation and assimilating all the fine achievements of the civilization progress of human beings...

... Schools and other educational institutions shall guarantee the participation of teachers and staffs in democratic management and supervision through the organic form such as the teachers and staffs congress mainly consisting of teachers in accordance with relevant provisions of the state (article 30)...

... Article 50 Students shall enjoy preferential treatment as to public cultural and sport facilities such as libraries, museums, science and technology centres, cultural centres, art galleries, gymnasiums and stadiums, historical or cultural spots and revolutionary commemoration halls or places so that education receivers can be offered convenience for education.

Radio and TV station shall design education programmes and promote the improvement of students in aspects of ideology, morale, cultural and scientific capacity...

Article 84 The present Law shall come into effect as of September 1, 1995.

ANNEXURE V

Sports Law of the People's Republic of China

(The People's Republic of China Order of the President of the fifty-fifth)

CHAPTER I
GENERAL PROVISIONS

Article 1: In order to sports development, enhance people's health, improve the level of sports to promote socialist material civilization and spiritual civilization, This Law is formulated in accordance with the Constitution.

Article 2: State develops physical culture and promotes mass sports activities to improve the whole nation 's health, physical education, exercise activities, the implementation of the development of the popularization and improvement of the combination, and promote the coordination of various sports.

Article 3: The State adhere to the sport for economic construction, national defense construction and social development services. Sports should be included in the cause of the economic and social development plan. Countries to promote sports management system. The state encourages enterprises, institutions, social organizations and citizens to set up and support to sports.

Article 4 of the sports administration of the State Council department in charge of the national sports work. Other relevant departments under the State Council within their respective mandates, managing sport. Sports administration department of local people's governments above the county level or the people's government authorized agencies in charge of the administrative area of sports.

Article 5: The State shall be given special protection and young people, children's sports activities, enhance the physical and mental health of young people, youth, and children.

Article 6: The State shall support ethnic minority areas to the development of sports, culture in ethnic sports. Scientific and technological achievements of the seventh national development of physical education and sports science research, promotion of advanced, practical sports, relying on scientific and technological development of sports.

Article 7: The state shall contribute to organizations and individuals in the sports career will be awarded.

Article 8: The state shall encourage the overseas sports exchanges.

Article 9: Foreign sports exchanges to adhere to the principles of independence, equality and mutual benefit, mutual respect, safeguarding national sovereignty and dignity, and to comply with the international treaties concluded or acceded to by the People's Republic of China.

CHAPTER II
Social Sports

Article 10: The state encourages citizens to participate in social and sports activities to enhance physical and mental health. Social sports activities should adhere to the amateur, voluntary, small and diverse, and follow the local conditions and principles of science and civilization.

Article 11: The state promotes the national fitness program, the implementation of standards for physical training, fitness monitoring. The state hierarchy of social sports instructors. Social sports instructors to guide social sports activities.

Article 12: Local people's governments should be for citizens to participate in social sports activities create the necessary conditions to support and assistance to carry out mass sports activities. The urban residents' committees and other community-based organizations should play a role in organizing residents to carry out sports activities. Rural villagers' committees, the role of the primary cultural and sports organizations should play, to carry out sports activities suitable for rural characteristics.

Article 13: State organs, enterprises and institutions shall carry out a variety of sports activities, organized mass sports competitions.

Article 14 trade unions and other social organizations shall, in accordance with their own characteristics, organized sports activities.

Article 15: The State encourages, supports the excavation of the nation, folk sports, organize and improve.

Article 16 of the whole society should be concerned about support for the elderly, people with disabilities participate in sports activities. The people's governments at all levels shall take measures to provide convenience for the elderly, the disabled to participate in sports activities.

CHAPTER III
School Sports

Article 17: The education administrative departments and schools should be the sport as an integral part of school education, cultivating the moral, intellectual and physical aspects of the comprehensive development of talent.

Article 18: The schools offering physical education and physical education as a subject of the assessment of student academic achievement. The school should create the conditions for the sick student organizations sports activities suited to their characteristics.

Article 19: Schools must implement national standards for physical training, the guarantee is given to students during the school day for sports activities.

Article 20: Schools shall organize various forms of extra-curricular sports activities, extracurricular training and athletic competition, and a whole-school sports will be held each school year, according to the conditions.

Article 21: School should be in accordance with relevant state regulations, with the qualified physical education teachers, to protect the physical education teachers enjoy their work characteristics related to treatment.

Article 22 of the school should be configured in accordance with the standards of the education administrative department under the stadium, the facilities and equipment. The school sports ground must be used for sports activities, shall not be used for other purposes.

Article 23: Schools shall establish a system of students' physical health checks. Education, sports and health administrative departments shall strengthen the monitoring of the physical fitness of students.

CHAPTER IV

Article 24: The State of the fourth chapter of the competitive sports of athletic sports development, to encourage athletes to improve sports level, to create excellent results in sports competitions, and win glory for the country.

Article 25: The State encourages and support for amateur sports training to develop excellent sports reserve talents.

Article 26 of the athletes and teams to participate in major domestic and international sports competitions, and shall, in accordance with the fair, the principle of merit selection and the formation of Specific way by the State Council administrative department of sports.

Article 27 of the train athletes must practice strict training and management of science, civilization, athletes patriotism, collectivism and socialist education, as well as moral and discipline.

Article 28 of the state elite athletes to give preferential treatment in employment or further education.

Article 29: The national sports federations of the athletes of the project to implement the registration management. Registered athletes, according to the provisions of the sports administration department under the State Council, to participate in the movement of persons between the sports competitions and sports teams.

Article 30: State athletes technical level, technical grade referee and coaches of professional and technical job hierarchy.

Article 31: The State classified management levels of sports competition. National Games by the State Council administrative department of sports management or sports administration department under the State Council in conjunction with the organization and management. Responsible for managing the national individual sports competition by the sport's national association. Comprehensive local sports and local individual sports competition management approach developed by the local people's governments.

Article 32: The State applies the system of sports competitions the national record for approval. The national record recognized by the sports administration department under the State Council.

Article 33 of the disputes in sports activities, responsible for the mediation, arbitration by the Arbitration for Sport. The establishment of sports arbitration body approach and the scope of arbitration by the State Council separately.

Article 34 sports competitions to implement the principle of fair competition. Sports competition organizers and athletes, coaches, referees shall abide by the sportsmanship, not fraud, malpractice. Prohibited the use of banned drugs and methods in sport. Disable drug testing institutions shall strictly check the banned drugs and methods. Any organizations and individuals engaged in gambling activities, sports competitions is strictly prohibited.

Article 35 of the major sports competitions held in China, the name, emblem, flag and mascot logo to be protected in accordance with relevant state regulations.

CHAPTER V

Article 36: The State of the fifth chapter of the sports community groups to encourage, support to sports and social groups in accordance with its charter, the organization of sports activities, and promote the development of sports.

Article 37: National Sports Associations at all levels is to contact the unity of athletes and sports workers mass sports organizations, should play a role in the development of sports.

Article 38: The Chinese Olympic Committee is to develop and promote the Olympic Movement is the main task of sporting organizations, to represent China to participate in international Olympic affairs.

Article 39 of the sports science community groups is a sports science and technology workers in academic mass organizations, should play a role in the development of sports science and technology.

Article 40: The national movement of the sports federations administering the popularization and improvement of work to represent China in the appropriate international sports federations.

CHAPTER VI

Article 41: The people's governments at or above the county level in the sixth chapter of the protection conditions should be funding for sports in sports capital construction funds included in the budget and infrastructure investment plans, and gradually increase with the development of the national economy on sports career input.

Article 42: The state encourages enterprises, institutions and social groups, self-financing the development of sports, to encourage organizations and personal donations and sponsorships of sports in

Article 43 of the state departments concerned should strengthen the management of sports funds to any organization or individual shall misappropriate, embezzle sports funds.

Article 44 above the county level sports administration departments of governments at all levels of fitness, athletics and other sports activities for the content of the business activities in accordance with relevant state regulations should strengthen management and supervision.

Article 45 above the county level, local people's governments shall, in accordance with the provisions of the national norms and criteria of the city's public sports facilities, land, urban public sports facilities into urban construction planning and land use planning, rational distribution, unified arrangement. Cities in the planning of businesses, schools, streets and residential areas should be sports facilities into, to the construction plan. Townships, nationality townships and towns shall be as economic development, and gradually build and improve sports facilities.

Article 46: Public sports facilities should be open to the community, convenient for people to carry out sports activities for students, the elderly, the disabled, a preferential approach to improve the utilization of sports facilities. No organization or individual may appropriate, destruction of public sports facilities. Due to special circumstances require the temporary occupation of sports facilities must be approved by the sports administration and the construction planning, and timely restitution; stadium land use change under the Town Planning shall, in accordance with the relevant provisions of the State, the first choice of the new repayment.

Article 47 for national and international sports competitions, sports equipment and supplies, must be validated by the designated agency of the sports administration department under the State Council.

Article 48: The state develops physical professional education, the establishment of the professional institutions of various types of sports, the Department, Division, training exercise, training, teaching, scientific research, management and engaged in mass sports professionals. The state encourages enterprises, institutions, social organizations and citizens in accordance with the law organizing sports professional education.

CHAPTER VII
LEGAL RESPONSIBILITY

Article 49 engaged in fraud and other violations of the rules of discipline and sports in competitive sports, to be punished in accordance with the articles of association; on the national staff of the persons directly responsible shall be given administrative sanctions by the sports and social groups.

The use of banned drugs and **Article 50** in the sport by the sports and social groups to be punished in accordance with the articles of association; on the national staff of the persons directly responsible shall be given administrative sanctions.

Article 51: The use of competitive sports to engage in gambling activities, the sports administration department to assist the public security organs shall be ordered to stop illegal activities, be punished by public security organs in accordance with the relevant provisions of the Regulations on Administrative Penalties for Public Security. Competitive sports activities, bribery, fraud, organization of gambling behavior constitutes a crime, be held criminally responsible.

Article 52 of the occupation and destruction of public sports facilities, sports administration departments ordered to make corrections and shall bear civil liability. Any of the acts enumerated in the preceding paragraph, the offender be punished by public security organs in accordance with the relevant provisions of the Regulations on Administrative Penalties for Public Security; constitute a crime, be held criminally responsible.

Article 53 in sports activities, disturb, disturb public order, given criticism and education and be stopped; the offender be punished by public security organs in accordance with the provisions of the Security Administration Punishment Act; constitute a crime shall be prosecuted for criminal responsibility.

Article 54 violation of national financial systems, financial systems, misappropriate, embezzle part of sports funds by the higher authorities shall order deadline to return the misappropriated, withheld funds and directly in charge and other directly responsible personnel shall be given administrative sanctions; constitute a crime, shall be held criminally responsible.

CHAPTER VIII
SUPPLEMENTARY PROVISIONS

Article 55 of the army of sports activities in a specific way by the Central Military Commission enacted in accordance with this Law.

Article 56: This Law shall enter into force on 10 January 1995.

ANNEXURE VI

Computer Information Network and Internet Security, Protection and Management Regulations

(Approved by the State Council on December 11 1997 and promulgated by the Ministry of Public Security on December 30, 1997)

CHAPTER ONE
COMPREHENSIVE REGULATIONS

Section 1—In order to strengthen the security and the protection of computer information networks and of the Internet, and to preserve the social order and social stability, these regulations have been established on the basis of the "PRC Computer Information Network Protection Regulations", the "PRC Temporary Regulations on Computer Information Networks and the Internet" and other laws and administrative regulations.

Section 2—The security, protection and management of all computer information networks within the borders of the PRC fall under these regulations.

Section 3—The computer management and supervision organization of the Ministry of Public Security is responsible for the security, protection and management of computer information networks and the Internet. The Computer Management and Supervision organization of the Ministry of Public Security should protect the public security of computer information networks and the Internet as well as protect the legal rights of Internet service providing units and individuals as well as the public interest.

Section 4—No unit or individual may use the Internet to harm national security, disclose state secrets, harm the interests of the State, of society or of a group, the legal rights of citizens, or to take part in criminal activities.

Section 5—No unit or individual may use the Internet to create, replicate, retrieve, or transmit the following kinds of information:

(1) Inciting to resist or breaking the Constitution or laws or the implementation of administrative regulations;
(2) Inciting to overthrow the government or the socialist system;
(3) Inciting division of the country, harming national unification;
(4) Inciting hatred or discrimination among nationalities or harming the unity of the nationalities;
(5) Making falsehoods or distorting the truth, spreading rumors, destroying the order of society;

(6) Promoting feudal superstitions, sexually suggestive material, gambling, violence, murder,
(7) Terrorism or inciting others to criminal activity; openly insulting other people or distorting the truth to slander people;
(8) Injuring the reputation of state organs;
(9) Other activities against the Constitution, laws or administrative regulations.

Section 6—No unit or individual may engage in the following activities which harm the security of computer information networks:

(1) No-one may use computer networks or network resources without getting proper prior approval
(2) No-one may without prior permission may change network functions or to add or delete information
(3) No-one may without prior permission add to, delete, or alter materials stored, processed or being transmitted through the network.
(4) No-one may deliberately create or transmit viruses.
(5) Other activities which harm the network are also prohibited.

Section 7—The freedom and privacy of network users is protected by law. No unit or individual may, in violation of these regulations, use the internet to violate the freedom and privacy of network users.

CHAPTER TWO
Responsibility for Security and Protection

Section 8—Units and individuals engaged in Internet business must accept the security supervision, inspection, and guidance of the Public Security organization. This includes providing to the Public Security organization information, materials and digital document, and assisting the Public Security organization to discover and properly handle incidents involving law violations and criminal activities involving computer information networks.

Section 9—The supervisory section or supervisory units of units which provide service through information network gateways through which information is imported and exported and connecting network units should, according to the law and relevant state regulations assume responsibility for the Internet network gateways as well as the security, protection, and management of the subordinate networks.

Section 10—Connecting network units, entry point units and corporations that use computer information networks and the Internet and other organizations must assume the following responsibilities for network security and protection:

(1) Assume responsibility for network security, protection and management and establish a thoroughly secure, protected and well managed network.

(2) Carry out technical measures for network security and protection. Ensure network operational security and information security.
(3) Assume responsibility for the security education and training of network users
(4) Register units and individuals to whom information is provided. Provide information according to the stipulations of article five.
(5) Establish a system for registering the users of electronic bulletin board systems on the computer information network as well as a system for managing bulletin board information.
(6) If a violation of articles four, five, six or seven is discovered than an unaltered record of the violation should be kept and reported to the local Public Security organization.
(7) According to the relevant State regulations, remove from the network and address, directory or server which has content in violation of article five.

Section 11—The network user should fill out a user application form when applying for network services. The format of this application form is determined by Public Security.

Section 12—Connecting network units, entry point units, and corporations that use computer information networks and the Internet and other organizations (including connecting network units that are inter-provincial, autonomous region, municipalities directly under the Central Government or the branch organization of these units) should, within 30 days of the opening of network connection, carry out the proper registration procedures with a unit designated by the Public Security organization of the provincial, autonomous region, or municipality directly under the Central Government peoples' government.

The units mentioned above have the responsibility to report for the record to the local public security organization information on the units and individuals which have connections to the network. The units must also report in a timely manner to Public Security organization any changes in the information about units or individuals using the network.

Section 13—People who register public accounts should strengthen their management of the account and establish an account registration system. Accounts may not be lent or transferred.

Section 14—Whenever units involved in matters such as national affairs, economic construction, building the national defense, and advanced science and technology are registered, evidence of the approval of the chief administrative section should be shown.

Appropriate measures should be taken to ensure the security and protection of the computer information network and Internet network links of the units mentioned above.

CHAPTER THREE
SECURITY AND SUPERVISION

Section 15—The provincial, autonomous region or municipal Public Security agency or bureau, as well as city and county Public Security organizations should have appropriate organizations to ensure the security, protection and management of the Internet.

Section 16—The Public Security organization computer management and supervision organization should have information on the connecting network units, entry point unit, and users, establish a filing system for this information, maintain statistical information on these files and report to higher level units as appropriate.

Section 17—The Public Security computer management and supervision organization should have establish a system for ensuring the security, protection and good management of the connecting network units, entry point unit, and users. The Public Security organization should supervise and inspect network security, protection and management and the implementation of security measures.

Section 18—If the Public Security computer management and supervision organization discovers an address, directory or server with content in violation of section five, then the appropriate units should be notified to close or delete it.

Section 19—The Public Security computer management and supervision organization is responsible for pursuing and dealing with illegal computer information network activities and criminal cases involving computer information networks. Criminal activities in violation of sections four or section seven should according to the relevant State regulations, be handed over to the relevant department or to the legal system for appropriate disposition.

CHAPTER FOUR
LEGAL RESPONSIBILITY

Section 20—For violations of law, administrative regulations or of section five or section six of these regulations, the Public Security organization gives a warning and if there income from illegal activities, confiscates the illegal earnings.

For less serious offenses a fine not to exceed 5000 RMB to individuals and 15,000 RMB to work units may be assessed.

For more serious offenses computer and network access can be closed down for six months, and if necessary Public Security can suggest that the business operating license of the concerned unit or the cancellation of its network registration. Management activities that constitute a threat to public order can be punished according to provisions of the public security management penalties articles. Where crimes have occurred, prosecutions for criminal responsibility should be made.

Section 21—Where one of the activities listed below has occurred, the Public Security organization should order that remedial action should be taken with a specific period and give a warning; if there has been illegal income, the income should be confiscated; if remedial action is not taken within the specified period, then a fine of not more than 5000 RMB may be assessed against the head of the unit and persons directly under the unit head and a fine of not more than 15,000 RMB against the unit; in the case of more offenses, the network and equipment can be closed for up to six months. In serious cases Public Security may suggest that the business license of the organization be canceled and its network registration canceled.

(1) Not setting up a secure system
(2) Not implementing security techniques and protection measures
(3) Not providing security education and training for network users
(4) Not providing information, materials or electronic documentation needed for security, protection and management or providing false information
(5) For not inspecting the content of information transmitted on behalf of someone else or not registering the unit or individual on whose behalf the information was transmitted
(6) Not establishing a system for registering users and managing the information of electronic bulletin boards.
(7) Not removing web addresses and directories or not closing servers according to the relevant state regulations.
(8) Not establishing a system for registering users of public accounts
(9) Lending or transferring accounts

Section 22—Violation of section four or section seven of these regulations shall be punished according to the relevant laws and regulations.

Section 23—Violations of section eleven or section twelve of these regulations or not fulfilling the responsibility or registering users shall be punished by a warning from Public Security or suspending network operations for six months.

CHAPTER FIVE
ADDITIONAL REGULATIONS

Section 24—These regulations should be consulted with regards to the implementation of the security, protection and management of computer information networks connecting to networks in the Hong Kong Special Administrative Region as well as with networks in the Taiwan and Macao districts.

Section 25—These regulations go into effect on the day of promulgation.

Select References

Primary Sources

China Olympics Committee, Documents, URL: http://en.olympic.cn/

Information Office of the State Council of the People's Republic of China (1992), *White Paper on Tibet- Its ownership and human rights situation* [Online: web] Accessed on 02 August 2008, URL: http://www.china.org.cn/e-white/tibet/index.htm

Taiwan Affairs Office & Information office State Council People's Republic of China (1993), *White Paper on The Taiwan question and Reunification of China* [Online: web] Accessed on 02 August 2008, URL: http://www.china.org.cn/e-white/taiwan/index.htm

Information Office of the State Council of the People's Republic of China (1998), *White Paper on New progress in human rights in the Tibet Autonomous Region* [Online: web] Accessed on 02 August 2008, URL: http://www.china.org.cn/e-white/last/index.htm

____ (2000), *White Paper on National Minorities Policy and its Practice in China* [Online: web] Accessed on 02 August 2008, URL: http://www.china.org.cn/e-white/4/index.htm

____ (2001), *White Paper on Tibet's March Towards Modernisation* [Online web] Accesses 02 August 2008, URL: http://www.china.org.cn/e-white/20011108/index.htm

____ (2005), *White Paper on Regional autonomy for ethnic minorities in China,* [Online: web] Accessed on 02 August 2008, URL: http://www.china.org.cn/e-white/20050301/index.htm

____ (2009), *White Paper on Fifty years of democratic reform in Tibet,* [Online: web] Accessed on 04 April 2009, URL: http://www.china.org.cn/government/whitepaper/node_7062754.htm

Hu Jintao's address to Boao Forum [Online: web] Accessed on 24 December 2008, URL: http://www.chinadaily.com.cn

Party press statement, *'Hold High the Great Banner of socialism with Chinese characteristics and strive for new victories in building a moderately prosperous society in all respects'*, [Online: web] Accessed on 25 October 2008, http://news.xinhuanet.com/english/2007-10/24

Sports Federation of China, Documents, URL: http://www.sport.org.cn/

Books

Abanti Bhattacharya, 'Chinese Nationalism: the Impact on Policy', Ph.D. Thesis, (Unpublished) New Delhi: Jawaharlal Nehru University, 2004.

Andrew D. Morris, *Marrow of the Nation, A history of Sport and Physical Culture in Republican China*, Los Angeles: University of California Press, 2004.

Benedict Anderson, *Imagined communities—Reflections on the Origin and Spread of Nationalism*, Verso, London & New York, 1983.

Chiang Kai-Shek, *Soviet Russia in China: A Summing-up at Seventy*, Farrar Straus and Company, New York, 1957.

Christopher Hughes, *Chinese Nationalism in the Global Era*, Routledge, New York, 2006.

Chris Berry and Mary Farquhar, *China on Screen: Cinema and Nation*, Columbia University Press, New York, USA.

Chu Yingchi, *Hong Kong Cinema: Colonizer, motherland and self*, Routledge Curzon, London & New York, 2003.

David Bonavia, *The Chinese*, Allen Lane, Harper and Row, USA, 1980.

David Shambaugh, *The Modern Chinese State*, Cambridge University Press, Cambridge, 2000.

Deng Xiaoping, "we are confident" and "No one can shake Socialist China" Selected Works III, Beijing: Foreign Language Press, 1984.

Dittmer and Kim, *China's Quest for National Identity*, Cornell University Press, London and Ithaca, 1993.

E.H. Carr, *What is History?* Palgrave, UK, 1961.

E.J. Hobsbawm, *Nations and Nationalism since 1780; Programme, Myth, Reality*, Cambridge University Press, London, 1990.

Eugene Anschel, *Homer Lea, Sun Yatsen, and the Chinese Revolution*, Praeger Publishers, USA, 1984.

Francoise Mengin, 'Cyber China: Reshaping National identities in the age of information', Palgrave & Macmillan, 2004.

Franz Michael, *China Through the Ages*, Westview Press, USA, 1986.

Haraprasad Ray, *Chinese sources of South Asian History in Translation, Volume 1*, The Asiatic Society, Kolkata, 2004.

Harold Harrison, *China: Inventing the Nation*, Oxford University Press, London, 2001.

Harumi Befu, "Introduction", in Befu (ed.) *Cultural Nationalism in East Asia: Representation and Identity*, University of California, Berkeley, 1993.

Herman and Chomsky ed, *Manufacturing Consent: The Political Economy of the Mass Media'*, Pantheon books, New York, 1988.

Hu Sheng, *Imperialism and Chinese Politics*, Foreign Language Press, Beijing, 1981.

Hutchinson and Smith, *Nationalism—Critical Concepts in Political Science*, Volume I, Routledge Publishers, London and New York, 2007.

Jacques Garnet, *A History of the Chinese Civilization*, Cambridge University Press, USA, 1982.

Jeniffer Hargreaves, *Sport, Culture and Ideology*, Routledge and Kegan Paul, London, 1985.

Jonathan Unger, *Chinese nationalism*, Armonk, New York, 1996.

Joseph Levenson, *Confucian China and Its Modern Fate: The problem of intellectual continuity*, University of California Press, Berkeley, 1958.

Jürgen Habermas, The Structural transformation of the Public Sphere: An Inquiry into a Category of Bourgeois Society, The MIT Press, Cambridge Massachusetts (English Translation 1989).

Keiji Furuya, Chiang Kai Shek—Life and Times, New York: St. John's University, 1981.

Lowell Dittmer, *China Under Reform; Politics in Asia and the Pacific: Interdisciplinary Perspectives*,Westview Press, San Fransico, 1994.

Luke Goode, *Jurgen Habermas, Democracy and the Public Sphere*, Pluto Press, London, 2005.

Ma Jisen, *The Cultural Revolution in the Foreign Ministry of China*, The Chinese University Press, Hong Kong, 2004.

Mao Zedong, *On Diplomacy*, Foreign Language Press, Beijing, 1998.

Mao Zedong, *Selected Works of Mao Zedong* Vol. V, Foreign Language Press Beijing, 1977.

Mao Zedong, *Selected Works of Mao Zedong*, Vol. II, Foreign Language Press, Beijing, 1965.

Maria Hsia Chang, *Return of the Dragon—China's Wounded Nationalism*, West View Press, USA, 2001.

National Uprising of Tibet 2008, Tibetan Parliamentary and Policy Research Centre, New Delhi, 2008.

Prasenjit Duara, *Rescuing History from the Nation—Questioning Narratives of Modern China*, University of Chicago Press, 1995.

Rebecca Karl, *Situating the world—Chinese Nationalism at the Turn of the Twentieth Century*, Duke University Press, Durham and London, 2002.

Ross Terill, *The New Chinese Empire,* Basic Books, New York, 2003.

Simon Shen, *Redefining Nationalism in Modern China: Sino-American Relations and the Emergence of Chinese Public Opinion in the Twentieth Century,* Palgrave Macmillan, Basingstoke, Hants, 2007.

Suisheng Zhao, *Chinese Foreign Policy: Pragmatism and Strategic Behavior,* Armonk, Me Sharpe, New York and London, 2004.

Suisheng Zhao, *Nation State by Construction: Dynamics of Modern Chinese Nationalism,* Stanford University Press, Stanford, 2004.

Susan Brownell, *Training the Body for China: Sports in the Moral Order of the People's Republic,* University of Chicago Press, Chicago, 1995.

Susan. L Shirk, *China—A Fragile Superpower,* Oxford University Press, New York, 2007.

Tadao & Ohara, *The Alleged Nanking Massacre, Japan's Rebuttal to China's Forged Claims,* Meisei-sha, Tokyo, 2007.

Tan Chung, *China and the Brave World,* Allied Publishers Private Limited, New Delhi, 1978.

Thomas Metzger, *Escape from Predicament: Neo-Confucianism and China's Evolving Political Culture,* Columbia University Press, New York, 1977.

Tom Nairn, *Janus Revisited,* Verso, London, 1998.

Tu ki Min, *Men and Ideas in Modern Chinese History,* Seoul National University Press, Korea, 1997.

Tu Wei-Ming ed, *The Living Tree: The Changing meaning of being Chinese today,* Stanford University Press, 1994.

Yongnian Zhang, *Globalisation and State Transformation in China,* Cambridge University Press, Cambridge, 2004.

Index